Positive Behavior Interventions & Supports

A Collection of Articles

From *TEACHING Exceptional Children*

ISBN 0-86586-449-7

Copyright 2010 by Council for Exceptional Children, 1110 North Glebe Road, Suite 300, Arlington, Virginia 22201-5704

Stock No. P5953

All rights reserved.

No part of this publication may be reproduced, stored in a retrieval system, or transmitted, in any form or by any means, electronic, mechanical, photocopying, recording, or otherwise, without prior written permission of the copyright owner.

Printed in the United States of America

10 9 8 7 6 5 4 3 2 1

Contents

Acknowledgments v

Introduction vii
    Alec F. Peck and Stan Scarpati

1   CEC's Policy on Safe and Positive School Climate 1

Schoolwide Practices

2   Improving the Way We Think About Students With Emotional
and/or Behavioral Disorders 7
    Kelley S. Regan

3   Creating Home–School Partnerships by Engaging Families
in Schoolwide Positive Behavior Supports 19
    *Howard S. Muscott, Stacy Szczesiul, Becky Berk, Kathy Staub, Jane Hoover,
and Paula Perry-Chisholm*

4   Wraparound As a Tertiary Level Intervention for Students
With Emotional/Behavioral Needs 33
    *Lucille Eber, Kimberli Breen, Jennifer Rose, Renee M. Unizycki,
and Tasha H. London*

5	Schoolwide Positive Behavior Supports: Primary Systems and Practices	45
	Brandi Simonsen, George Sugai, and Madeline Negron	
6	Cooperating Initiatives: Supporting Behavioral and Academic Improvement Through a Systems Approach	61
	Michael D. Coyne, Brandi Simonsen, and Michael Faggella-Luby	
7	Evaluating School Climate and School Culture	71
	Andrew T. Roach and Thomas R. Kratochwill	
8	High School Peer Mentoring That Works!	85
	Judith Dopp and Tara Block	

Classroom Strategies

9	Making It Work: Differentiating Tier Two Self-Regulated Strategies Development in Writing in Tandem With Schoolwide Positive Behavioral Support	101
	Karin N. Sandmel, Mary Brindle, Karen R. Harris, Kathleen Lynne Lane, Steve Graham, Jessica Nackel, Rachel Mathias, Annette Little	
10	Classwide Interventions: Effective Instruction Makes a Difference	123
	Maureen A. Conroy, Kevin S. Sutherland, Angela L. Snyder, and Samantha Marsh	
11	Classwide Secondary and Tertiary Tier Practices and Systems	135
	Sarah Fairbanks, Brandi Simonsen, and George Sugai	
12	Using Positive Behavioral Support to Manage Avoidance of Academic Tasks	149
	Nina Zuna and Dennis McDougall	
13	Teaching Transitions: Techniques for Promoting Success Between Lessons	161
	Kent McIntosh, Keith Herman, Amanda Sanford, Kelly McGraw, and Kira Florence	

Acknowledgments

The Council for Exceptional Children would like to extend a special thank you to Alec Peck and Stan Scarpati for their continuing contribution to the field as stewards and editors of *TEACHING Exceptional Children*. It is under their leadership that these articles were selected and brought forth to be published. CEC would also like to extend appreciation to George Sugai, Brandi Simonsen, and Robert H. Horner who served as the guest editors for *TEACHING Exceptional Children's* special issue which focused entirely on positive behavior interventions and supports published August 2008.

Introduction

Alec F. Peck and Stan Scarpati

This book presents a series of articles about principles and procedures that can be implemented in schools and classrooms to improve the quality of behavioral interventions and behavioral support planning and, in turn, the quality of life for all students. Each of these articles was published in *TEACHING Exceptional Children* within the past few years.

CURRENT CHALLENGES TO SCHOOLS

Teachers and school administrators are continually challenged to create opportunities for all students to be academically and socially successful. During this era of inclusive school practices, the unique learning and behavioral characteristics exhibited by many students has sharpened this challenge. Demands for higher achievement in literacy and mathematics and for improved performance on the high stakes tests mandated for all students, including those who are disabled or English language learners, has further exacerbated the challenge. Teachers and other school personnel must plan and perform at a level that is higher than ever to ensure the outcomes demanded by the public.

These are not the only critical issues faced by school personnel. While schools strive to meet academic challenges, many face another set of formidable tasks in the creation and maintenance of a safe and respectful learning environment. Arranging school and class environments for learning while simultaneously dealing with ongoing discipline problems and safety issues is a frustrating issue in many schools. In some, suspensions, expulsions, violence, and drug usage further complicate the scenario.

RESPONSE TO DISCIPLINE AND SAFETY ISSUES

The challenge to develop effective strategies to respond to discipline and safety demands in schools has typically been met by developing and using appropriate positive or negative consequences. Many schools react to discipline and safety issues as they appear, on a case-by-case basis. However, the reality is that the effect of these strategies tends to be short lived, if they are effective at all. These reactive strategies are limited in their ability to enable students to demonstrate newly learned behavior beyond the situation in which it is learned.

In individual classrooms, consequence-based management strategies have also been the hallmark of many behavior management systems, with an emphasis on the functional relationship between student behavior and what is likely to either encourage that behavior to continue or to diminish or disappear altogether. While many of these procedures have merit and have been included in the research on effective treatment, they have also been proven limited in effect and may be inappropriate within integrated settings. Furthermore, they are often invasive and inappropriate, or are ineffective in teaching students meaningful alternatives to their behavior.

We know, of course, that behavior change is complex and is vulnerable to many unexpected and uncontrollable influences that often suppress the most well designed and logically implemented behavior management plan. For many, to focus solely on the consequence stage of behavior change limits the opportunity for teaching new skills and appropriate social behavior. Focusing on consequences alone reduces behavior management conceptually (and in practice) to an ongoing set of small, moderately effective "quick fix" techniques that are not likely to be maintained or generalized. Opportunities to understand what influences student behavior prior to its occurrence are often missed when consequence-based behavior management is used exclusively. Furthermore, understanding events in their natural context, i.e., in the setting in which the behaviors occur, are missed or at least are not fully included when interventions are organized around consequences.

POSITIVE BEHAVIOR SUPPORT

As schools organize to build their capacity to meet the behavioral needs of all students, attention has shifted to the definitions, features, and uses of positive behavior interventions and support (PBIS). The term refers to a systematic application of behavioral interventions that are designed to produce socially acceptable behaviors in all students. While many of the strategies included within the PBIS framework are not new to the field of behavioral interventions, they are applied from a new perspective. PBIS also extends the influence of research-based practice from classrooms and schools to communities, parents, and families. Ultimately, a sustainable link is established where each environment (e.g., classroom and home) is viewed as a context in which a behavior serves a function or purpose. Under the PBIS model, efforts are made to adapt behavior in order to achieve that function or purpose in a manner that meets the appropriate contextual expectations. For example, learning the socially appropriate skill of "turn-taking" during competitive situations has one type of payoff for students in school and another when the student is at home.

The validity of the PBIS approach is that it is justified by the outcomes produced and by the fact that these outcomes are acceptable to members of the school and related communities. We suggest that the reader keep in mind that PBIS is a decision making framework that relies on data to guide the design and implementation of evidence-based practices, and that these practices are focused on improving outcomes for all students. PBIS is not just for students with disabilities. It is truly a system designed to benefit all students.

For additional detail and technical assistance concerning PBIS we refer you to the Center on Positive Behavioral Interventions and Supports established by the Office of Special Education Programs, U.S. Department of Education (www.pbis.org).

ABOUT THIS BOOK

Prior to the articles about PBIS, we present the Council for Exceptional Children's (CEC) policy on safe and positive school climates and how safe learning environments contribute to cognitive, academic, social-emotional and ethical development of all students. You will see that this policy is closely aligned with the philosophy of PBIS and provides a professional basis for the strategies and practices that unfold in the articles that follow. The articles, culled from previous issues of *TEACHING Exceptional Children,* are organized into two groups; *schoolwide practices* are followed by articles that describe effective *classroom strategies*.

SCHOOLWIDE PRACTICE

Effective interventions begin with an accurate understanding by teachers and other school personnel of the students who consistently exhibit emotional and/or behavioral disabilities. In *Improving the Way We Think About Students With Emotional and/or Behavioral Disorders,* Kelly S. Regan describes how pre-service and experienced teachers in general and special education settings share the challenge at one time or another of working with students who present emotional and behavioral disabilities (EBD). She then focuses on teacher behavior as the locus of concern and explores four guidelines for improving the way teachers think about the student with EBD in the classroom.

Engaging parents and families is a significant strength of implementing PBIS practice as part of a schoolwide intervention. In *Creating Home–School Partnerships by Engaging Families in Schoolwide Positive Behavior Supports,* Howard S. Muscott, Stacy Szczesiul, Becky Berk, Kathy Staub, Jane Hoover, and Paula Perry-Chisholm feature the importance of using evidence-based strategies when partnering with parents. These authors demonstrate how they utilize Epstein's model of "Family Involvement for School and Family Partnerships" as a framework and describe state and school-level strategies designed to address family engagement via a three-tier "Responsiveness to Family Engagement Practices" model.

Wraparound services are often hailed as key components when effective school-to-community practices are designed. Lucille Eber, Kimberli Breen, Jennifer Rose, Renee M. Unizycki, and Tasha H. London, in *Wraparound As a Tertiary Level Intervention for Students With Emotional/Behavioral Needs,* describe a continuum of wraparound practice for students with the most significant EBD needs. They include specific engagement techniques to ensure that the design of supports and interventions reflects the voice and perspectives of the family, student, and teacher(s). In addition to a brief history of wraparound, they provide an illustration from a school that built these services into a comprehensive schoolwide PBIS plan.

Using the professional literature along with the evidence that establishes the foundation for PBIS, Brandi Simonsen, George Sugai, and Madeline Negron discuss how a three-tier continuum of support can lead to successful interventions. In *Schoolwide Positive Behavior Supports: Primary Systems and Practices,* they use a case study to demonstrate the application of the PBIS principles. The continuum logically advances from primary interventions that support all students to a tertiary level that is designed to meet the needs of students who require the most intensive services in order to be successful.

Continuing to address a schoolwide systems approach to PBIS, Michael D. Coyne, Brandi Simonsen, and Michael Faggella-Luby outline three important guiding principles in *Cooperating Initiatives: Supporting Behavioral and Academic Improvement Through a Systems Approach.* They include a model for schoolwide initiatives that shares a common language and organization. They also use examples of beginning reading improvement and schoolwide positive behavior supports to illustrate how this model can accommodate multiple efforts from different domains.

Given the reality that any successful PBIS effort must involve all school personnel in planning and implementation, it is necessary that the school climate reflect an atmosphere of cooperation and agreement. School climate, and how to assess it, is presented by Andrew T. Roach and Thomas R. Kratochwill in *Evaluating School Climate and School Culture.* Using an historical approach, practitioners are directed to assessment options such as written questionnaires, ethnographic methods and focus groups, along with procedures for their effective use. These tools assist in developing a framework when PBIS practices and interventions are initially designed.

From a related (yet not strictly PBIS) perspective, Judith Dopp and Tara Block approach the inclusion of students with learning disabilities by involving peers as change agents for cooperative learning. In *High School Peer Mentoring That Works!* They describe a high school program that trained peer leaders to systematically use positive communication and problem solving with their classmates. They share results that indicate how all students were more likely to become class leaders, to model positive skills, and to reduce behavior problems.

CLASSROOM STRATEGIES

When PBIS is applied to classroom instruction, it becomes the focal point for effective practice. In *Making It Work: Differentiating Tier Two Self-Regulated Strategies Development in Writing in Tandem With Schoolwide Positive Behavioral Support,* Karin N. Sandmel, Mary Brindle, Karen R. Harris, Kathleen Lynne Lane, Steve Graham, Jessica Nackel, Rachel Mathias, and Annette Little present a tiered model of instruction to meet the needs of three case study students. How these students were identified as having both behavioral and writing difficulties and selected to receive more intensive, tier two instruction and support is explained. The article concludes with a careful illustration of how self-regulated strategies development (SRSD) for teaching writing and self-regulation strategies was differentiated to match the strengths and needs of the students described.

Another application of the three tier approach to classroom instruction designed to manage student behavior is presented by Maureen A. Conroy, Kevin S. Sutherland, Angela L. Snyder, and Samantha Marsh in their article entitled *Classwide Interventions: Effective Instruction Makes a Difference.* They provide an overview of several evidence-based classwide interventions that can be used to manage the behavior of all students in the classroom and increase classwide student engagement. They include descriptions and illustrations of each classwide intervention.

As described in the two preceding articles, a progressive approach that employs a sequence of interventions becomes more challenging when the practices are designed to meet the needs of students at the secondary and tertiary level of PBIS. Sarah Fairbanks, Brandi Simonsen, and George Sugai address this in their article, *Classwide Secondary and Tertiary Tier Practices and Systems.* They describe the typical features, the steps required to implement, and the intervention pre-requisites for secondary and tertiary intervention systems within classroom settings. They finish with an example that incorporates the logic of primary, secondary, and tertiary interventions in the classroom.

Finally, the last two articles focus on specific techniques that can be embedded in any classroom PBIS scheme. First, in *Using Positive Behavioral Support to Manage Avoidance of Academic Tasks,* Nina Zuna and Dennis McDougall describe how managing behavior by utilizing schemes that are linked to behavior antecedents can be effective. The authors demonstrate that understanding the function of a behavior can assist in designing antecedent practices.

Finally, Kent McIntosh, Keith Herman, Amanda Sanford, Kelly McGraw, and Kira Florence point to a systems approach that effectively improves how students transition from one activity or classroom to another. In *Teaching Transitions: Techniques for Promoting Success Between Lessons,* these authors discuss teaching routines, modeling appropriate behavior, monitoring student progress, and providing effective feedback as strategies that can mitigate problem behaviors when students move between activities.

Positive behavior interventions and support has been shown to evolve into an effective system when special and general educators cooperatively plan to improve the educational experiences of students vulnerable to academic and behavioral difficulties. Within a framework of positive and safe school practice, public policy and daily classroom practice can be shaped by the ongoing research on PBIS. These practices can ultimately become the cornerstone of a positive relationship between educators and their students, the parents and families involved with the school, and their communities. We anticipate that the articles in this book will assist in supporting that relationship, and will promote the development of high quality PBIS models.

1

CEC's Policy on Safe and Positive School Climate

The Council for Exceptional Children (CEC) recognizes the important impact a safe and positive school climate has on the personal development and academic achievement of all students. Research has shown that schools implementing supportive and positive school climate strategies are more successful in creating environments conducive to learning. Recent incidents of school violence, including harassment directed at students with disabilities and/or gifts and talents, have drawn attention to the unacceptable cost of not assuring a safe and positive climate in our schools for all students. Furthermore, students with disabilities may be more at risk because they do not necessarily have the ability to understand and report what is happening to them.

Such incidents, as well as surveys of students and faculty regarding safety, document continuing and pervasive harassment and bullying experienced by students and reveal that these actions are more likely to be perpetrated on the basis of appearance and actual or perceived differences in ethnicity, race, language, abilities, gender, sexual orientation, gender expression, or religion.

As student enrollment becomes increasingly diverse, schools are challenged to assure that all students feel valued and supported. Available research confirms that students feel safer and learn better when schools have clear policies prohibiting harassment and discrimination and when all members of the school community (students, parents, educators, administrators, and other school personnel) actively uphold the right of every student to a safe learning environment. Harassment can take many forms, including cyber bullying and other technological/electronic methods. In addition, although overt acts easily come to the attention of schools, it is essential that covert acts are recognized and addressed. CEC believes that all members of the school community have a critical role to play in assuring that students have access to a safe and supportive school environment.

In light of legal mandates and professional standards that promote the use of evidence-based practices to increase positive academic and social-emotional behaviors among students, CEC believes that special educators must acquire and use a knowledge base of effective practices for promoting supportive school climates in ways that support human and civil rights and promote social justice for the diverse student populations in today's schools.

Discrimination or harassment directed at students or adults on the basis of ethnic and racial backgrounds, language, age, abilities, family status, gender, sexual orientation, socioeconomic status, religious and spiritual values, and geographic location violates the human and/or civil rights of individuals who are the targets of such behavior.

To ensure the creation of safe learning environments that contribute to all students' cognitive, academic, social-emotional, and ethical development, it is the policy of the Council for Exceptional Children that:

- All schools should have clear policies that prohibit harassment and discriminatory behaviors of any kind, including those related to ethnic background, language, age, abilities, family status, gender, sexual orientation, socioeconomic status, religious and spiritual values, and geographic location. Students and staff should be clearly informed of such policies and procedures, including data collection, reporting, sanctions, and indemnity to those reporting incidents. Educational efforts at the federal, provincial, state, and local levels should promote policies, guidelines, and universal interventions designed to reduce or prevent discrimination or harassment as well as to create a school climate that is conducive to respect and dignity for all individuals.

- Because bullying and harassment create emotional wounds that amplify the hardships of exceptionality as well as jeopardize the emotional and mental well-being of students, teachers, administrators, and other school support personnel with knowledge of harassment or bullying carry the responsibility to report these behaviors to relevant authorities and school personnel similar to the professional obligation to report child abuse.

- In recognition that students' families, professionals, and staff may also be at risk of experiencing discrimination on the basis of factors including ethnic and racial backgrounds, language, age, abilities, family status, gender, sexual orientation, socioeconomic status, religious and spiritual values, and geographic location, school policies, activities, and interventions related to a positive school climate should address the needs and safety of adults as well as students.

- School-based implementation of antidiscrimination policies must equally support and provide open access for the participation of students in activities and student-led groups designed to enhance a respectful, safe, and positive school climate and to promote respect for diversity in general or with respect to one or more diversity elements.

- To support antidiscrimination policies, schools should provide students, staff, and administrators with access to a range of resources, including designated professionals with expertise in intercultural and diversity-related counseling and human relations.

- School policies should promote practices and curricula that build a sense of community and understanding for and among all students in recognition of the positive relationship between school climate, learning environments, and educational outcomes for all individuals.

- Professional development for educators and educational administrators should build schools' capacity to implement a diversity-rich curriculum as well as to respond effectively to instances of harassment, bullying, or intimidation. To this end, such activities should enhance educators' skills and strategies for effectively delivering culturally-sensitive educational experiences within the context of current standards-based curricula. Similarly, professional development for administrators should develop their leadership skills and strategies for developing and implementing antidiscrimination policies and for ensuring positive learning environments for all students. Schools should provide opportunities for parent education to complement professional development for educators.

- Teacher and educational leadership preparation programs should prepare educators, administrators, and related services personnel to create safe learning environments and to intervene effectively in the event that harassment or discriminatory behaviors occur. This includes understanding about the range of ways that schools can evaluate school climate comprehensively using evidence-based practices as well as how school climate findings can be used to build authentic learning communities that support positive youth development and academic achievement.

REFERENCE

Council for Exceptional Children 2008 Policy Manual.

DATE ADOPTED

Approved by the Council for Exceptional Children Board of Directors April 2008.

To access CEC's Policy on Safe and Positive School Climate *online, go to www.cec.sped.org > Policy & Advocacy > CEC Professional Policies. For further information, contact Deborah A. Ziegler, Associate Executive Director, Policy and Advocacy Services, Council for Exceptional Children, 703-264-9406 (P), 703-243-0410 (F), 800-224-6830 (Toll free), 866-915-5000 (TTY) (E-mail: debz@cec.sped.org).*

Schoolwide Practices

2

Improving the Way We Think About Students With Emotional and/or Behavioral Disorders

Kelley S. Regan

Creating a positive classroom setting is exciting for teachers. At the beginning of the school year, before even meeting the students, anticipation mounts and teachers begin to consider every possible detail. The event is much like that of arranging a party. First, the host must consider the environment. She selects the colors, the place settings, and images to post, the seating arrangements, and the visual effects to enhance the setting for all those attending. She also thinks about who will be seated next to each other and considers the structure or flow of the party—when will the band begin to play? And when will the guest of honor make a toast?

Second, unless everyone is aware of her role, a party can be uncomfortable for both the host and the attendees. The primary objective of the party is for everyone to learn more about one another. The host must consider her own role in arranging the party. Will she take the lead and facilitate mingling among those attending while remaining on the periphery of the small groups? Will a best friend or family member be on hand to share in the lofty burden of maintaining a successful event? Or will she want to be the center of the party? And what role should the members of the party take on? Clear, specific details could be described on the invitation—what to bring, what to wear, and the timeframe for the party. Expectations lead to minimal surprises—communicating clearly will govern a successful evening.

Finally, the host considers the food to serve the guests. These choices are endless, and a considerable amount of time is required to learn all the various

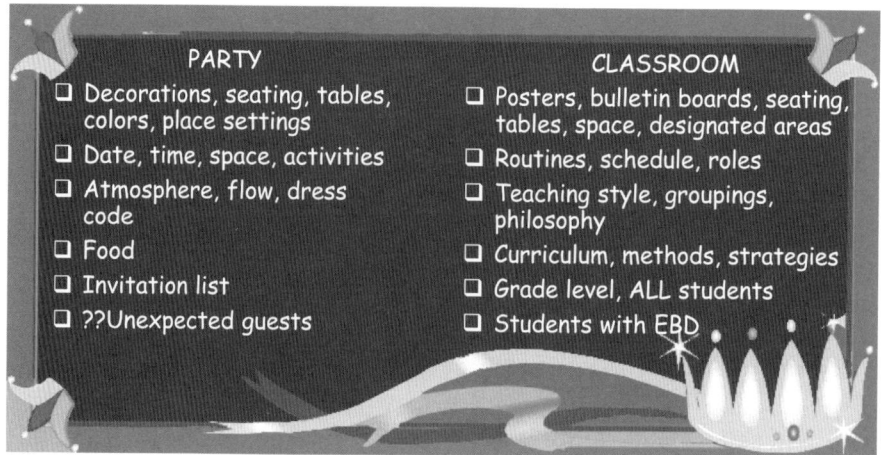

selections in addition to the essential items that everyone will need to access. Once the host understands the comprehensive list of vendors, she makes a selection after considering each individual's needs. Some may prefer seafood, others may prefer spicy selections or light finger foods. So, the host differentiates according to the preferred eating "style." A stand-up or sit-down event? Plastic dinnerware? Fine china?

And the most obvious preplanning component for a party is to make a list of everyone to invite. How are they selected? The host presumably has a positive relationship with everyone attending her engaging party. However, when those attending are given the option to bring one selected "guest," the host's ability to be proactive in achieving an ideal guest list is affected. The unexpected may drift in, and if so the host may have a nagging concern about the possibility of an unfamiliar guest challenging her harmonious environment. The dynamic will certainly be altered, and some of those attending may be unable to meet the objective of the party. What does the host do? What does a teacher do to maintain a positive learning environment while still supporting a student with an emotional and/or behavioral concern?

We can never fully prepare for the unexpected—be it a party event or a classroom event. Teacher preparation programs provide preservice teachers with evidence-based teaching strategies, skills of behavior management, and various field experiences. The greatest learning however, is acquired the very first year of instruction in the teacher's own classroom. Teaching students with emotional and/or behavioral disorders (EBD) may prove to be the most challenging for preservice teachers. However, when teachers begin to take a proactive role in shaping their perceptions and subsequent behaviors toward a student with EBD, looking closely for the student hiding underneath these behaviors, a positive learning environment and a positive student-teacher relationship ensues. One cannot exist without the other.

The supervision of novice teachers in the field illuminates four considerations that may improve the way we think about students with EBD as members of our positive learning environment: *reflection, relationships, roles,* and *resources.*

1. Before managing the behaviors of others, adults must be able to manage their own. Foremost, a teacher of a student(s) with EBD should be a *reflective* practitioner, that is, she should consider her mindsets, biases, and perceptions of students with EBD.
2. The teacher should develop a *relationship* with every student in order to establish trust and a commitment to the established ground rules.
3. The teacher should strengthen the teacher-student relationship by empowering students with a sense of belonging and clarity in an environment that has clearly defined *roles* for learning, playing, and participating.
4. The teacher should provide and use creative *resources* to support the learning and behavior of the individual with EBD.

GUIDING CONSIDERATION 1: REFLECTION

Well-qualified teachers enter the classroom believing that all students should be valued, can learn, and have an innate need to belong. These ideals of the first-year teacher can be diminished when atypical student behaviors surface. Teachers initially trust the practical tools they acquire from preparation programs detailing how to create a positive behavior management system in the classroom. When these tools fail to demonstrate any success with a particular student, teachers may feel inadequate, incompetent, and helpless, often resorting to traditional means of behavior management (i.e., punishment; Sugai & Horner, 2002). They may claim that they have exhausted all tools and therefore find insult to their futile attempts to engage a learner. In fact, high stress and a lack of preparation in the area of behavior management may be a leading contributor to attrition in the field of special education (Billingsley, 2004). When struggling to manage the behaviors of a particular student or class, reflecting on our own perceptions and skills is necessary. A lack of self-awareness may actually lead to problematic student behaviors and negatively affect classroom management and learning (Richardson & Shupe, 2003; Sutherland & Wehby, 2001).

A mindset often preventing the progress of novice teachers is that of "control" versus "manage." Beliefs about behavior will certainly affect how we respond to behavior. Consider that everything a teacher and a student does is behavior—behavior is both purposeful and motivated. For new and experienced teachers, behavior management may be misconstrued as control—a need for fulfilling their own ego. Ego, unfortunately, is often a culprit hindering a positive classroom environment. Reflecting and considering our own ego is a task central in life but is particularly salient in the classroom, where power can sometimes validate our self-efficacy beliefs. No one can

> **What Are Positive Behavioral Interventions and Supports (PBIS)?**
>
> Elementary and high schools in more than 30 states and the District of Columbia have employed features of PBIS in order to reduce problem behaviors and enhance learning environments. The Office of Special Education Programs (OSEP) funded Technical Assistance Center on Positive Behavioral Interventions and Supports (PBIS) provides methods to teach staff and all students how to establish behavioral expectations (school-wide and/or individually), acknowledge appropriate behavior, use ongoing data to make decisions, and establish a continuum of consequences for violating behavioral expectations. PBIS has been positively associated with a decrease in discipline referrals, an increase in instructional time, and an increase in perceived school safety (Sugai & Horner, 2006). The state of Maryland reports that 467 schools trained to use features of PBIS attribute their successful implementation to the investment in technical assistance, staff development activities, and behavior support coaches (Barrett, Bradshaw, & Lewis-Palmer, 2008).
>
> Although elements of PBIS suggest a positive impact for students in both general and special education, the federal government has mandated that those students with individualized educational programs (IEPs) receive a functional assessment of behavior. Problematic behaviors of students tend to be progressive throughout schooling and given the significance of discipline problems and aggression in schools, the federal government has mandated that student IEPs should include a functional behavioral assessment (FBA) with a proactive positive behavioral intervention plan (BIP; Individuals With Disabilities Education Act, 2004).

control another individual's behavior. However, we as teachers can attempt to *manage* student behaviors.

When a teacher is struggling with a particular student behavior or an emotional concern, she should look critically at the behavior a student displays —assess the pattern of the situation and determine the function of the behavior, collect objective data, and consider replacement behaviors. Practical and reputable solutions have been developed by the Center on Positive Behavioral Interventions and Supports. Positive behavioral interventions and supports (PBIS) feature evidence-based interventions and supports across varying levels of intensity and settings (e.g., districtwide, statewide, schoolwide, classroomwide, and individually) to prevent the development and intensification of problem behaviors and subsequently maximize academic success for all students (National Technical Assistance Center on Positive Behavior Interventions and Supports, 2008). For students with EBD or students with characteristics similar to those of a child with EBD, the behavioral management systems may need to be individualized. See boxes, "What Are Positive Behavioral Interventions and Supports (PBIS)?" and "What Is a Functional Behavioral Assessment (FBA) and What Is a Behavioral Intervention Plan (BIP)?"

Thoughtful reflection and productive collaborations with individuals in the school building (e.g., counselors, behavioral specialists, special educa-

> **What Is a Functional Behavioral Assessment (FBA) and What Is a Behavioral Intervention Plan (BIP)?**
>
> An FBA is a process in which a team of individuals (a) identifies a problematic behavior to target and (b) observes the environmental events that precede and follow the behavior in order to develop a hypothesis statement as to why the problematic behavior is occurring (Scott, Anderson, & Spaulding, 2008). An example of a hypothesis statement may resemble the following cloze example from Scott et al.: "In [description of a specific routine], when [antecedent] occurs, the student will [explicit behavior observed]. When this happens, [consequences] occurs. Thus, the function of the behavior is [specific function of behavior is described]."
>
> When an effective hypothesis is formed, the team may then act on the design and execution of a BIP, sometimes referred to as a behavioral support plan. The design of the BIP, very much contingent on the effectiveness of the FBA, is fluid in its development, with the ultimate goal being to teach an alternative skill or replacement behavior to the targeted problem behavior (Maag & Katsiyannis, 2006). Maag and Katsiyannis emphasize that the BIP include a summary of the findings from the generated hypothesis, a clear description of the operationalized behavior (include the type of data used to evaluate the behavior), a summary of all modifications to the plan, instructional strategies, positive and differential consequences, and future replacement behaviors.

tors) allow teachers to become engaged in this diagnostic process rather than reluctant to work with a particular child and/or resistant to the possibility of change.

Another response would be to start reflecting within—closely examine the established mindsets and perceptions one may have about a child who appears unmotivated with a low self-concept, a negative attitude, or a reluctance to participate. The teacher's preconceptions and ego should be removed from the equation—the child's reaction is not necessarily about the teacher. Children with EBD often display their hurt outwardly to others without discretion as to the recipient of their anxiety or aggression. Focusing on our own reaction is manageable and productive in effecting change in others. The psychoeducator Nicholas Long embraces the notion of adjusting teacher behavior with the Conflict Cycle paradigm. (The conflict cycle is a component of one theoretical model to explain challenging behaviors. Multiple approaches should be considered when working with students with EBD).

The Conflict Cycle model (Figure 1) asserts that students with EBD tend to come to the school environment with irrational beliefs—beliefs that are grounded in their personal experiences and poor self-concept (Long & Morse, 1996). These beliefs persist, causing the stress to affect their thoughts and feelings. Their irrational thoughts foster their feelings, yet the teacher tends to enter their world only when the child's thoughts and feelings enfold into an exhibited behavior. Students with EBD are characterized by internalizing (e.g., anxiety, fear, depression, social withdrawal) and externalizing

Figure 1. Conflict Cycle

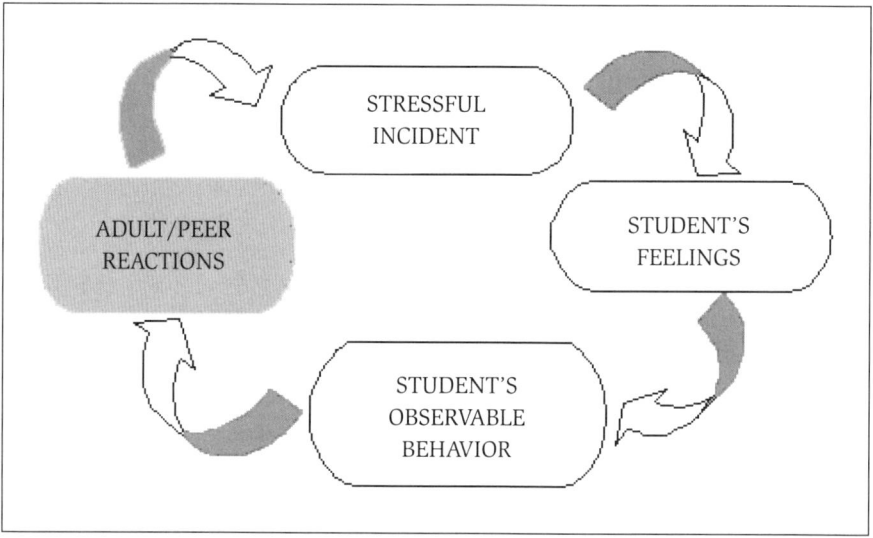

behaviors (e.g., aggression, overactivity, noncompliance, and delinquency; Coleman & Webber, 2002). During the child's time of crisis, teachers have the ability to feed into the student's irrational beliefs (e.g., ALL teachers are against me) or choose to manage their behaviors and proceed in a different direction. With the goal of maintaining a positive learning environment, a teacher can alter her response to a student with EBD and choose to not perpetuate the cycle of irrational beliefs of the child. Depending on the individual situation, such responses may include providing clear choices for the child, planned ignoring, providing the child with a direction and then moving away, and/or reminding the child of his goals. Our responses are most effective when there is an established relationship with a child and when we free ourselves from our own ego. Looking beyond the child's veil of surface behaviors, we may proceed with an empathic way of thinking.

GUIDING CONSIDERATION 2: RELATIONSHIPS

A frequent adult reaction to conflict in classrooms is to redirect a child and to deliver expectations. Choosing words with care is essential because one comment can create or destroy a positive student relationship. A student's self-control, social competence, and even academic performance can often indicate the depth of the interpersonal relationship between the child and the teacher(s) in the school (Murray & Greenberg, 2006). Students with EBD are characterized by their inability to develop and maintain positive interpersonal relationships with others. Peers may reject them, and their reputations may precede them from one grade to the next. No one can argue that positive energy can empower others. For example, increasing the rate of a teacher's behavior-specific praise to a child with EBD can increase the on-task behavior of that child (Sutherland, Wehby, & Copeland, 2001).

The teacher of a child with EBD has the task of building trust with that student. Trust can be fostered by the teacher's sincerely demonstrating that she/he values the child, provides for their needs, and sets them up for success. The child should know that despite all misgivings on a particular day, the next day is anew and the routine and the trust will persist.

Students with EBD have a low self-concept, and despite attempts of teachers to overflow their insatiable buckets with positive reinforcement, they often continue to seek more. This need can be exhausting for teachers considering class size and schedules—and the reality that one individual cannot be a solid figure for every student. Just like teachers, children are only human; relating to just one adult may be all they are able to do initially. Consider finding at least one other adult who can connect with that student— someone who will provide his time, energy, and care.

Teachers and facilitators of the classroom environment should also arrange opportunities for students with EBD to develop positive relationships with their peers. Identifying these students' strengths can give them unique roles in the classroom so that they are perceived positively by others in their community of learners. Every arrangement made should be carefully thought out with the intent of optimal success. If a child has difficulty understanding integers, teach them. If a child has difficulty with spelling, provide him with tools to support this area. If a child has difficulty with social skills, teach them social skills, model them, and provide opportunities for the child to generalize these skills. Educating is about making connections and teaching others how to do so.

GUIDING CONSIDERATION 3: ROLES

The roles of the teacher and the student in a classroom need clarity. From one lesson to the next, the roles vary; For example, a cooperative group exercise establishes very different roles for the teacher and the students in comparison with a direct instruction lesson. Likewise, roles vary during an interactive writing lesson versus an independent writing exercise. An accurate assessment of a student's ability is necessary when establishing the roles of both teacher and student. Often, students with EBD are reluctant to perform independently of the teacher. This reluctance is a reflection of limited academic achievement across all areas of instruction and again, a reflection of such students' irrational beliefs—for example, "I will not succeed at this math test because I am horrible at math." Accurate assessment of a student's ability enables a teacher to plan for and design the optimal role for him that can contribute to a positive experience.

In addition, clarity of expectations for everyone's role supports the success of student learning. Cooperative learning methods (i.e., peer tutoring,

Figure 2. A Visual Self-Monitoring Checklist for a Lesson's Agenda

(Check off items as they occur.)

Objective: To measure and draw right, acute, and obtuse triangles using the appropriate tools.

1) Find an angle in 2 minutes and TAG IT! ❑
2) Motivate: Geo Riddle mania ❑
3) Group Roles – Share Job Tasks ❑
4) SMART BOARD class review ❑
5) Group TRY It! ❑
6) Respond in Math Journals ❑
7) Wrap-up ❑

peer-assisted learning strategies) of instruction have been conducive to positive social and academic outcomes for participants with disabilities, as in this role, they overcome many obstacles to learning when provided structured student roles and an opportunity to learn with others (Ginsburg-Block, Rohrbeck, & Fantuzzo, 2006). When using cooperative learning methods, teachers should support students with EBD by verbally rehearsing the routines of all individuals involved. Posting a visual reminder of the sequenced tasks to be followed supports students' clear understanding of the expectations. All students can use such a posted listing not only for self-regulation but for assisting peers as well.

Communicated expectations, both verbalized and displayed visually, support students with EBD. A teacher can support all students when she provides a visual schedule for each school day, refers to it, and uses it to share what is expected in the environment. Task-analyzing this support system means to also provide an agenda for each lesson within that school day (Figure 2). Students with EBD may need even further supports by hearing the expectations of each activity within an individual lesson. Frequent reminders and a system of referring back to these posted and verbalized expectations can act as anchors for classroom teachers to minimize behavioral disruptions that can lead instruction and focus astray. Communicated expectations limit surprises and reinforce everyone's learning.

Academic and behavioral self-regulatory techniques are specific tools used to support and empower students who respond to structure and routine. These techniques include self-monitoring checklists with a written guide that cues the student to complete sequenced steps of a specific task (Reid, Trout, & Schartz, 2005). Students can take a role in planning for their day, recording the events of the day, and even making self-evaluations of their performance. Frequent and consistent feedback encourages desired behaviors and empowers students as they gain skills of independence.

GUIDING CONSIDERATION 4: RESOURCES

Just as food selection is a crucial component of a party's success, the resources teachers use can be a crucial component of a harmonious classroom setting—of rich learning. Selected resources can enhance or alter student learning. A "resource" is a broad term that certainly varies from one county to the next and sometimes from one school to the next. However, one consistency is that any student identified with EBD will have an IEP, and this documentation is the first step when identifying resources for the student to be successful in the classroom. The modifications and accommodations provided on the student's IEP support his access to the general curriculum. Such modifications may include adapting the length or type of paper-pencil tasks, using assistive technology, and/or permitting intermittent breaks while a student is working on a particular task.

The IEP will also indicate other individuals who will be working with this student—individuals who are rich resources for the teacher to use to best meet the needs of the student. For example, the student may be receiving services from a school counselor or services from a speech and language therapist. Although consultation and collaboration among personnel within special education is routine, the notion can be somewhat challenging to translate into practice. Often, individuals may be underutilized. Any individual who interacts with a student is a resource. When defeat feels just around the corner and the teacher has tried everything to engage the child, communicating with a parent, a counselor, another teacher, or the art/music/physical education teacher may bring new insight into the situation.

Resources commonly used by teachers include consumable materials, basal readers, textbooks, and/or programmatic materials (e.g., SRA/Corrective Reading, Englemann et al., 1999; Read Naturally®, 2001; Step Up to Writing®, 2007). Many research-based commercialized programs are adopted by the county, so teachers may or may not have options about using all or components of the specified program. However, teachers generally have autonomy when selecting methods of instruction. Varying the methods of instruction and employing differentiated curriculum enhancements (i.e., mnemonics, text-structure analysis, peer tutoring, ample practice; Scruggs & Mastropieri, 2007) can ensure that the teacher is meeting the needs of diverse learners in the classroom. Creative materials that support the vast methods of instruction are one way to accommodate student preference for perceptual input. The four modalities of perceptual input include visual, auditory, and the often underutilized kinesthetic and tactile modalities. Children with EBD are often resistant to paper-pencil tasks and respond favorably to hands-on activities that involve active participation and experiential learning. Integrating a variety of methods tends to foster the internalization of new material for students with disabilities in contrast with more traditional modes of instruction (e.g., science content, Scruggs & Mastropieri; social studies content, Spencer, Scruggs, & Mastropieri, 2003).

A third resource to consider is yourself! Self-evaluation is often used to promote teacher introspection and to identify the crucial aspects of teaching. Teacher behavior, such as asking high-quality questions and providing positive praise, affects student behavior and can result in increased on-task behavior and lower levels of inappropriate behavior (Good & Brophy, 1994; Kauchak & Eggen, 2007; Sutherland & Wehby, 2001). Self-evaluation seems pertinent if we have the student's interest in mind. For example, teachers can record frequency data on the occurrences of positive reinforcement in the classroom, occurrences of opportunities to respond, and additional teacher behaviors that may encourage or suppress productive learning environments. Feedback is central to the process of learning any skill, and because teaching is often conducted in isolation, teachers may need to generate this feedback in creative ways.

Just as we would consider how to collect data regarding the function of a student's behavior, the same tools can be used for self-evaluation. For example, teachers may audiorecord 20 to 30 minutes of a classroom session, videotape a 50-minute lesson, and/or ask another teacher to observe her classroom. An audiorecording could monitor the use of language—perhaps the teacher's most powerful tool in the classroom (e.g., How often am I praising Jamal? Do I ask Mary multiple questions back to back? Do I frequently elicit student responses?).

Whether you are the host of a party or the lead teacher of a lesson, the desired outcome should be a positive experience for everyone. When teachers consider reflection, relationships, roles, and resources, not only are students with EBD supported, but all students are given the opportunity for high achievement. All participants enjoy the party.

REFERENCES

Barrett, S. B., Bradshaw, C. P., & Lewis-Palmer, T. (2008). Maryland state-wide PBIS initiative systems, evaluations, and next steps. *Journal of Positive Behavior Interventions, 10,* 105–114.

Billingsley, B. (2004). Special education teacher retention and attrition: Critical analysis of the research literature. *Journal of Special Education, 38,* 39–55.

Coleman, M. C., & Webber, J. (2002). *Emotional and behavioral disorders: Theory and practice* (4th ed.). Boston: Allyn & Bacon.

Englemann, S., Becker, W., Carnine, L., Eisele, J., Haddox, P., Hanner, S., Johnson, G., Meyer, L., Osborn, J., & Osborn, S. (1999). *Corrective Reading Series.* Columbus, OH: McGraw-Hill.

Ginsburg-Block, M. D., Rohrbeck, C. A., & Fantuzzo, J. W. (2006). A meta-analytic review of social, self-concept, and behavioral outcomes of peer-assisted learning. *Journal of Educational Psychology, 98*(4), 732–749.

Good, T. L., & Brophy, J. E. (1994). *Looking in classrooms* (6th ed.). New York: Harper Collins.

Individuals With Disabilities Education Act of 2004, 20 U.S.C. 1401-82 (2004).

Kauchak, D. P., & Eggen, P. D. (2007). *Learning and teaching: Research based methods* (5th ed.). Boston: Pearson.

Long, N. J., & Morse, W. C. (1996). *Conflict in the classroom.* (5th ed.) Austin, TX: Pro-Ed.

Maag, J. W., & Katsiyannis, A. (2006). Behavioral intervention plans: Legal and practical considerations for students with emotional and behavioral disorders. *Behavioral Disorders, 31,* 348–363.

Murray, C., & Greenberg, M. T. (2006). Examining the importance of social relationships and social contexts in the lives of children with high-incidence disabilities. *Journal of Special Education, 39*(4), 220–233.

National Technical Assistance Center on Positive Behavior Interventions and Supports. (2007). Retrieved June 1, 2008, from www.PBIS.org/main.htm

Read Naturally® Repeated Reading Program. (2001). St. Paul, MN: Read Naturally, Inc.

Reid, R., Trout, A. L., & Schartz, M. (2005). Self-regulation interventions for children with attention-deficit hyperactivity disorder. *Exceptional Children, 71,* 361–378.

Richardson, B. G., & Shupe, M. J. (2003). The importance of teacher self-awareness in working with students with emotional and behavioral disorders. *TEACHING Exceptional Children, 36,* 8–13.

Scott, T. M., Anderson, C. M., & Spaulding, S. A. (2008). Strategies for developing and carrying out functional assessment and behavior intervention planning. *Preventing School Failure, 52,* 39–49.

Scruggs, T. E., & Mastropieri, M. (2007). Science learning in special education: A case for constructed versus instructed learning. *Exceptionality, 15,* 57–74.

Spencer, V., Scruggs, T. E., & Mastropieri, M. A. (2003). Content area learning in middle school social studies classrooms and students with emotional and behavioral disorders: A comparison of strategies. *Behavioral Disorders, 28,* 77–93.

Step Up to Writing®. (2007). Longmont, CO: Sopris West Educational Services.

Sugai, G., & Horner, R. H. (2002). Introduction to the special series on positive behavior support in schools. *Journal of Emotional and Behavioral Disorders, 10,* 130–135.

Sugai, G., & Horner, R. H. (2006). A promising approach for expanding and sustaining school-wide positive behavior support. *School Psychology Review, 35,* 245–259.

Sutherland, K. S., & Wehby, J. H. (2001). The effect of self-evaluation on teaching behavior in classrooms for students with emotional and behavioral disorders. *Journal of Special Education, 35,* 161–171.

Sutherland, K. S., Wehby, J. H., & Copeland, S. R. (2001). Exploring the relationship between increased opportunities to respond to academic requests and the academic and behavioral outcomes of students with emotional and behavioral disorders. *Journal of Emotional and Behavioral Disorders, 22*(2), 113–121.

Originally published in *TEACHING Exceptional Children,* Vol. 41, No. 5, pp. 60–65.

3

Creating Home–School Partnerships by Engaging Families in Schoolwide Positive Behavior Supports

Howard S. Muscott, Stacy Szczesiul, Becky Berk, Kathy Staub, Jane Hoover, and Paula Perry-Chisholm

Schoolwide positive behavior supports (SWPBS) is a culturally responsive set of systems, practices, and data-based decision-making features designed to achieve socially important behavior change. One important feature of SWPBS is the evidence-based practice of engaging families as partners in schooling. Statewide initiatives, early childhood education programs, and K–12 schools engaged in SWPBS can establish and use home–school partnerships as leverage for school improvement. How can schools foster family engagement in developing, implementing, and sustaining SWPBS? What are the challenges associated with such engagement? What barriers do schools face? What effective state- and school-level strategies enhance family engagement and home–school partnerships?

Our nation's schools are faced with complex and deep-rooted challenges such as poverty, discrimination, weak school–family relationships, low student motivation, and high student mobility. These challenges must be overcome if children and youth are to meet their needs for belonging, mastery, independence, and generosity (Brendtro, Brokenleg, & Van Bockern, 1990); experience social competence and academic achievement in school; and ultimately enjoy a high quality of life. To support families, schools must utilize evidence-based approaches to teaching and learning. Moreover, these approaches must be embedded in efficient systems that allow practitioners to implement them with fidelity and cross the research-to-practice divide, which historically serves as a deterrent to school reform efforts.

One promising approach to school reform that is gaining significant traction across the country is schoolwide positive behavior supports (SWPBS), a culturally responsive set of evidence-based interventions designed to achieve socially important behavior change and improve academic achievement (U.S. Department of Education, 2000). SWPBS involves creating a set of universal behavior support features for proactively and systematically (a) identifying, teaching, and reinforcing valued social behaviors and (b) identifying and responding effectively to challenging behaviors that undermine teaching, learning, and social relationships (Sugai & Horner, 1999). Using systems to support adults, practices to support students, and data for decision making, SWPBS arguably has grown in popularity like no other school reform effort in educational history (Sugai & Horner, 2006). Research and program evaluations have shown that schools implementing SWPBS with fidelity experience improvements in school climate; reductions in problem behaviors that would have led to office referrals, suspensions, and expulsions; increased opportunities for academic-engaged time; and gains in student achievement (Bradshaw, 2006; Horner, Sugai, Eber, Phillips, & Lewandowski, 2003; Muscott, Mann, & LeBrun, in press).

BARRIERS TO FAMILY ENGAGEMENT AND HOME–SCHOOL PARTNERSHIPS

In *Playing Their Parts* (Public Agenda, 1999), a national survey of parents and public school teachers revealed that most parents considered their children's teachers as accessible and caring, and teachers were more likely to be complimented than criticized. However, when it came to engagement in decision making, Public Agenda found most parents uncomfortable in leadership roles and most teachers uncomfortable having parents in those roles. In fact, despite federal policy (the No Child Left Behind Act of 2001, NCLB; Individuals With Disability Education Improvement Act of 2004, IDEA) that clearly mandates family and community engagement, most teachers and administrators "still think of themselves as individual leaders of classrooms, schools, or districts with little attention to the importance of teamwork and collaboration with parents and community partners" (Epstein & Sanders, 2006, p. 82). As noted by the National Association of State Mental Health Program Directors and the National Association of State Directors of Special Education, "Successful interagency partnerships make every effort to include family members in the decisions and actions that affect their own children. Parents and family members are the experts on their own children, and insofar as possible, they must be allowed, encouraged and supported to participate actively in every aspect of decision making regarding their families' children" (2002, p. 25).

Major barriers include (a) one-side power relationships between schools and families (Nogera, 1999); (b) inadequate teacher preparation regarding establishing and sustaining relationships with parents (Epstein & Sanders,

2006); (c) limited time and material resources for engaging parents; and (d) pressure from underresourced national and state accountability measures. Finally, teachers' and administrators' attitudes about parent engagement are often shaped by the cultural filter of White, middle-class values, assumptions, and experiences and do not align with those of some families and the neighborhood (Henderson, Johnson, Mapp, & Davies, 2006). When these barriers cannot be addressed satisfactorily, regression to blaming and scapegoating is common, and the likelihood of disengagement increases significantly.

Families that are challenged by poverty, single parenthood, language and literacy barriers, and cultural differences are no longer likely to be dismissed outright by school personnel as dysfunctional (Leistyna, 2002). However, unless schools make concerted efforts, family engagement is more likely to occur with some families—those from more educated, more economically stable backgrounds—than with others—those from less educated, working class backgrounds (Sheldon, 2003). The result of such circumstances is predictable: parents who understand the system act on a sense of entitlement and make requests for scarce resources. In turn, teachers and administrators satisfy the active parents' requests to diminish the potential for confrontation, leaving the students of less savvy and empowered parents with fewer advantages.

Schools that answer the call to purposefully reenvision the role of parents in creating better learning environments for children strive to empower *all* parents—regardless of their educational or socioeconomic backgrounds—to be active partners in their children's school experience. Such schools productively channel the advocacy efforts of typically active parents and effectively mitigate feelings of marginalization, inferiority, or uncertainty in parents who have traditionally felt less empowered. In both cases, parents are recognized as important members of the school community, increasing the likelihood of improvements in academic achievement and social competence for all children.

MOVING TOWARD A PARTNERSHIP MODEL

Expanding the definition of "family engagement" is the first step for schools in creating more inclusive, productive places of learning for students and adults. Engagement is predicated on building trusting relationships with family members; that is to say, relationships in which teachers and parents respect one another, believe in each other's ability and willingness to fulfill their responsibilities, have high personal regard for one another, and trust each other to put children's interests first (Bryk & Schneider, 2005; Henderson et al., 2006). Relationship building is enhanced when schools use family-centered practices that respect the uniqueness and personal circumstances of *all* families (Keenan, 2004), including those who have children with disabilities (Muscott, 2002), and provide opportunities for leadership (Epstein, 2002).

Epstein (2002) provides an expansive framework through which educators must think deeply about how they support and facilitate parenting, learning at home, communicating, volunteering, participating in decision making, and collaborating with community. Schools on the path to meaningful inclusion of families recognize parents (and grandparents or guardians) as being engaged in their children's educational experiences when they provide for their child's basic physical and psychological needs, promote the child's learning at home, volunteer in the classroom, advocate on behalf of the child with teachers and administrators, participate on decision-making committees, become active in community organizations that promote the work of schools and the welfare of all children, or some combination thereof (see box, "Additional Resources").

Many New Hampshire schools involved in SWPBS, via the Positive Behavioral Interventions and Supports-NH (PBIS-NH) initiative, have begun using Epstein's (2002) framework to shift how teachers and families think about partnerships related to students' academic and social-emotional growth (see box, "What Does the Literature Say about SWPBS?"). They do not assume that families who have traditionally been considered disengaged are making a conscious choice not to get involved in their child's school experience. Rather, schools are recognizing that a range of challenges may prohibit well-intentioned families from effective engagement. As a result, they are embedding proactive and responsive systems and practices that address a wide range of needs and challenges.

RESPONSIVENESS TO FAMILY ENGAGEMENT

Educators in PBIS-NH schools think about parent engagement in terms of Epstein's (2002) framework and a multi-tiered approach that addresses responsiveness to family engagement through three tiers of support: universal, targeted, and intensive. Once schools identify the range of behaviors and actions that constitute engagement, the next logical step is determining what families need to know or access to "engage." Thus, teachers and administrators implicitly recognize their responsibility to meet families at their own level with regard to engaging in their child's education experience. Schools that perform a focused assessment of parents' needs understand what strategies or supports will be necessary to (a) sharpen a wide range of parents' basic skills, (b) establish consistent systems of two-way communication, (c) create a spectrum of volunteering opportunities, (d) teach families how to support students' academic progress by exposing them to new academic and behavior content and skills, (e) expand the influence of families by sharing power in decisions about teaching and learning at their schools, and (f) tap into the resources and strengths available in the community.

Being responsive to all families requires that educators understand the range of readiness for engagement that exists and be able to match strategies to each family's place on the continuum. Although engagement needs for

Additional Resources

Alliance for School Mental Health. (2006). *PBIS school-family-community-partnership toolkit*. Long Island, NY: Author. Available from the Office of PBIS, District 75, NYC Public Schools, 400 First Avenue, New York, NY 10010.

Beach Center on Disability. (2007). *Family research instruments and toolkits*. Available at http://www.beachcenter.org/families/family_research_toolkit.aspx

Bouffard, S. M., & Stephen, N. (2007). Promoting family involvement in middle and high schools. *Principal's Research Review, 2*(6), Reston, VA: NASSP. Available at http://www.gse.harvard.edu/hfrp/projects/fine/resources/research/nassp.html

Caspe, M., & Lopez, M. E. (2006). *Lessons from family-strengthening interventions: Learning from evidence-based practice*. Cambridge, MA: Harvard Family Research Project. Available at http://www.gse.harvard.edu/hfrp/projects/fine/resources/research/lessons.html

Kentucky Commissioner of Education's Parents Advisory Council. (2007). *The missing piece of the proficiency puzzle: Recommendations and a rubric for involving families and community in improving student achievement*. Lexington, KY: Department of Education.

National Center on School, Family and Community Partnerships at Johns Hopkins University: http://www.csos.jhu.edu/P2000/center.htm

National Parental Information Resource Center Coordination Center: http://www.nationalpirc.org/

Public Education Network (2004). *School–parent compact: Action guide for parent and community leaders*. Washington, DC: Author.

PBIS-NH School Contacts

For more information about how schools implemented the programs described in this article, contact:

Dublin Consolidated School
Main St., Box 1006
Dublin, NH 03444-1006
May Clark, Principal
(603) 563-8332
mclark@conval.edu

East Derry Memorial School
18 Dubeau Drive
Derry, NH 03038-4807
Sue Devine, Third Grade Teacher
(603) 432-1260
sdevine@derry.k12.nh.us

Hillside Middle School
112 Reservoir Avenue
Manchester, NH 03104
Stephen Donohue, Principal
(603) 624-6352
sdonohue@mansd.org

Lakes Region Community Child Services Center
22 Strafford Street, Unit 4
Laconia, NH 03246
Marti Ilg, Program Coordinator
(603) 524-1235
martiilg@hotmail.com

Mastricola Lower Elementary School
7 School Street, Merrimack, NH 03054
John Fabrizio, Principal
(603) 424-6218
john.fabrizio@merrimack.k12.nh.us

Southern New Hampshire Head Start
P.O. Box 5040, 40 Pine Street
Manchester, NH 03108-5040
Pam Lane, Family Services Manager
(603) 668-8010
plane@snhs.org

> **What Does the Literature Say About SWPBS?**
>
> SWPBS particularly emphasizes the relationship between school and home, making educators and family members prominent agents in transforming students' educational experiences. Not surprisingly, SWPBS draws on a robust research literature to validate its emphasis on home–school partnerships. The literature suggests that such partnerships improve attendance, homework completion, and student achievement (Christenson & Sheridan 2001; Henderson, Johnson, Mapp, & Davies, 2006), particularly in urban areas (Nogera, 1999), and independent of family background (Keith et al., 1993). Family engagement has also been shown to decrease school violence (Boulter, 2004), improve graduation rates, and increase the likelihood that early adolescents will enroll in higher education (Deslandes & Bertrand, 2005).

most will be satisfied by universal strategies, some families will need more targeted forms of support. For example, most families might only need basic information regarding how they might engage in their child's education effectively. For many of these parents, information provided through traditional communication systems (e.g., newsletters, open houses, resource lists, and parent conferences) will suffice. However, for some families, a second tier of targeted supports may be required to support effective engagement in their child's education. These families may need information in their native language, provided by a translator, or personal contact by a school staff member with whom there is mutual trust and respect, rather than a mass e-mail or newsletter. Positive relationships hold the key to success.

At the intensive tier, a small number of families may be disengaged from their child's school because of, for example, their own failed school experiences, an ineffective relationship with their child, personal challenges, or previously compromised relationships. Unpleasant relationships or experiences promote escape and avoidance behaviors, which make school and family engagement difficult. In these cases, teachers and administrators must adopt a highly individualized and respectful approach that requires, at its core, an understanding of families' unique needs, fluency with specialized interaction and relationship-building skills, and knowledge and access to targeted resources and supports. These families may not feel they have the power or capacity to effect change for their children and see disconnecting from the school as the only viable option. Schools that operate with an approach that is expanded, proactive, and organized along a continuum of intensifying parent support and engagement, however, are more likely to experience mutually beneficial outcomes associated with family–school partnerships (Keenan, 2004). For example, schools involved in the Mental Health and Schools Together: New Hampshire initiative (e.g., Peterborough Elementary and Littleton High School; see www.nhcebis.seresc.net/family_engagement_article2008) have linked with local community mental health centers and developed a facilitated referral process to help families access appropriate and culturally responsive mental health supports in a timely fashion.

Before getting involved with the PBIS program, I found myself yelling, fighting and having no patience with my two daughters, Natalie, age 4, and Nicole, age 2. As a result of our involvement with the Black Bear Tracks program, my husband and I now work better with the girls. The girls now pick up their own toys, put their own dirty clothes away and we can sit down at the dinner table without them getting out of their chairs. One big improvement is that I am not always yelling and losing my patience and we have more bonding times together.

—Dawn Johnson
Parent, Lakes Region Child Care Center

PBIS-NH AND FAMILY ENGAGEMENT

Since the inception of the PBIS-NH systems change initiative in the fall of 2002, SWPBS has been systematically introduced and comprehensively supported in 141 public and private preschools and K–12 schools; the PBIS-NH initiative reaches more than 40,000 New Hampshire children, 98% of whom attend public schools. To date, PBIS initiatives are actively underway in 17% of New Hampshire's public schools, reaching 16% of public school students in the state; and teachers, administrators, and families in these schools are experiencing a number of important educational outcomes. For example, program evaluations reveal that PBIS-NH early childhood education (ECE) programs and schools experience decreases in problem behaviors resulting in less office discipline referrals and suspensions and increases in time for teaching, learning, and leadership activities, which result in improvements in academic achievement (Muscott et al., in press; Muscott et al., 2004; New Hampshire Center for Effective Behavioral Intervention and Supports, 2008). In school year 2006 to 2007, ECE and K–12 schools in multiple cohorts had 1,088 (7.2%) fewer office discipline referrals and 260 (16%) fewer suspensions than the previous school year. Of 27 elementary, middle, and multilevel schools analyzed over a 2-year timeframe, 24 (89%) showed improvement in mean reading scores and 11 (41%) showed improvement in mean math scores on the New Hampshire state test. More important, 16 (59%) made gains in reading proficiency levels and 14 (52%) made gains in math proficiency levels.

PBIS-NH State-Level Practices for Family Engagement

By articulating concrete values, identifying evidence-based practices, establishing transparent linkages with area organizations, and outlining the specific criteria and expectations for school-based teams, PBIS-NH lays the groundwork for families and educators to develop relationships and cultivate productive partnerships. These exceptional partnerships, in turn, serve to bolster the mission of PBIS-NH to support the social-emotional well-being and achievement of all New Hampshire's students. We began our efforts by creating linkages with statewide family and youth leadership organizations (e.g., National Alliance on Mental Illness-NH, Granite State Federation of Families, Parent Information Center, Alliance for Community Supports, Main Street Academix) that resulted in state-level policy, shared trainings and presentations, and joint grant proposals.

These state-level partnerships produced consensus on a definition of a family-friendly school as a place where all families (a) feel welcomed, valued, and respected; (b) have opportunities for their opinions to be heard and their input known and acted upon; (c) have varied and authentic opportunities to be involved in activities of decision-making; and (d) feel satisfied with these elements (New Hampshire Family Engagement Work Group, 2004).

To operationalize these values, the Family Engagement Work Group identified the features of a family-friendly school as a place where families (a) are informed of school activities in a variety of ways, (b) have access to information about how they can support their child's learning, (c) have access to information about how they can be involved in supporting learning in school through volunteering and assisting, and (d) know what resources are available and how to access those resources. As a second outcome, the group articulated a skill set for family members who serve on the universal leadership team (see www.nhcebis.seresc.net/family_engagement_article2008). The group also ratified the policy of the New Hampshire Center for Effective Behavioral Interventions and Supports that all ECE programs and schools be required to have at least one family member on their universal leadership team. Finally, the group agreed with the recommendation that schools regularly assess responsiveness to family engagement using the Family Engagement Checklist (Mann & Muscott, 2004) and develop an action plan to address any areas not fully implemented.

PBIS-NH School-Level Family Engagement Practices

Engaging Families Through Parenting and Learning at Home. Many New Hampshire ECEs and K–12 schools have developed engagement activities related to parenting and learning at home that are delivered at open houses or in more formal workshops. One type of activity involves helping parents become fluent in using PBIS strategies to create a home climate that is conducive to studying, completing projects, and doing homework. Another typical activity involves helping families design a behavioral matrix based on home routines that is consistent with the expectations used in the SWPBS system. For example, the Southern New Hampshire Head Start in Nashua was the first ECE in the PBIS-NH initiative to support parents with basic parenting skills using an adapted home matrix based on their Heads Up program (Be Safe, Be Kind, and Take Care of Our Things). Family workers visited families to help them create positively stated, observable behaviors for home routines such as bedtime, mealtime, and peer play.

To enhance connections between school and home, the Lakes Region Child Care Services Center surveyed parents to assess interest and barriers, and partnered with another local agency, UpStream, to offer a five-part parenting series. Educators and family members involved in creating and delivering the "Parenting Series" considered the universal needs of the families by conducting surveys; providing training, materials, practice, and feedback in natural settings; including parents in decision making and leadership; and emphasizing positive behavioral expectations (Be Safe, Be Kind, and Take Care). Results included high and consistent attendance, high graduation rates from the training series, continued participation after the training concluded, reports of improved family functioning, and creation of a community of leaders and learners. One father, for example, noted that the bedtime routine had become much more peaceful since they implemented the ideas: "We don't have to fight with him at bedtime anymore, we just look at the matrix and know what to do."

 My children love this school—the school has been a phenomenal support for me and my kids. I can communicate with the school staff about anything. When you have the support you need, you succeed.

—Parent of a student
at South Meadow Middle School, Peterborough

Engaging Families Through Two-Way Home–School Communication. Historically, schools have used unilateral forms of communication with families by disseminating pertinent information through irregular administrative letters, parent handbooks, newsletters, report cards, or infrequent phone calls. According to Epstein (2002), a defining element of school–home partnerships is establishing effective *two-way* communication systems. Through the reciprocal exchange of information, families are better equipped to engage in school programs and understand their children's progress—and schools become more aware of parental strengths and concerns.

Schools such as Mastricola Lower Elementary, Hillside Middle, and Dublin Consolidated Elementary (see box, "Additional Resources"), which we spotlight in this article, recognize the role that communication plays in creating partnerships with families. They created a number of universal communication systems, such as monthly newsletters with a write-in parent advice section, initial SWPBS activities to introduce the program to parents, periodic open houses with aligned activities, an interactive Web site, and a parent liaison who solicits information from families and brings questions and suggestions to school meetings.

Mastricola's monthly school newsletter features a SWPBS column to inform and engage parents, listing the upcoming "Behavior Skill of the Week" and offering suggestions for fostering common approaches in "The Big 3" (safety, respect, and responsibility; see www.nhcebis.seresc.net/document/filename/369/Mastricola_ES_Nov_newsletter_revised_highlighted.pdf). Every 6 weeks, members of Hillside Middle School's parent–teacher organization (PTO) edit and print their *Beak Speaks* parent newsletter (see www.nhcebis.seresc.net/document/filename/365/Beak_Speaks_pages_combined.pdf). During the first year of the SWPBS initiative, the newsletter included articles about the adoption of the program and an explanation of what it would mean to students. Additional articles clarified the dress code, changes to the tardiness policy, details of the Hillside High-Five acknowledgment program, and data summaries.

The use of interactive rollout activities to introduce the SWPBS program to students and families and open houses to create ongoing, two-way dialogue about the program are typical in PBIS-NH ECE centers and K–12 schools. Dublin Consolidated School, a small, rural elementary school, used a consistent schedule of open houses to achieve two-way communication with families and creatively sustain the momentum for SWPBS implementation. During one such open house, *An Evening of ABCs,* families participated in four different activities that highlighted the important aspects of the program. According to Principal May Clark:

> Fifth graders wrote and performed skits showing families how students exhibit the ABCs in three locations: arrival/dismissal, lunch, and physical education classes. A Jeopardy! game that had been used in a school activity with students was used to inform and assess families' knowledge of the ABCs. The ABC song was performed by second graders and taught to families. Finally, students shared their responses to a writing prompt related to respect in four small groups so families had the opportunity to hear the work done by students of all ages. The open house was attended by more than 90 family members.

Viewed through Epstein's (2002) framework, this form of engagement provided an opportunity for two-way communication within the context of a fun, interactive hour of activities. Events were made relevant by (a) using discipline data to identify the specific routines needing additional behavior support (i.e., arrival/dismissal, lunch, and physical education classes); (b) maximizing opportunities for students to design and perform at open houses; (c) emphasizing activities that actively involved parents and students; and (d) showcasing student products (e.g., written essays, posters) that highlighted the integration of academics with behavior support and contributed to a positive school climate.

Periodic and brief surveys are also a good way to gauge whether families feel connected to the school and understand their child's experiences. Some families do not respond to paper surveys; schools might employ a second-tier attempt through a telephone poll. Volunteers with clipboards can also administer surveys at school events. Mastricola Elementary, for example, developed and distributed a survey to assess parent awareness of their "The Big 3" program. The leadership team used findings from the survey to develop articles for their newsletters. (See www.nhcebis.seresc.net/document/filename/366/Mastricola_ES_PBIS_Survey__05.pdf for surveys from Mastricola Elementary School.)

Family members who do not speak English, have limited reading skills, and/or lack educational resources at home may need additional supports and different communication mechanisms. Without adequate and accurate translators and translations, some children may misunderstand and/or miscommunicate school messages. Investments in computer-based translation systems, third-party liaisons, translated materials, automated phone messages, and so forth are worthwhile to bridge the language divide between educators and non-English-speaking families.

Engaging Families Through Volunteering and Shared Decision Making. Traditionally, parental involvement in schools has been unsystematic, voluntary, and limited (e.g., chaperoning field trips, participating in fundraisers, tutoring), and perceived by some educators as time-consuming and obligatory rather than helpful. Educators in PBIS-NH schools have moved family engagement toward Epstein's (2002) vision in which recruitment is systematic, opportunities for volunteering are available to all families, and family engagement is influential to student success.

When schools view parents as partners and engage them in decision-making processes that are mutually respectful, they realize higher levels of student achievement and greater public support. PBIS-NH schools are required to have at least one family member on the universal leadership team to attend trainings, participate in team meetings, bring the family perspective to decision making, support rollout activities, serve as a liaison to family organizations, and encourage other family members to become active.

For example, Mastricola and East Derry Memorial actively recruit family members to serve as equal partners on SWPBS teams that make decisions affecting teachers, administrators, students, and families. At Mastricola, Maureen Tracy, the parent member, has done more than serve as a liaison for the team, PTO, and parent volunteer program. She has set up information tables during parent conferences, coordinated a SWPBS section in the annual Merrimack Christmas parade in conjunction with the student council, and developed a SWPBS Parent Hotline to provide answers and information for families. Similarly, Leah Manchester, parent member on East Derry Memorial's universal leadership team, takes her role seriously.

> I was the outsider, the noneducator in the group, but I wanted to truly be part of the team. So, I try to attend all meetings and special events, and I offer to help in any way I can.

For the most part, my role as parent representative has been primarily as an information conduit, helping parents understand what SWPBS is and how [it] works. . . . At each PTA meeting, Vice Principal Lidia Desrochers and I provide an update of what behaviors the students are working on, their accomplishments, our celebrations and what to expect next. Our monthly PTA newsletter reaches a larger audience.

I am glad to part of the SWPBS team. We have made progress in helping families understand what we are trying to accomplish and how they can use and reinforce the [program] at school, at home and in the community. Parents have found that the tenets . . . are helpful in enhancing parenting skills and creating a positive environment at home. Our goal over the next 2 years is to improve two-way communication and involve more families and the community in evaluating and measuring the success of the program. It will be wonderful to see that opportunity expanded so that other parents and community members can participate. We believe that providing a wide range of family engagement practices will continue to be important as the [program] becomes even more a part of our culture in the next few years.

Although volunteers should not be involved in disciplining students, they can certainly receive training to participate in other aspects of the program, including teaching expectations and providing acknowledgment when students exhibit desired behaviors. However, family members, like staff, also should receive training on confidentiality, appropriate social interactions, handling conflicts, seeking assistance/advice, and so on. Mastricola Elementary's behavioral matrix supports the expectations that school volunteers exhibit safe, respectful, and responsible behaviors while in the school, further strengthening school climate and the idea that family members are role models for children even at school. The matrix is a part of the Volunteer Handbook and used during training (see www.nhcebis.seresc.net/family_engagement_article2008).

LOOKING AHEAD

Educators in PBIS-NH schools are working diligently to create safe, successful, and satisfying teaching and learning climates that support students' social competence and academic achievement. They purposefully work on establishing trusting relationships with families that form the basis for a wide range of engagement practices. No matter how well intentioned the effort, there are clear barriers to engagement between schools and families. Whether schools choose to acknowledge their role in mitigating the barriers will, no doubt, make a difference in the quality of a child's educational experience. Fortunately, empirical evidence suggests that educators and parents can overcome barriers that obstruct well-intentioned families from engaging in their children's educational experiences when schools choose to endorse and implement responsive, multi-tiered interventions and supports that address the wide range of engagement needs.

The family engagement strategies we describe give testament to the emerging power of reform efforts in New Hampshire using SWPBS to support adults, evidence-based practices to support students, and data-based decision making to assess effectiveness. The true test will be whether the effective family engagement practices being used in many PBIS-NH ECE programs and K–12 schools can be sustained with fidelity and ultimately expanded across the state. It is likely that increasing the engagement of families as authentic partners within the culture of SWPBS will significantly improve the probability that students experience increased social competence and academic achievement in school and ultimately enjoy a higher quality of life.

REFERENCES

Boulter, L. (2004). Family–school connection and school violence prevention. *The Negro Educational Review, 55*(1), 27–40.

Bradshaw, C. (2006, July). *Project Target: An evaluation of PBIS in Maryland*. Presentation at meeting of OSEP Project Directors, Baltimore, MD.

Brendtro, L. K., Brokenleg, M., & Van Bockern, S. (1990). *Reclaiming youth at risk: Our hope for the future*. Bloomington, IN: National Education Service.

Bryk, A., & Schneider, B. (2005). *Trust in schools: A core resource for improvement*. New York: Russell Sage Foundation.

Christenson, S. L., & Sheridan, S. M. (2001). *Schools and families: Creating essential connections for learning*. New York: Guilford Press.

Deslandes, R., & Bertrand, R. (2005). Motivation of parent involvement in secondary-level schooling. *The Journal of Educational Research, 98*, 164–175.

Epstein, J. L. (2002). *School, family and community partnerships: Your handbook for action*. Thousand Oaks, CA: Corwin Press.

Epstein, J. L., & Sanders, M. G. (2006). Prospects for change: Preparing educators for school, family, and community partnerships. *Peabody Journal of Education, 81*(2), 81–120.

Henderson, A., Johnson, V., Mapp, K., & Davies, D. (2006). *Beyond the bake sale: The essential guide to family/school partnerships*. New York: The New Press.

Horner, R. H., Sugai, G., Eber, L., Phillips, D., & Lewandowski, C. A. (2003). *Illinois positive behavioral interventions and supports project: 2002–2003 progress report*. Chicago: ISBE EBD/PBIS Network.

Keenan, S. (2004). *Family and professional partnerships within a system of care: Exploring the role of families in pre-service and in-service development and training*. Washington, DC: American Institutes for Research, Technical Assistance Partnership for Child and Family Mental Health.

Keith, T. Z., Keith, P. B., Troutman, G. C., Bickley, P. G., Trivette, P. S., & Singh, K. (1993). Does parental involvement affect eighth-grade students' achievement? Structural analysis of national data. *School Psychology Review, 22*, 474–496.

Leistyna, L. (2002). Extending the possibilities of multicultural community partnerships in urban public schools. *The Urban Review, 34*(1), 1–23.

Mann, E., & Muscott, H. S. (2004). *The family engagement checklist.* Bedford, NH: New Hampshire Center for Effective Behavioral Interventions and Supports.

Muscott, H. S. (2002). Exceptional partnerships: Listening to the voices of families. *Preventing School Failure, 46,* 66–69.

Muscott, H. S., Mann, E., Benjamin, T. B., Gately, S., Bell, K., & Muscott, A. J. (2004). Positive behavioral interventions and supports in New Hampshire: Preliminary results of a statewide system for implementing schoolwide discipline practices. *Education and Treatment of Children, 27,* 453–475.

Muscott, H. S., Mann, E., & LeBrun, M. (in press). Positive behavioral interventions and supports in New Hampshire: Effects of large-scale implementation of school-wide positive behavior support on student discipline and academic achievement. *Journal of Positive Behavioral Interventions.*

National Association of State Mental Health Program Directors, and the National Association of State Directors of Special Education. (2002). *Mental health, schools and families working together for all children and youth: A shared agenda.* Alexandria, VA: Author.

New Hampshire Center for Effective Behavioral Intervention and Supports. (2008). *PBIS-NH: 2006–2007 report to the NH DOE.* Bedford, NH: Author.

New Hampshire Family Engagement Work Group. (2004). *Family-friendly schools.* Bedford, NH: New Hampshire Center for Effective Behavioral Interventions and Supports.

Noguera, P. (1999). Transforming urban schools through investments in the social capital of parents. *Motion Magazine.* Retrieved April 14, 2008, from www.inmotionmagazine.com/pncap1.html

Public Agenda (1999). *Playing their parts: What parents and teachers really mean by parental involvement.* Retrieved April 12, 2008, from www.publicagenda.org/specials/parent/parent.htm

Sheldon, S. (2003). Linking school–family–community partnerships in urban elementary schools to student achievement on state tests. *The Urban Review, 25*(2), 149–165.

Sugai, G., & Horner, R. H. (1999). Discipline and behavioral support: Preferred processes and practices. *Effective School Practices, 17,* 10–22.

Sugai, G., & Horner, R. H. (2006). A promising approach for expanding and sustaining school-wide positive behavior support. *School Psychology Review, 35,* 245–259.

U.S. Department of Education. (2000). *Twenty-second annual report to Congress on the implementation of the Individuals With Disabilities Act.* Washington, DC: Author.

Originally published in *TEACHING Exceptional Children,* Vol. 40, No. 6, pp. 6–14.

Wraparound As a Tertiary Level Intervention for Students With Emotional/Behavioral Needs

Lucille Eber, Kimberli Breen, Jennifer Rose, Renee M. Unizycki, and Tasha H. London

Robert, a fifth-grader with a history of behavior problems, has become more belligerent to his teacher in the past few weeks, refusing to complete tasks, disrupting instruction, and now threatening other students—who have become less tolerant of his outbursts. The social worker feels suspending him will "make things worse"; she knows his mother is struggling with him at home as well. Robert reports his father is getting out of prison next week, is anxious to have his dad back in his life, and wishes his dad and mom would reunite after being divorced for many years. The principal, also reluctant to keep suspending Robert, feels Robert "needs much more" than a functional behavioral assessment and behavior intervention plan and has asked for a special education referral. She feels a placement in a setting where "he will get more attention from staff" is in everybody's best interest. The teacher agrees that a special education referral is needed because behavior plans developed by the school's positive behavior support team "have not worked."

Sound familiar? If a student has multiple behavior problems that escalate over time and across different settings, school-based problem-solving teams can become quickly overwhelmed, especially when educators identify "setting events" for problem behaviors that have occurred outside of school and are beyond the control of school personnel. Instead of resorting to exclusion or restrictive placements, schools need to be able to implement proactive interventions that match the complexity and intensity of the student's needs. A function-based individualized behavior intervention plan (BIP) has been described as an important foundation for tertiary tier support (Crone & Horner, 2003); however, identifying the function and designing a specific behavior support plan around problem behavior may be insufficient to prevent more failure—and may be potentially more restrictive or punitive for students such as Robert. Schools need to (a) know when it is necessary to move to the highest level of intervention planning for such students and (b) have the skills to quickly provide a level of support commensurate with the demonstrated needs of such students.

The wraparound process is a comprehensive intervention for the 1% to 2% of students with the highest level of emotional/behavioral need. As the most complex intervention in the schoolwide positive behavior support (SWPBS) response-to-intervention continuum (Eber et al., in press), wraparound includes specific engagement techniques to ensure that the design of supports and interventions incorporate the voice and perspectives of the family, student, and teacher. The strength-based wraparound approach deliberately builds constructive relationships and support networks among the student, family, and other key adults, including teachers. Addressing the needs of the adults (e.g., family and teacher) is considered critical to ensuring success for the student at school, at home, and in the community.

WRAPAROUND: A HISTORY

A value-based approach for supporting students with complex mental health needs, wraparound originated as a grass-roots practice, as mental health and other practitioners struggled to provide realistic options for youth with serious emotional/behavioral disorders (EBD) who had traditionally been placed in highly restrictive settings with limited success (Eber & Keenan, 2004); whose families had typically been excluded from intervention planning; and who generally experienced poor outcomes (Burchard, Bruns, & Burchard, 2002). Wraparound (see box, "Additional Resources") is grounded in the System of Care movement, which began in the 1980s as mental health and related youth-serving agencies attempted to more effectively work in concert with families to identify the supports most likely to help youth attain positive outcomes, both socially and academically. The core System of Care principles espoused through wraparound include: (a) families and children are full-participants in planning and selecting interventions, (b) services involve multiple providers across all of the domains relevant to the child's needs, and (c) the process is culturally relevant (Stroul, 2002; Stroul & Friedman, 1986, 1996).

Concurrent with the emergence of wraparound in the System of Care field in the 1980s, an individualized application of positive behavior supports (PBS) known as person-centered planning (PCP) surfaced as part of the advocacy movement for persons with developmental delays (Risley, 1996; Wehmeyer, Baker, Blumberg, & Harrison, 2004). Focused on reducing problem behaviors in persons with developmental disabilities without resorting to

> **Additional Resources**
> 1. Kansas Institute for Positive Behavior Support: http://www.kipbsmodules.org
> 2. Illinois PBIS Network: http://www.pbisillinois.org/
> 3. National Technical Assistance Center on Positive Behavioral Interventions and Supports: http://www.pbis.org/main.htm
> 4. National Wraparound Initiative: http://www.rtc.pdx.edu/nwi/
> 5. Substance Abuse and Mental Health Service Administration (SAMHSA) Systems of Care: http://www.systemsofcare.samhsa.gov/
> 6. University of Kansas, Center on Developmental Disabilities—Positive Behavior Support: http://uappbs.apbs.org/
> 7. Eber, L. (2005). Wraparound: Description and case example. In G. Sugai & R. Horner (Eds.), *Encyclopedia of behavior modification and cognitive behavior therapy: Educational applications* (pp. 1601–1605). Thousand Oaks, CA: Sage.

aversive techniques (Horner et al., 1990), the goals and approach of PCP parallel the value base, process, and desired outcomes for wraparound: (a) full participation in the community, (b) participation in healthy interpersonal relationships, (c) right to self-determination, (d) access to meaningful education, (e) opportunity for gainful employment, and (f) ongoing opportunities for growth (Risley).

As with function-based behavior supports identified through PCP, wraparound recognizes the influence of environment (e.g., settings and persons) on behavior. Successful implementation of both PCP and wraparound relies upon team collaboration, considers the youth's wants and needs, and recognizes the importance of family voice and choice when planning interventions. The concept of contextual fit, central to functional behavior assessment (FBA), BIP, PCP, and wraparound, examines the degree of compatibility or "goodness of fit" between multiple elements of an intervention plan (Albin, Lucyshyn, Horner & Flannery, 1996, p. 82). In particular, the match between the proposed intervention and the values, skills, and knowledge of implementers, family members, and the child is crucial. The FBA process must be streamlined for educators by balancing the need for accurate behavioral data and the constraints of the practitioner's environment (Scott, Nelson, & Zabala, 2003). Families and educators can reach consensus on the priorities for intervention, and the strategies planning is engaging, collaborative, and considerate of "real-life" conditions.

THE WRAPAROUND PROCESS

As a philosophy and a process, wraparound supports the student, family, and teacher by proactively organizing and blending natural supports, interagency services, PBS, and academic interventions. As previously mentioned, a critical feature of the wraparound process is a specific focus on engaging the student, family, and teacher equally in a proactive team process. The student, family, teacher(s), and others who may have ongoing contact and interaction with the student are key members of the strength-based team that determines and prioritizes needs and designs and implements strategies likely to improve quality of life for all involved.

A team facilitator (typically a school social worker [SSW], psychologist, counselor, or other clinical staff), who is trained in this family-centered, strength-based philosophy and approach, leads the wraparound process. The facilitator needs to be able to (a) engage students, families, and teachers who have experienced failed interventions and therefore may feel frustrated, disillusioned, or angry; (b) translate student, family, and teacher "stories" into need statements and strength inventories that guide the design of interventions; (c) bring together student, family, teacher, and natural supports to form a team; (d) ensure voice and ownership of interventions by those who are involved in implementation; and (e) organize and use multiple levels of data to guide the development and monitoring of interventions by the team on a regular basis.

As the most complex intervention within the tertiary tier of SWPBS, wraparound requires forming a unique team that reflects the strengths and needs of the individual student. Natural support persons are included as key team members who can ensure contextual fit, increasing the likelihood that the supports and interventions will have positive effects. An uncle or older sibling, a teacher from a previous school year who had a positive relationship with the student, and a music teacher who appreciates a student's talent are all examples of critical natural supports. Wraparound teams develop unique supports and interventions that increase the student's opportunity to experience success at home, at school, and in the community.

Other key features of the wraparound process include a focus on (a) improvements in quality of life instead of only a reduction in problem behaviors; (b) regular progress monitoring using school data and the perspectives of teacher(s), student, and family; and (c) frequent meetings to carefully design unique strategies that reflect the strengths and voice/choice of the student, family, and teacher.

WRAPAROUND: A CASE STUDY

Staff members at "Sunshine Elementary School" have begun the process of creating and implementing a full continuum of positive behavior supports (i.e., primary, secondary, and tertiary tiers). The Universal PBIS Team addresses primary tier supports, including overall school climate and the supports needed by all students. The Secondary Tier Team monitors the implementation of three types of support: (a) generically delivered check-in, check-out (CICO) intervention for students whose behaviors are not sufficiently responsive to primary tier interventions; (b) an individualized version of CICO, known as check-and-connect, for students whose behaviors need more than the generic version of CICO; and (c) small group social skills instruction for students with significant social skills deficits. The Tertiary Planning Team adopts a system focus to ensure that students who require highly individualized function-based interventions to succeed actually receive these interventions and progress satisfactorily. This team continuously monitors the progress of individualized interventions and does not design or implement the actual individualized interventions. The Tertiary Planning Team enforces the requirement that each student at the Tertiary level has his or her own uniquely designed team who creates and implements interventions, monitors increments of change, and revises the plan as needed based on data (Eber et al., in press).

"Henry," a student at Sunnyside Elementary School, had extremely poor attendance, failing grades, and poor homework completion. He had experienced trouble with the law in the community, which resulted in a court-assigned probation officer and a mandated Department of Children and Family Services (DCFS) counselor. Based on this information, the Tertiary Planning Team identified Henry as having complex needs and requiring a comprehensive wraparound plan. The SSW, who had been trained as a wraparound facilitator, approached Henry's mother to see if she would be interested in an individualized, strength-based wraparound team to support his transition back to school.

During the first phase of wraparound, **engagement and team preparation** (see Table 1), the student's family is introduced to the wraparound program. When Henry's mother shared a pamphlet she had been given for a short-term residential treatment center, the SSW started the conversation by offering Henry's mother the opportunity to develop a comprehensive support plan so Henry could experience success in his natural home, school, and community settings. In addition, the SSW explained that the process included developing a uniquely designed wraparound team to meet Henry's needs and take advantage of his strengths and the most natural supports possible. She asked his mother for suggestions of positive, supportive, and helpful team members to design this strength-based plan.

Initial team members included Henry, his mother, the SSW, his primary classroom teacher, the school principal, the bilingual liaison, and the district SWPBS tertiary-tier coach. Each person was chosen for a specific role on the team. Henry had a strong connection with his primary teacher, who also would implement certain interventions. The principal genuinely liked Henry, was invested in his success, and could assist with modifying system variables to ensure Henry's progress. The mother had a good relationship with the bilingual liaison and also needed her support as a translator. The tertiary coach was on the team to guide and support the SSW as she learned to lead the wraparound process.

Table 1. The Wraparound Process

Phase I: Engagement and Team Preparation

Facilitator . . .
- meets with family and key team members to gather their perspectives.
- guides family to generate a strengths list (multiple settings and perspectives) and a list of needs.
- generates a team member list, which includes natural supports, with the family.
- documents and shares baseline data about student's strengths/needs.

Phase II: Initial Plan Development

Team . . .
- begins regular meeting schedule.
- documents and reviews strengths and needs data (home/school/community).
- chooses a few needs for team to focus action planning, with special priority assigned to family concerns.
- develops an intervention plan (including function-based behavior supports as needed) to respond to home, school, and community strengths/needs.
- assesses community supports/resources available to meet needs identified by family.

Phase III: Plan Implementation and Refinement

Team . . .
- documents accomplishments of student and team at each meeting.
- meets frequently, checking follow-through and assessing progress of different interventions.
- receives regular documentation including data and plan updates.
- facilitates ongoing communication among those providing interventions in home, school, and community.

Phase IV: Transition

Team . . .
- discusses transitioning out of wraparound.
- considers the concerns of all team members in transition planning.
- communicates methods for future access to services to all team members.
- negotiates methods of introducing student and family to future teachers or providers.

The team evolved as additional team members were identified to ensure a consistent and seamless support plan for Henry and his mother. Specifically, his mother felt that "these people should probably be part of a team that's doing so much to help Henry": She identified a DCFS counselor who had been assigned to provide in-home support as someone to invite to team meetings. She also suggested that Henry's probation officer should be involved; although she thought that the probation officer should be provided with updates from the team, she did not feel it would be helpful to Henry to have him present at team meetings.

In the second phase of wraparound, **initial plan development**, the team identified and documented Henry's strengths and needs. Henry's strengths included a good relationship with his teacher, responsiveness to positive attention from adults he liked, leadership among his peers, and effective self-advocacy. The SSW helped the team identify two big needs for Henry: (a) "Henry needs to feel as if he fits in with the other kids at school" and (b) "Henry needs to feel successful at school." Henry's mother and school staff also wanted Henry to be "invested in his education," so that he would want to be at school and attend school willingly. By focusing on *needs* rather than *problems*, Henry's team changed the tone of both meetings and interventions from reactive to proactive. Rather than using preexisting interventions or services that are more deficit-oriented, the team designed interventions to respond to Henry's unique strengths and needs.

Because Henry had a positive relationship with his teacher, he was included in the check-and-connect intervention being delivered to other students in the school, some of whom were not on wraparound plans (Anderson, Christenson, Sinclair, & Lehr, 2004; Crone, Horner, & Hawken, 2004). Henry's teacher would greet him each morning by saying, "Thank you for coming; I am so glad you are here today." Henry and his teacher would talk about the individual behavior goals listed on his daily point card. This intervention was selected because Henry's expected behavior could be "corrected" in advance and positive behavior encouraged in other settings, with extra support or reminders as needed.

Henry's plan included strategies that he selected along with his family and teachers and that were based on his expressed strengths and needs. For example, he joined the school safety patrol, with the goal of acting as a positive role model; this helped him monitor and improve his own behavior in the hallways.

In the third phase of wraparound, **plan implementation and refinement**, the team focused on (a) regularly using data for decision making; (b) checking with the family, student, and teacher(s) to ensure that the plan was working; (c) adjusting the wraparound plan based on feedback from team members; and (d) addressing additional needs that may have been identified but were not priorities at the onset of the wraparound process. During this phase, Henry's principal was able to facilitate completion of benchmark testing (Dynamic Indicators of Basic Early Literacy Skills, DIBELS; Good & Kaminski, 2002) even though Henry was not at school when others were tested. To address the truancy problem, the principal also arranged for the school bus to pick up Henry in front of his home rather than on the corner (where he was frequently distracted by people he knew and then did not get on the bus). Classroom interventions included homework adjustments, fewer spelling words, checking that Henry understood directions, and extra reading support in class from the Title I teacher. In addition, the team designed unique progress criteria for Henry so he could be eligible for the schoolwide Student of the Month recognition. His classroom duties included putting stickers on the homework chart for everyone in the class. The school also referred Henry and his family to a local interagency network so they could receive financial support to participate in community recreation activities.

The wraparound team monitored Henry's progress through a variety of data sources, including office discipline reports, attendance/tardy record, grades, DIBELS scores, and CICO behavior card points. Team member perspectives about Henry's strengths, needs, and progress were collected using the Illinois Systematic Information Management for Educational Outcomes (SIMEO; see Illinois State Board of Education, 2005) data system. For example, SIMEO's Educational Information Tool collected teacher ratings of classroom academic and behavioral performance; the Home, School, Community Tool helped in assessing Henry's strengths and needs across multiple settings and life domains (e.g., safety/basic emotional, behavioral, and social needs/strengths).

Small increments of improvement were recognized, celebrated, and built upon. For example, from second quarter to third quarter, with wraparound in progress, Henry's grades began to improve (spelling: 15%–40%, math: 15%–48.5%, and reading: 20%–63%). During the previous school year, Henry's attendance was 22%. As wraparound was introduced, his attendance increased from 15% for the first quarter of the school year (attending 6 out of 41 days—he did not register until there were 10 days left in this quarter) to 60% in the second quarter (25 out of 42 days), and 75% (12 out of 16 days) at the beginning of the third quarter. His DIBELS score increased from 55 words per min in the fall to 67 words per min in the winter.

Figure 1 illustrates SIMEO data shared at team meetings to document improvements in the team's perception of Henry's placement risk, which went from minimal to no risk at home, high to minimal risk at school, and high to moderate risk in the community.

SIMEO data in Figure 2 were used by the team to identify increments of increased strengths across home/school/community, and improved behavior at school.

During the fourth phase, **transition**, Henry's accomplishments will continue to be reviewed and celebrated. The team will develop a transition plan to ensure success as it adjusts to less frequent team meetings and/or moves to natural supports without the ongoing wraparound team. As Henry's school performance improved, the team had to plan for increasing the use of natural supports and for ensuring successes during and after summer break.

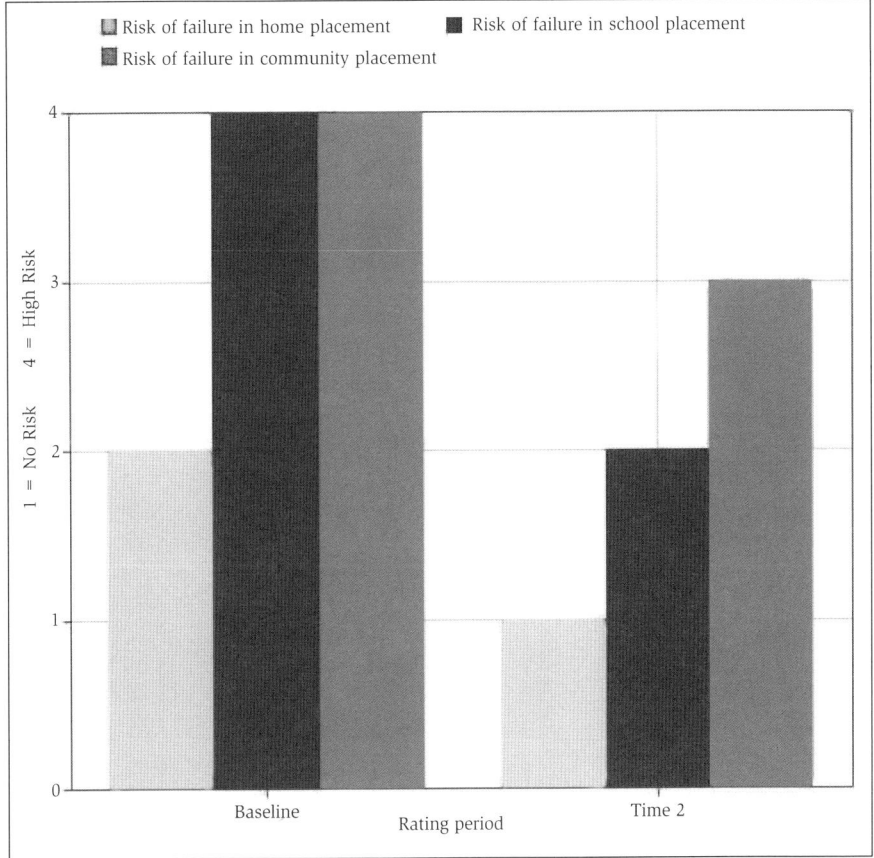

Figure 1. Data on Henry's Placement Risk Across Settings

SUPPORTING WRAPAROUND IMPLEMENTATION

To ensure Henry's success, his team dedicated planning time for the wraparound facilitator (the SSW) to meet with Henry, his family, and his teachers to hear their stories and perspectives, gather and review data about strengths and needs, and facilitate regular team meetings. The principal allowed time for school team members to participate in team meetings. In addition, the SSW checked in with the teacher at least twice a week to monitor progress, assess implementation fidelity, answer questions, celebrate successes, and make intervention adjustments. This flexibility and the allocation of the SSW's time were supported by the school and district.

Designated personnel must be adequately trained to facilitate comprehensive wraparound teams, and time must be allocated and protected to participate in planning team meetings. In addition, schools need to designate personnel who will facilitate wraparound team meetings, have ongoing conversations with the family and other team members, and collect and share

Figure 2. Data on Henry's Improvements/Strengths Across Settings

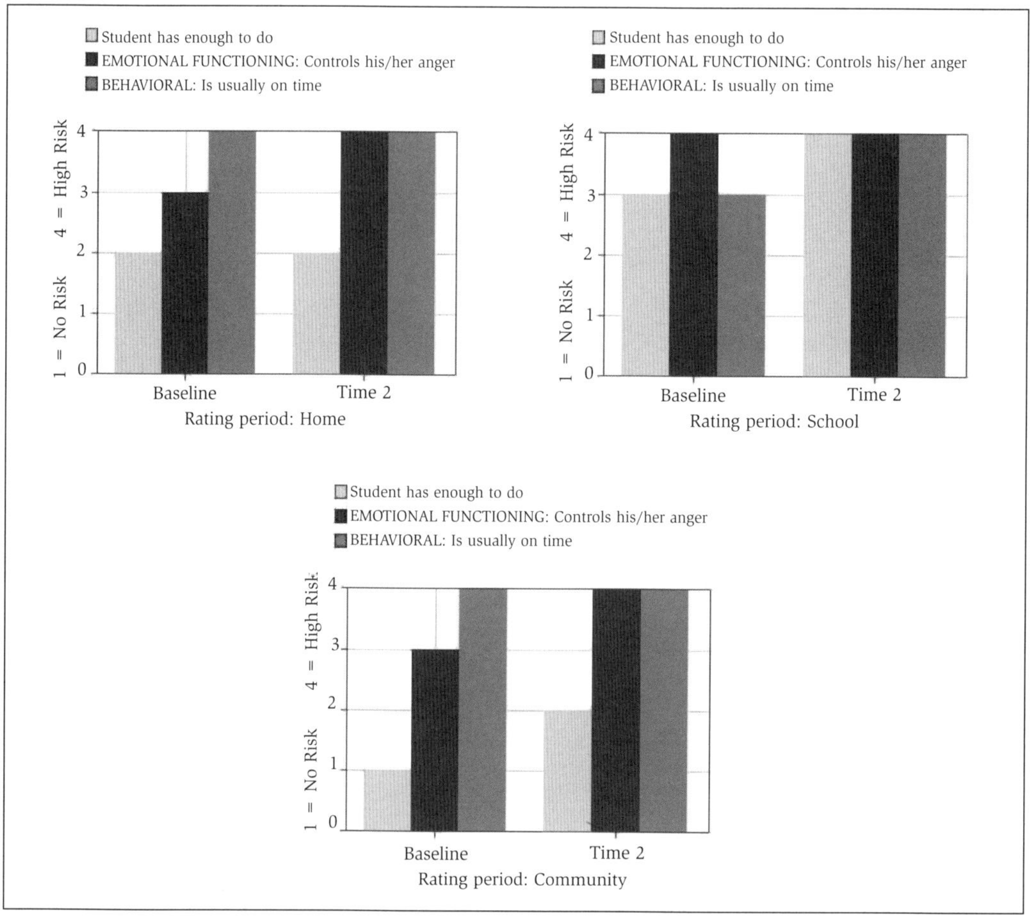

[Bar charts showing ratings (1 = No Risk to 4 = High Risk) at Baseline and Time 2 for three categories: "Student has enough to do," "EMOTIONAL FUNCTIONING: Controls his/her anger," and "BEHAVIORAL: Is usually on time" across three settings — Home, School, and Community.]

data and monitor progress. In Henry's situation, the SSW was supported administratively to engage in ongoing communication and follow-up activities. Both the SSW and the bilingual liaison were available to meet with Henry's mother after work. From mid-October through early February, Henry's mother met with the facilitator three times for conversations at the public library, once at home, and twice at school with the whole team. Henry's teacher was provided with a substitute so he could attend some meetings or was permitted to divide his classroom and send the smaller groups to other classrooms.

FINAL THOUGHTS

Although the wraparound process may be new to schools, oftentimes the interventions that result from wraparound are actually variations of existing primary and secondary interventions, tailored to ensure the student is successful. This strength-based and family-centered intervention process requires careful attention to developing a unique team for each student; the team focuses on the needs of all stakeholders, providing supports to the teacher as well as to the student and family. Teachers only implement strategies with which they agree and have had a voice in designing; they receive support from other team members throughout the process, and, along with the family and student, determine whether the plan is working.

A student's individualized wraparound team can address issues that occur outside of school, which often immobilize typical intervention teams in schools. Henry's story illustrates how the wraparound team addressed triggers to behavior occurring outside of school, as well as how teams can engage and include other agencies involved with a family. Typical school intervention processes may leave these people out, leading to disconnected parallel processes that inadvertently stifle progress.

Implementing wraparound as a stand-alone intervention might seem costly and daunting to school personnel. But when the wraparound process is embedded in a coherent system of graduated support, many of the systems needed to support this level of intervention are in place and the increased personalization and intensity are natural extensions of the multi-tiered support logic.

REFERENCES

Albin, R. W., Lucyshyn, J. M., Horner, R. H., & Flannery, K. B. (1996). Contextual fit for behavioral support plans. In L. K. Koegel, R. L. Koegel, & G. Dunlap (Eds.), *Positive behavioral support: Including people with difficult behavior in the community* (pp. 81–98). Baltimore: Brookes.

Anderson, A. R., Christenson, S. L., Sinclair, M. F., & Lehr, C. A. (2004). Check & Connect: The importance of relationships for promoting engagement with school. *Journal of School Psychology, 42,* 95–113.

Burchard, J. D., Bruns, E. J., & Burchard, S. N. (2002). The wraparound approach. In B. Burns & K. Hoagwood (Eds.), *Community treatment for youth: Evidence-based interventions for severe emotional and behavioral disorders* (pp. 69–90). New York: Oxford University Press.

Crone, D., Horner, R., & Hawken, L. (2004). *Responding to problem behavior in schools: The Behavior Education Program.* New York: Guilford Press.

Crone, D. A., & Horner, R. H. (2003). *Building positive behavior support systems in schools: Functional behavioral assessment.* New York: Guilford Press.

Eber, L., Hyde, K., Rose, J., Breen, K., McDonald, D., & Lewandowski, H. (in press). Completing the continuum of school-wide positive behavior support: Wraparound as a tertiary level intervention. In W. Sailor, G. Dunlap, G. Sugai, & R. Horner (Eds.), *Handbook of positive behavior support.* New York: Springer.

Eber, L., & Keenan, S. (2004). Collaboration with other agencies: Wraparound and systems of care for children and youths with emotional and behavioral disorders. In R. B. Rutherford, M. M. Quinn, & S. R. Mathur (Eds.), *Handbook of research in emotional and behavioral disorders* (pp. 502–516). New York: Guilford Press.

Good, R. H., & Kaminski, R. A. (Eds.). (2002). *Dynamic indicators of basic early literacy skills* (6th ed.). Eugene, OR: Institute for the Development of Educational Achievement. Available at http://dibels.uoregon.edu/

Horner, R. H., Dunlap, G., Koegel, R. L., Carr, E. G., Sailor, W., Anderson, J., et al. (1990) Toward a technology of "nonaversive" behavioral support. *Research and Practice for Persons With Severe Disabilities, 30*, 3-10.

Illinois State Board of Education. (2005). *Illinois PBIS network.* Available at http://www.pbisillinois.org/

Risley, T. (1996). Get a life! Positive behavioral intervention for challenging behavior through life arrangement and life coaching. In L. K. Koegel, R. L. Koegel, & G. Dunlap (Eds.). *Positive behavior support: Including people with difficult behavior in the community* (pp. 435-437). Baltimore: Brookes.

Scott, T. M., Nelson, C. M., & Zabala, J. (2003). Functional behavior assessment training in public schools facilitating systemic change. *Journal of Positive Behavior Interventions, 5*, 216-224.

Stroul, B. A. (2002). *Issue brief—System of care: A framework for system reform in children's mental health.* Washington, DC: Georgetown University Child Development Center, National Technical Assistance Center for Children's Mental Health.

Stroul, B. A., & Friedman, R. M. (1986). *A system of care for children and youth with severe emotional disturbances* (Rev. ed). Washington, DC: Georgetown University Child Development Center, CASSP Technical Assistance Center.

Stroul, B. A., & Friedman, R. M. (1996). The system of care concept and philosophy. In B. Stroul (Ed.), *Children's mental health: Creating systems of care in a changing society.* (pp. 1-22). Baltimore: Brookes.

Wehmeyer, M. L., Baker, D. J., Blumberg, R., & Harrison, R. (2004). Self-determination and student involvement: Innovative practices. *Journal of Positive Behavior Supports, 6*, 29-35.

Originally published in *TEACHING Exceptional Children,* Vol. 40, No. 6, pp. 16-22.

Schoolwide Positive Behavior Supports: Primary Systems and Practices

Brandi Simonsen, George Sugai, and Madeline Negron

"So, this is why I feel like all I do is deal with student behavior," said an administrator of an urban middle school, "5,367 office discipline referrals in one year!" While flipping through the latest stack of discipline referrals on her desk, the administrator noticed that students were being referred to the office for anything from tapping a pencil in class ("disruptive behavior") to fighting in the hallway ("physical aggression"). The administrator sighed, "Teachers should know how to manage some of these behaviors in their classrooms."

Like this administrator, many school personnel are becoming increasingly frustrated with the impact of student behavior on their schools. More than ever, the public perception is that student behavior is out of control. Although isolated instances of violence (e.g., school shootings) contribute to this perception, people are most concerned with the lack of discipline and control in schools (Rose & Gallup, 2005). As a result, schools establish policies that try to increase discipline and control, often by adopting "get tough" practices. In other words, schools set strict rules about the types of student behavior that are unacceptable and assign rather severe consequences for students who do not abide by the rules. When the initial policies prove ineffective, schools often respond by "getting tougher." That is, they invest in other security (e.g., metal detectors) and punitive measures (e.g., "zero tolerance" policies that result in expulsion) that actually have little impact on student behavior (Skiba & Peterson, 2000).

Simultaneously, schools are trying to close an ever-widening achievement gap and ensure that all students, including students with diverse academic abilities, make adequate yearly progress (AYP). Given the multiple competing initiatives and demands, schools need to invest in a proactive approach to organizing and managing resources. Specifically, schools need to identify clear and measurable *outcomes* (e.g., decrease problem behavior, increase academic achievement); collect and use *data* to guide their decisions; implement relevant, evidence-based *practices;* and invest in *systems* that will ensure that practices are implemented with fidelity and sustained over time.

Schoolwide positive behavior supports (SWPBS) is a proactive, systems-level approach that enables schools to effectively and efficiently support student (and staff) behavior. SWPBS specifically asks schools to select outcomes, data, practices, and systems—the four critical elements previously mentioned—that are contextually appropriate and meaningful for the school. When schools implement SWPBS, they typically experience decreases in inappropriate behaviors (as measured by decreases in discipline referrals, suspensions, and expulsions). In addition, schools that implement SWPBS often find that students' academic performance improves, as teachers are able to return to teaching academics after stabilizing the social behavior.

Unlike typical school practices, which often wait for a student to fail before providing support, SWPBS employs a three-tier approach to behavior support to (a) proactively address the social behavior needs of all students and (b) prevent social and academic failure (see Figure 1; Sugai & Horner, 2002; Sugai et al., 2000; Walker et al., 1996). The primary tier is designed to support all students and staff across all settings in the school. Meaningful outcomes are identified for all students and staff (e.g., increases in the percentage of students making AYP, decreases in the percentage of students receiving two or more office discipline referrals); aggregate data are examined to determine if outcomes are met; practices (e.g., establishing positively stated schoolwide rules, teaching social skills, developing a schoolwide reinforcement system) are implemented to maximize the success of all students; and systems are selected to ensure that practices are implemented with fidelity by staff. When implemented effectively and accurately, schools can expect most students (approximately 89%, 74%, and 71% of elementary, middle, and high school students, respectively) to respond to the primary tier intervention (Horner, 2007).

Even with effective primary tier intervention in place, a group of students (approximately 11%, 26%, and 29% of elementary, middle, and high school students, respectively) will require additional behavior support to experience success (Horner, 2007). The secondary tier is designed to support a targeted group of students who have not responded to primary tier interventions, but whose behaviors do not pose a serious risk to themselves or others. Outcomes are specific to the targeted group of students and often focus on preventing problem behaviors from becoming chronic. Data are collected to

Figure 1. The Three-Tiered Continuum of Support

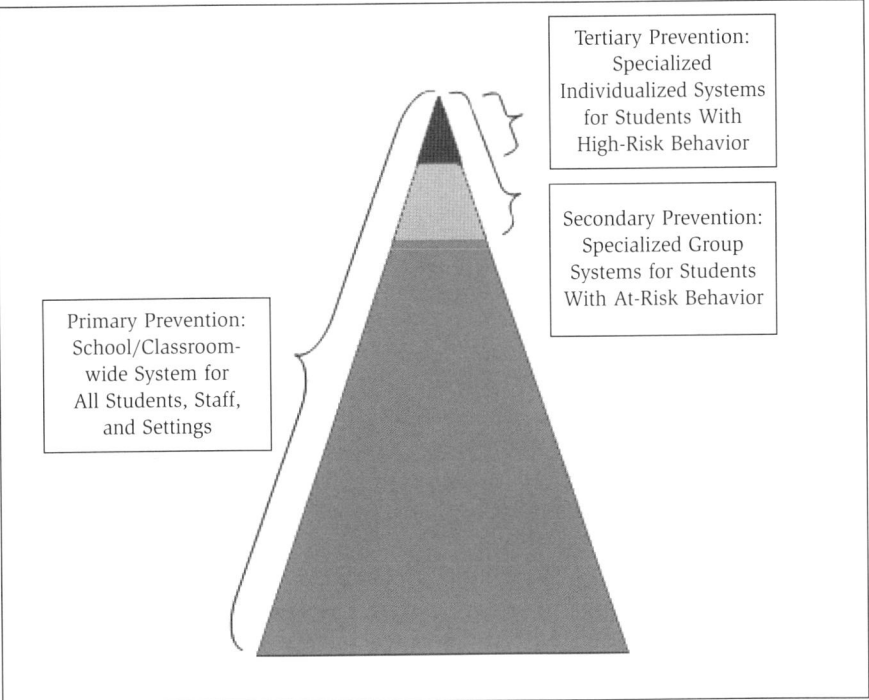

measure progress toward outcomes; data sources may include office discipline referrals, points earned for desired behavior (if using an intervention that employs a point system), attendance records, and other measures of appropriate behavior. Practices typically focus on intensifying the supports provided in the primary tier (i.e., increasing structure, providing more intensive social skills instruction, and delivering more frequent reinforcement); and systems (e.g., a team to run the selected secondary intervention) are established to ensure that adopted practices are implemented with fidelity and that data are regularly collected, reviewed, and used to make decisions.

Tertiary tier interventions are designed to support individual students (a) who require additional support to benefit from secondary or primary tier intervention (i.e., students who have not responded to secondary tier intervention) or (b) whose behaviors are serious enough to require more immediate and intensive support (i.e., students whose behaviors pose a risk and who are not appropriate for secondary tier intervention). Interventions at this level are highly individualized; thus, outcomes, data, and practices are identified for each student, and systems are designed to support the ongoing implementation of multiple individualized interventions within a school.

In this article, we focus on schoolwide implementation of the primary tier intervention. Subsequent articles in this issue focus on secondary and tertiary tier interventions, classwide interventions, and even more intensive supports. Specifically, we (a) briefly review the supporting literature, (b) describe the key implementation features, and (c) share an example of how one urban middle school implemented primary tier interventions in SWPBS.

LITERATURE SUPPORTING PRIMARY TIER INTERVENTIONS IN SWPBS

Research findings indicate that SWPBS creates an effective school environment where proactive behavioral practices can be implemented successfully (Kartub, Taylor-Greene, March, & Horner, 2000; Lewis, Powers, Kelk, & Newcomer, 2002). Specifically, individual research studies demonstrate that implementation of primary tier interventions is associated with increases in consistency among staff, increases in positive interactions, and decreases in office discipline referrals (Netzel & Eber, 2003; Safran & Oswald, 2003; Turnbull et al., 2002). Similarly, initial findings from randomized control trials, the "gold standard" for experimental research, indicate positive outcomes (e.g., increased fidelity of implementation and improved academic and behavior outcomes) for schools implementing SWPBS (Horner et al., in press; Leaf & Bradshaw, 2007). Thus, research indicates that SWPBS is an effective approach to schoolwide intervention.

In addition, research documents that SWPBS is an efficient approach to schoolwide intervention. For example, Scott and Barrett (2004) conducted cost–benefit analyses for schools implementing SWPBS; that is, they identified the amount of time saved by school staff and students who were no longer assigning and receiving, respectively, large numbers of office discipline referrals. They found that administrators saved, on average, 15¾ days of administrator time, and students saved, on average, 79½ days of instructional time per year following implementation of SWPBS. Although additional research is still needed, school staff can be confident that interventions in the primary tier are evidence-based and are likely to be effective when implemented with fidelity in their schools.

KEY IMPLEMENTATION FEATURES

The focus of primary tier interventions is improving school outcomes, as indicated by data, by implementing evidence-based practices to support *all* students across *all* settings. To implement primary tier interventions, schools need to (a) identify meaningful outcomes; (b) establish and invest in schoolwide systems; (c) select and implement contextually appropriate, evidence-based practices; and (d) collect and use data to make decisions.

Identify Meaningful Outcomes

Before implementing primary tier interventions, schools need to identify what they plan to achieve. Specifically, schools should review their school or district improvement plans to identify priority areas. To be implemented successfully, SWPBS should be among the top three initiatives listed in the school or district improvement plan. In addition, schools should review extant data sources (i.e., rates of office discipline referrals, suspensions, and expulsions; state or districtwide test scores; numbers of students referred for or served by special education; etc.) and other relevant information to identify areas for improvement. Based on these data, schools need to identify observable, measurable, specific, and achievable annual outcomes, which will become the metric by which success of an intervention is judged. Outcomes may include a reduction, by a certain percentage, in the number of students receiving multiple office discipline referrals, an increase in the number of students meeting criteria on the state or districtwide assessments, and other similar contextually important schoolwide improvements.

Establish and Invest in Schoolwide Systems

After schools have identified outcomes, the focus shifts to establishing the systems that facilitate the implementation of primary tier interventions. First, schools need to establish a representative team that guides the implementation process. Team membership should include a (a) school administrator who has the authority to commit school resources; (b) select group of teachers who are representative of the certified faculty; (c) representative of special services (i.e., counselor, school psychologist, school social worker, etc.) who brings behavioral expertise; (d) member of the support staff (i.e., paraprofessional, secretary, janitor, etc.); and (e) family member. The members of the team should be positive people with social influence. The goal is to start with a team that "works" (i.e., members are supportive of improving practices in the school and understand the importance of using data to make decisions).

Second, the team must identify someone who will act as the team coach. Coaches are responsible for ensuring the team meets regularly, develops and follows a data-based action plan, and adheres to the information gathered during training activities; often, we joke that coaches are the "positive nags" of the team because they provide regular supportive or positive reminders rather than negative punishers. Any member of the team may serve as the coach; however, the coach should have social influence over other team members (and the faculty at large).

Third, schools need to obtain 80% buy-in, or agreement from the faculty and staff, to implement SWPBS. Buy-in is often documented by a staff vote.

Fourth, schools need to ensure that they have a system that allows efficient input (i.e., data entry) and output (i.e., visual displays, or graphs) of data (i.e., office discipline referrals); data should be easily accessible and used for decision making. To make data more meaningful, many schools find that they need to redesign their office discipline referrals. For example, the behaviors listed on the referral are often ambiguous; schools may revise the names of behaviors listed and provide operational definitions of each.

Figure 2. Primary Tier Readiness Requirements: Systems

☑ Establish a representative SWPBS **team** that "works."
☑ Identify a team member who will serve as a **coach**.
☑ Secure **80% buy-in** from the school staff.
☑ Employ a **data system** that facilitates data entry and meaningful visual displays (graphs).
☑ Participate, as a team, in **SWPBS training**.

Finally, schools need to sign up for training in SWPBS. Training activities are offered locally in most states, and information about training can be found on the Web site of the Office of Special Education Program's National Technical Assistance Center on Positive Behavioral Interventions and Supports (http://pbis.org). Following each training event, the SWPBS team needs to efficiently disseminate the information to all faculty and staff. Typically, school teams spend a year attending training events and planning for implementation; then, they implement the planned activities during the second year. School teams should use a brief readiness checklist to determine if they have met these requirements for establishing SWPBS systems (see Figure 2).

Select and Implement Practices

Once a school has established the systems described in the previous section and is in the process of receiving training, the SWPBS team is ready to select and implement practices. To be clear, the majority of the work will be completed by members of the SWPBS team; however, the team members should actively recruit and incorporate feedback from the larger faculty at every step. The key steps to selecting and implementing practices are presented in Figure 3.

First, school faculty are asked to identify a small (three to five) number of positively stated schoolwide expectations. The expectations, or rules, should be broad enough to encompass the majority of desired behavior and be mutually exclusive (i.e., they should not overlap). For example, the expectations *Be Safe, Be Respectful, and Be Responsible* are broad enough to prompt all desired behavior, and most individual behaviors fit within only one of the expectations (e.g., "keeping hands, feet, and objects to self" fits within the broader expectation of "Be Safe"). Typically, posters are made of the expectations and displayed in all locations of the school—in both classroom and nonclassroom settings.

Second, the SWPBS team defines the selected expectations in the context of all settings and routines in the school (e.g., classroom, cafeteria, hallway, bathroom). Often, SWPBS teams use a matrix format; expectations are written as row headings, settings and routines are written as column headings,

Figure 3. Implementing Primary Tier SWPBS Interventions: Practices

- ☑ Establish a small number of positively stated **expectations**.
- ☑ Define the expectations in the context of **routines/settings**.
- ☑ Develop scripted **lesson plans** to teach expectations.
- ☑ Increase **active supervision** in classroom and nonclassroom settings.
- ☑ Establish a continuum of strategies to **acknowledge appropriate behavior**.
- ☑ Establish a continuum of strategies to **respond to inappropriate behavior**.
- ☑ Develop a **staff reinforcement system**.
- ☑ Develop an **action plan** to guide roll-out and **implement**.

and the description of what it "looks like" to follow each expectation within each setting/routine is documented, using a few bullet points, in the cross-sections of each row and column in the matrix (see Fairbanks in this issue for an example).

Third, the SWPBS team develops lesson plans to teach each expectation within each setting/routine. Like lesson plans developed to teach academic skills, social skills lesson plans follow a consistent format: (a) state the rule and routine; (b) provide students with a definition, or description, of what it looks like to follow the rule within the routine; (c) model the expected behavior; (d) engage students in an activity that allows them to practice the expected behavior in the natural setting (i.e., the place where the behavior is expected); and (e) assess to ensure students have acquired and are fluent with the social skill (the expected behavior). To ensure that all teachers deliver the lesson plans consistently, lesson plans should be scripted.

Fourth, the SWPBS team should identify a plan to increase active supervision in both classroom and nonclassroom settings. Active supervision includes three key staff behaviors: moving around the environment in unpredictable patterns so that students have the sense that they are always being watched, visually scanning the environment, and interacting with most students in the environment (Colvin, Sugai, Good, & Lee, 1997). During interactions, staff should provide specific praise or error corrections contingent on appropriate or inappropriate behavior, respectively.

Fifth, the SWPBS team should establish a continuum of strategies to acknowledge appropriate, or "expectation-following," behavior. At a minimum, the SWPBS team should ensure that school staff are consistently using specific and contingent praise to recognize instances of appropriate behavior (i.e., telling students exactly what they did well immediately after the desired behavior is observed). Many schools also choose to establish a more overt reinforcement system. For example, schools may create positive behavior tickets that recognize students for appropriate behavior. In some schools, tickets can be turned in for a lottery drawing; in other schools, tickets can be used as money in a school store. Regardless of how schools operationalize their reinforcement system, the key idea is to "catch kids being good."

Sixth, schools need to review the strategies they have in place to discourage inappropriate behavior. Specifically, schools should ensure that the first response to minor inappropriate behavior is a brief error correction that redirects the student back to the appropriate behavior (e.g., I saw X, and instead I would like to see Y). The second response should be to re-teach the desired behavior. In other words, school staff should treat social behavior errors just like academic errors; they should provide feedback and instruction as necessary. For more intense or chronic problem behaviors, the SWPBS team needs to ensure that a documented and predictable staff and administrator response is in place and applied consistently by all staff. Often, this process results in the SWPBS team modifying the discipline handbook and creating two levels of behaviors: minor behaviors that should be handled in the classroom with basic behavior interventions and major behaviors that are referred to the office for additional support.

Seventh, the SWPBS team should design a staff reinforcement system that recognizes staff for the efforts involved in implementing SWPBS. Like the system designed for students, expectations for staff (e.g., staff are expected to teach lesson plans on scheduled days and deliver X number of positive behavior tickets) should be clearly defined, and staff members should receive, at a minimum, specific social recognition. Some schools choose to design a more elaborate system for staff reinforcement, with staff receiving a variety of rewards (e.g., preferred parking, get-out-of-school-early coupon) contingent on specific behaviors.

Finally, after designing the practices, the SWPBS team needs to identify and implement a plan for "roll-out" of primary tier interventions. That is, they need to specify how the expectations will be introduced, where posters will be displayed, when and where social skills lessons will be taught, when and how the schoolwide reinforcement system will be implemented, and other similar steps. This action plan should be documented, disseminated, and clearly explained to all staff to ensure consistency; implementation should be given high priority.

Collect and Use Data to Make Decisions

While establishing and sustaining the implementation of primary tier interventions, the SWPBS team should actively collect and use data. A school that meets readiness requirements should already have a data system that facilitates data entry (input) and generates meaningful visual displays of data (e.g., graphs), which can be manipulated to answer questions generated by the SWPBS team (e.g., Where are students exhibiting problem behavior?). A system that meets these criteria is the Schoolwide Information System (www.swis.org). To ensure data are being used effectively, the SWPBS team should engage in the following steps (see Figure 4).

Figure 4. Monitoring Implementation Effectiveness and Fidelity: Data

- ☑ **Review data** at every SWPBS team meeting and **use data to make decisions.**
- ☑ **Share data** with the faculty and model data-based decision making.
- ☑ **Celebrate successes** with students and staff.
- ☑ **Share successes** with parents and other community members.

Step 1: The SWPBS Team Should Make Data Review a Priority at Every Regular Team Meeting. At the beginning of each SWPBS team meeting, the coach should facilitate a review and discussion of schoolwide data for the past month. In particular, the team should discuss the (a) overall rates (i.e., number per day) of office discipline referrals (or other schoolwide measures of student behavior), (b) percentage of students who have received multiple (two or more) office discipline referrals for major offenses and potential supports required for those students, (c) typical locations where problems are occurring, (d) time(s) of the day where problems are occurring, and (e) nature or type of behaviors. Based on these data, the SWPBS team can recommend modifications to their current interventions. For example, if a large percentage (e.g., 40%–60%) of students are receiving multiple office discipline referrals, the SWPBS team may decide to re-teach the expectations to all students in the school. Similarly, if the SWPBS team notes that most problem behaviors are happening in one location (e.g., the cafeteria), they may decide to increase prompting, active supervision, and reinforcement of school expectations in that setting. Thus, data are actively used to make decisions during team meetings.

Step 2: The SWPBS Team Should Share Data With the Faculty and Model Data-Based Decision Making. Because buy-in is required to sustain implementation of primary tier interventions over time, all faculty and staff must be informed of the schoolwide data and should receive brief updates from the SWPBS team at regular staff meetings. In addition, some schools choose to share data with their staff in a school newsletter or a visual display (e.g., bulletin board) in a staff area.

Step 3: The SWPBS Team Should Celebrate Successes Identified With Data. Specifically, when data patterns indicate that progress is being made toward one or more of the desired outcomes, the SWPBS team should work with administration to plan a celebration for the staff and students. Celebrations can range from social recognition at an assembly, staff meeting, or over the morning announcements to a tangible or activity reward (e.g., a party, lunch, fun item, etc.).

Step 4: The SWPBS Team Should Share Successes With Parents and the Broader Community. Family involvement is a key ingredient to the success of SWPBS implementation. As mentioned previously, a family member should serve on the SWPBS team, and all school families should be informed about the positive changes being made at the school. Therefore, parents should be invited to celebrate the successes of their students and the staff of the school. Again, sharing the success can range from informing parents during PTA/PTO meetings or via newsletters and asking them to congratulate their student to inviting parents to join a school assembly or event where the staff and students are celebrating the improvement. Similarly, the SWPBS team should share successes with other community members, including administrators in the district office, school board members, and others in the broader community (e.g., members of the Chamber of Commerce, service groups). This positive publicity helps maintain the momentum of SWPBS and may generate donations that the school can reinvest in its implementation efforts.

IMPLEMENTING SWPBS IN AN URBAN MIDDLE SCHOOL

The frustrated administrator described at the beginning of this article, reached the peak of her frustration when she realized that students in her school received 5,367 office discipline referrals in one year. Later that year, the administrator attended a regional conference, and she learned about SWPBS. As she listened to the presentation, she grew increasingly excited about the real possibility of shifting from a reactively driven discipline system to a preventive and positive approach in her school. A new sense of optimism grew as she heard stories about schools reducing their rates of office discipline referrals, reclaiming lost instructional minutes, improving school climate, and increasing academic scores on high-stakes tests because teachers had time to teach. Learning about how to get ready to adopt and implement SWPBS in her school became high priorities for the principal.

She started by working with her district administrator (who also was director of special services) to *contact the PBS coordinator* from her state, which was listed on the national Web site (http://pbis.org). Together, they arranged a meeting with school and district administrators, state PBS coordinator, and consultants from the local university. At this meeting, the administrator received information about readiness requirements and upcoming training activities.

After this initial orientation meeting, the administrator worked to *complete the readiness requirements* in time for the training activities. Specifically, she established a SWPBS team that "worked." She hand picked senior teachers and support personnel who had social influence with their peers and were likely to be supportive of SWPBS. She gathered schoolwide data (i.e., office discipline referrals) that her team would need to guide decisions about outcomes. Initially, she did not have district support to invest in a new data system (e.g., *Schoolwide Information System*); therefore, she worked with her existing system and generated the information she would need to help her team move forward. After the SWPBS team attended an initial training activity where they received a basic overview of SWPBS, team members presented the idea of SWPBS to the rest of the faculty and staff during grade level team meetings. Following the presentations, the SWPBS team conducted a staff vote, which resulted in greater than 80% buy-in. Thus, all readiness requirements were met, and the SWPBS team continued to attend training events throughout the year.

During the course of the training year, the SWPBS team *designed their primary tier intervention*, and all implementation steps were documented in a detailed action plan, which was reviewed and updated at each regular team meeting. Team members, with input from the faculty, identified three positive expectations for their school—Respect, Responsibility, and Pride—that they called the "Keys to Success." The team then identified all of the relevant settings/routines in their school and created a matrix that defined each "key" within each setting/routine (see Figure 5). The team then created lesson plans for each box in the matrix (i.e., each expectation within each routine). The matrix, lesson plans, reinforcement system, plan for implementation, and other relevant information were assembled in a PBS notebook, which was distributed to all faculty and staff prior to implementation.

To increase the likelihood of students following the rules, the PBS team developed a two-part schoolwide reinforcement system. First, they created behavior tickets that staff members were to give to students who demonstrated one of the Keys to Success. The tickets were preprinted with check boxes that allowed staff to indicate which key the student followed in which location. Second the team felt it was important to recognize students for both social and academic excellence, so they developed a card system. Students who received one or fewer discipline referrals were eligible for a yellow card; students who made the honor role but had multiple office discipline referrals were eligible for a silver card; and students who made the honor role and had one or fewer discipline referrals received the coveted gold card. Each card gave the students access to privileges in the school (e.g., sitting next to a friend at lunch) and the community (e.g., a free slice of pizza at a local restaurant and other donated items from local establishments). The schoolwide reinforcement was also documented in the PBS notebook.

To improve the reliability of discipline referral data, the team modified their office discipline referral form by defining behaviors and splitting them into two categories (major and minor) that corresponded to office and classroom managed behaviors, respectively. They also included a possible motivation (i.e., function) section on the form, which asked staff to identify what they believed the student was trying to access or escape by engaging in the problem behavior. In addition to modifying the form, the SWPBS team enhanced their discipline procedures and documented the new procedures in the PBS notebook. Specifically, they identified how teachers should respond

Figure 5. A Sample Matrix of Expectations Within Routines and Settings

	Hallway/Stairway	All Classrooms	Café	Bathroom/Water Fountain	Bus/Bus Stop/Walkers	Locker Room	Auditorium	Media Center
PRIDE	☐ Keep hands, feet and objects to yourself ☐ Use a quiet voice	☐ Keep hands, feet and objects to yourself ☐ Use a quiet voice ☐ Enter room quietly ☐ Be considerate of other people's belongings ☐ Be an active listener	☐ Keep hands, feet and objects to yourself ☐ Use a quiet voice ☐ Enter and exit in an orderly manner ☐ Be considerate of other people's belongings ☐ Stand in line as directed	☐ Keep hands, feet and objects to yourself ☐ Use a quiet voice ☐ Allow others their privacy ☐ Wait your turn at the sink or fountain ☐ Take care of school property	☐ Keep hands, feet and objects to yourself ☐ Use a quiet voice ☐ Be considerate of the bus driver and the bus ☐ Wait patiently to get on or off the bus ☐ Share your seat	☐ Keep hands, feet and objects to yourself ☐ Use a quiet voice ☐ Be considerate of other people's belongings	☐ Keep hands, feet and objects to yourself ☐ Use a quiet voice ☐ Stay seated until directed otherwise ☐ Respond to the speaker appropriately ☐ Listen with eyes on speaker	☐ Keep hands, feet and objects to yourself ☐ Use a quiet voice ☐ Enter room quietly ☐ Use media center materials and equipment appropriately
RESPONSIBILITY	☐ Walk facing forward, staying to the right ☐ Follow rules without adult reminders ☐ Walk directly to destination using appropriate route ☐ Have hall passes available ☐ Report all unsafe behavior and vandalism	☐ Respond to quiet signal immediately ☐ Be on time and be prepared ☐ Follow classroom procedures ☐ Report all unsafe behavior and vandalism	☐ Sit in designated areas ☐ Respond to quiet signal immediately ☐ Report all unsafe behavior and vandalism	☐ Walk directly to destination using appropriate route ☐ Report all unsafe behavior and vandalism ☐ Wash and dry hands ☐ Return to class immediately	☐ Have belongings ready to enter and exit ☐ Remain seated at all times ☐ Report all unsafe behavior and vandalism ☐ Follow bus rules at all times ☐ Get on and off bus at correct stop ☐ Stay off private property	☐ Be prepared for gym class ☐ Respond to quiet signal immediately ☐ Report all unsafe behavior and vandalism	☐ Respond to quiet signal immediately ☐ Sit in designated areas ☐ Enter and exit in an orderly manner ☐ Be prompt ☐ Report all unsafe behavior and vandalism	☐ Respond to quiet signal immediately ☐ Follow media center procedures ☐ Report all unsafe behavior and vandalism ☐ Return materials on time
RESPECT	☐ Use polite language ☐ Keep hallways and stairways clean	☐ Use polite language ☐ Do your own work ☐ Do your best work at all times ☐ Keep work areas clean	☐ Use polite language ☐ Keep table and floor clean and place trash into barrels ☐ Leave area as you found it or better	☐ Use polite language ☐ Keep area clean ☐ Throw paper towels in trash cans ☐ Flush appropriately ☐ Keep water fountains clean	☐ Use polite language ☐ Throw trash in waste basket	☐ Use polite language ☐ Leave area as you found it or better	☐ Use polite language ☐ Treat speaker as a welcome guest ☐ Treat furniture appropriately ☐ Leave area as you found it or better	☐ Use polite language ☐ Keep your work area clean ☐ Leave area as you found it or better

to the problem behaviors now defined as classroom managed, and they articulated how administrators should respond to the behaviors classified as office managed.

The SWPBS team also designed a staff reinforcement system, which delineated a variety of ways in which staff would be recognized (e.g., lunch with administrator, doughnuts for a grade-level team) contingent on specified behaviors (e.g., exceeding expectations for delivering coupons). They also established opportunities for all staff to be recognized when the school met certain benchmarks. For example, they brought in cookies when they achieved 80% buy-in.

After documenting the various systems in the PBS notebook, the SWPBS team *designed a plan for roll-out* at the beginning of the next school year. At this school, SWPBS was a top priority, and the team decided that they would dedicate the first four days of the school year entirely to SWPBS. They developed a schedule to facilitate activities, and they clearly communicated that all teachers would teach social skills lesson plans to all students in the natural settings. They created a "passport" so that each student could receive a stamp for participating in each lesson. For example, a teacher would take his class out to the busses, which came back to the school in the middle of the day so that the lesson could occur on the bus, deliver a lesson on how to follow the keys to success on the bus, and stamp each student's passport once they had demonstrated each key on the bus. This plan was communicated to staff, and the team provided training in how to implement the plan (i.e., how to teach lessons, how to use the reinforcement systems, etc.) during a series of professional development activities. Thus, all staff members were ready for the roll-out of SWPBS on the first day of the school year; they even had t-shirts that stated the keys to success.

The SWPBS team *monitored implementation* of their action plan, and *reviewed schoolwide data* at their regular team meetings. When they noticed an area for improvement, they made a data-based decision. For example, the school administrators noted that they were receiving multiple reports of students fighting on one staircase during a particular passing period. Rather than increasing punishment for those students, a "get tough" approach that may have been used in the past, the administrators increased active supervision. Specifically, the principal and two vice principals each positioned themselves at the top, middle, and bottom of the stairs; the fighting was prevented. By taking 5 minutes of their day to supervise a transition, they saved hours in processing discipline referrals and suspensions for students fighting.

As a result of implementing SWPBS, the administrator can now allocate her time to more proactive and preventative approaches and be an instructional leader, rather than a disciplinarian. Within one year, the school was implementing SWPBS with high fidelity (i.e., they achieved a score of 98% of the Schoolwide Evaluation Tool, a measure of implementation fidelity). As a result, they experienced a decrease in the number of office discipline referrals, and the students and staff reported that they enjoyed the reinforcement systems. The school staff has now shifted focus to adopting other initiatives to improve academics, is continuing to provide their staff with professional development to continue to enhance their skills, and is shifting their attention to improving their practices and systems for students whose behaviors are nonresponsive to primary tier interventions. In other words, because the school adopted a proactive and efficient approach to intervention, they have been able to pursue other initiatives and further improve the quality of education provided to students.

CONCLUDING COMMENTS

This article describes the essential practices and systems of a schoolwide primary tier intervention. Specifically, we emphasized the importance of six key elements: (a) common vision and approach to schoolwide discipline, (b) small number of schoolwide expectations that are operationalized into observable or behavioral terms, (c) formal procedures or lesson plans for teaching these behavioral expectations across real school settings, (d) continuum of practices for acknowledging students who display these behavioral expectations, (e) continuum of consequences for rule violations (both classroom and office managed), and (f) systems for collecting and reviewing data for decision making.

We emphasized the importance of systems that establish and sustain consistent accurate implementation across all staff, students, and settings, including for example, team-based leadership and coordination; documented staff commitments and agreements; district-level endorsements and supports (e.g., coordination, coaching, initiative integration); and investments in useable and efficient data storage and output systems.

When done consistently and accurately, school staff can experience improved disciplinary climate, more available instructional minutes, enhanced academic achievement, greater family and community relations, and improved capacity to address the needs of students who need more intensive behavior and/or academic supports to be successful.

REFERENCES

Colvin, G., Sugai, G., Good, R. H., III, & Lee, Y. (1997). Using active supervision and precorrection to improve transition behaviors in an elementary school. *School Psychology Quarterly, 12,* 344–363.

Horner, R. H. (2007). *Discipline prevention data.* Eugene, OR: OSEP Center on Positive Behavioral Interventions and Supports, University of Oregon.

Horner, R. H., Sugai, G., Smolkowski, K., Todd, A., Nakasato, J., & Esperanza, J. (in press). A randomized control trial of school-wide positive behavior support in elementary schools. *Journal of Positive Behavior Interventions.*

Kartub, D. T, Taylor-Greene, S., March, R. E., & Horner, R. H. (2000). Reducing hallway noise: A systems approach. *Journal of Positive Behavior Interventions, 2,* 179–182.

Leaf, P., & Bradshaw. (2007). *Project Target*. Retrieved January 16, 2008 from Johns Hopkins University, Center for the Prevention of Youth Violence Web site: http://www.jhsph.edu/preventyouthviolence/Research/Project_Target.html

Lewis, T. J., Powers, L. J., Kelk, M. J., & Newcomer, L. L. (2002). Reducing problem behaviors on the playground: An investigation of the application of school-wide positive behavior supports. *Psychology in the Schools, 39*(2), 181–190.

Netzel, D. M., & Eber, L. (2003). Shifting from reactive to proactive discipline in an urban school district: A change of focus through SWPBS implementation. *Journal of Positive Behavior Interventions, 5*(2) 71–79.

Rose, L. C., & Gallup, A. M. (2005, September). 37th annual Phi Delta Kappa/Gallup poll of the public's attitudes toward the public schools. *Kappan*, 41–59.

Safran, S. P., & Oswald, K. (2003). Positive behavior supports: Can schools reshape disciplinary practices? *Exceptional Children, 69*, 361–373.

Scott, T. M., & Barrett, S. B. (2004). Using staff and student time engaged in disciplinary procedures to evaluate the impact of school-wide PBS. *Journal of Positive Behavior Interventions, 6,* 21–27.

Skiba, R. J., & Peterson, R. L. (2000). School discipline at a crossroads: From zero tolerance to early response. *Exceptional Children, 66*, 335–346.

Sugai, G., & Horner, R. H. (2002). The evolution of discipline practices: School-wide positive behavior supports. *Child and Family Behavior Therapy, 24*, 23–50.

Sugai, G., Horner, R. H., Dunlap, G. Hieneman, M., Lewis, T. J., Nelson, C. M., et al. (2000). Applying positive behavioral support and functional behavioral assessment in schools. *Journal of Positive Behavior Interventions, 2,* 131–143.

Turnbull, A. P., Edmonson, H., Griggs, P., Wickham, D., Sailor, W., Freeman, R., et al. (2002). A blueprint for schoolwide positive behavior support: Implementation of three components. *Exceptional Children, 68*, 377–402.

Walker, H. M., Horner, R. H., Sugai, G., Bullis, M., Sprague, J. R., Bricker, D., et al. (1996). Integrated approaches to preventing antisocial behavior patterns among school-age children and youth. *Journal of Emotional and Behavioral Disorders, 4*, 194–209.

Originally published in *TEACHING Exceptional Children*, Vol. 40, No. 6, pp. 32–40.

6

Cooperating Initiatives: Supporting Behavioral and Academic Improvement Through a Systems Approach

Michael D. Coyne, Brandi Simonsen, and Michael Faggella-Luby

Many teachers and administrators find it difficult to work toward multiple schoolwide goals simultaneously. They describe the effort as almost schizophrenic because attention and energy must be constantly shifted and compete between very different initiatives and mandates, each of which seems to place unrealistic demands on teachers' limited time and capacity. Although this scenario is all too familiar in schools, the question is whether educational initiatives with different goals have to compete.

This article presents a model in which educational initiatives do not compete but cooperate. We provide examples of efforts designed to improve behavioral outcomes and examples designed to increase academic achievement to illustrate how seemingly very different initiatives can be conceptualized and implemented within the same coherent and coordinated model of schoolwide improvement. This article provides a conceptual framework that outlines guiding principles that should anchor all school improvement efforts as well as model descriptions for conceptualizing and implementing schoolwide initiatives that share a common language and logic. We also provide examples of beginning reading and SWPBS to illustrate how this model can accommodate multiple efforts with different goals.

A COMPREHENSIVE CONCEPTUAL FRAMEWORK

A school's approach for supporting educational change in any area should be guided by a comprehensive conceptual framework for school improvement.

There are several guiding principles fundamental to the success of schoolwide educational initiatives, regardless of the goals (e.g., behavioral or academic improvement). These guiding principles include (a) promoting evidence-based practices, (b) supporting change at the systems level, and (c) developing local capacity to sustain effective practices over time. When schools anchor improvement efforts within a comprehensive conceptual framework, they ensure that different initiatives share fundamental assumptions, a common vision, and important outcomes.

School Improvement Efforts Should Promote Evidence-Based Practices

A large and growing body of converging multidisciplinary research evidence can inform educational practice. For example, knowledge about assessment and intervention practices for improving social behavior in schools is growing because research has been and is being conducted by behavior analytic researchers (Bambara & Kern, 2005; Carr et al., 2002; Safran & Oswald, 2003; Sugai & Horner, 2002; Sugai et al., 2000). Similarly, in beginning reading, a substantial and compelling scientific knowledge base related to the nature of reading development and effective instructional practices exists to support improved reading outcomes (Adams, 1990; McCardle & Chhabra, 2004; National Reading Panel, 2000; National Research Council, 1998). To ensure reliable and meaningful educational improvement, school improvement efforts should embrace a conceptually sound and methodologically rigorous scientific knowledge base.

School Improvement Efforts Should Support Change at the Systems Level

Although a large scientific knowledge base exists to inform educational improvement, implementing evidence-based practices is challenging and complex (Greenwood, Delquadri, & Bulgren, 1993; Peters & Heron, 1993). For example, it is unrealistic to expect teachers working independently to implement and sustain the host of evidence-based practices necessary to produce lasting academic and behavioral change. Instead, teachers need the support of larger organizational structures that work to coordinate and maintain practices at a systems level.

Moreover, students, teachers, administrators, and other school staff vary along any number of characteristics including culture, race, training, language, learning histories, socioeconomic status, staff size, and geographic location. Because schools and districts have such distinctive characteristics, each system must adopt and implement a unique combination of evidence-based practices to maximize the contextual fit between practices and the educational environment. Therefore, school improvement efforts should be organized at the systems level (e.g., school or district level) to ensure that educational improvement is feasible, consistent, and relevant to local needs.

School Improvement Efforts Should Develop Local Capacity to Sustain Effective Practices Over Time

The ultimate goal of school improvement efforts is the widespread, coordinated, and long-term implementation of effective evidence-based practices. For this to happen, schools and districts must develop the internal capacity to sustain practices over time through a process of continuous regeneration (Sugai, Horner, & McIntosh, 2008). When schools develop local capacity or the internal expertise to lead and manage school improvement efforts and effective practices become institutionalized, systems maintain high quality implementation by being responsive to inevitable changes in administration, personnel, and funding. For evidence-based practices to remain relevant, effective, and efficient for the long term, school improvement efforts need to focus on developing local capacity.

A COMMON LOGIC AND LANGUAGE

Even when schools embrace a comprehensive conceptual framework for school improvement, they still confront the challenging task of juggling the implementation of multiple initiatives and mandates. Although separate efforts may work toward important and meaningful goals, they most often compete for limited time and resources. Moreover, individual initiatives are typically conceived and presented as if existing in a vacuum with a unique theoretical framework, terminologies, and expected outcomes. The reality, however, is that initiatives must be implemented in concert with other efforts that have their own unique frameworks, terminologies, and expected outcomes.

We believe that schools and districts can work smarter and more efficiently than they currently are by promoting a common logic and language for both behavioral and academic improvement that transcends disciplinary domains. A single coherent logic for school improvement creates efficiencies by allowing schools to focus on the strategic integration of multiple initiatives. A common approach to behavioral and academic change can be operationalized within a prevention model, used in public health literature, that conceives of supports along a continuum (Simeonsson, 1994; Walker et al., 1996). This continuum of supports (see Figure 1; Sugai, 2001) is similar to multi-tiered approaches (Vaughn & Klingner, 2007) and response to intervention (RTI) approaches (Fuchs & Fuchs, 2006; Kame'enui, 2007).

Every tier of the continuum considers four central dimensions of support: outcomes, data, practices, and systems. These dimensions, articulated by the Office of Special Education Programs (OSEP) Center on Positive Behavioral Interventions and Supports (2004), can be applied across (a) three tiers of support (universal, targeted, and individual) and (b) different domains (i.e., academic and social/behavioral). When conceptualizing and implementing school improvement efforts, schools should (a) identify desired social or

Figure 1. A Schoolwide Model of Instructional and Behavioral Supports

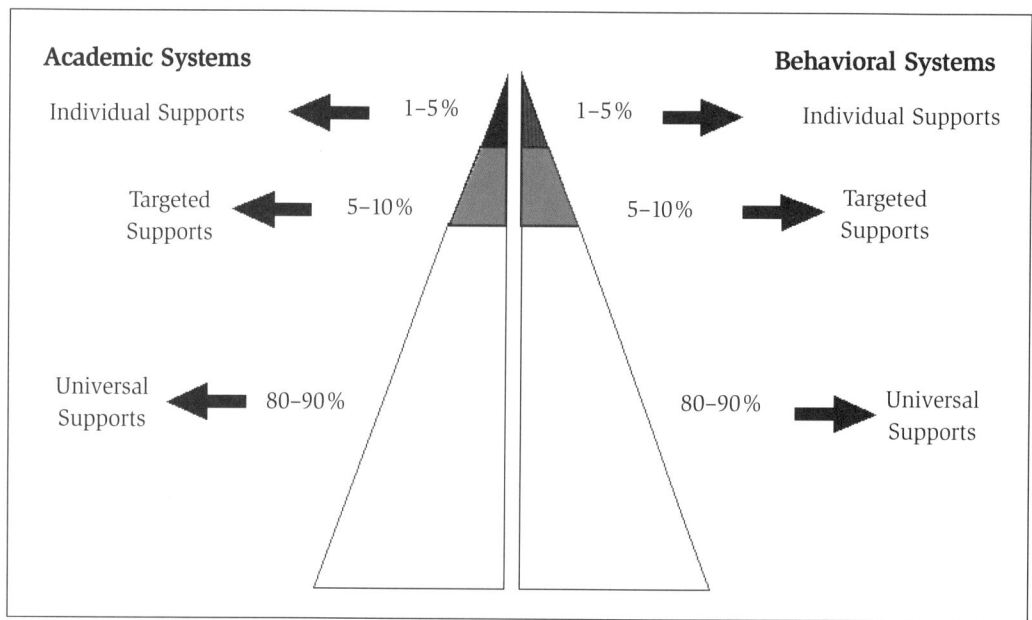

academic outcomes; (b) use assessment data as the basis for making decisions; (c) choose, implement, and modify selected practices based on evidence of efficacy; and (d) develop systems to support the implementation of practices. Figure 2 illustrates the interplay among these principles.

ACCOMMODATING MULTIPLE EFFORTS WITH DIFFERENT GOALS

Schools work smartly when they embrace a common language and logic for school improvement. The following sections illustrate how the four dimensions of supports underscore similarities across beginning reading and SWPBS efforts at each tier of the continuum. Moreover, in this model, similar systems work to support teachers and staff implementing behavioral and academic practices.

Universal Supports

Universal supports, outcomes, data, practices, and systems focus on the whole school (i.e., all environments, all students, and all staff). Universal supports for both academic and social/behavior domains are presented in Figure 3.

Targeted Supports

Targeted supports focus on groups of students who require additional support to benefit from universal supports. For example, targeted supports might be

Figure 2. Critical Elements of Schoolwide Intervention

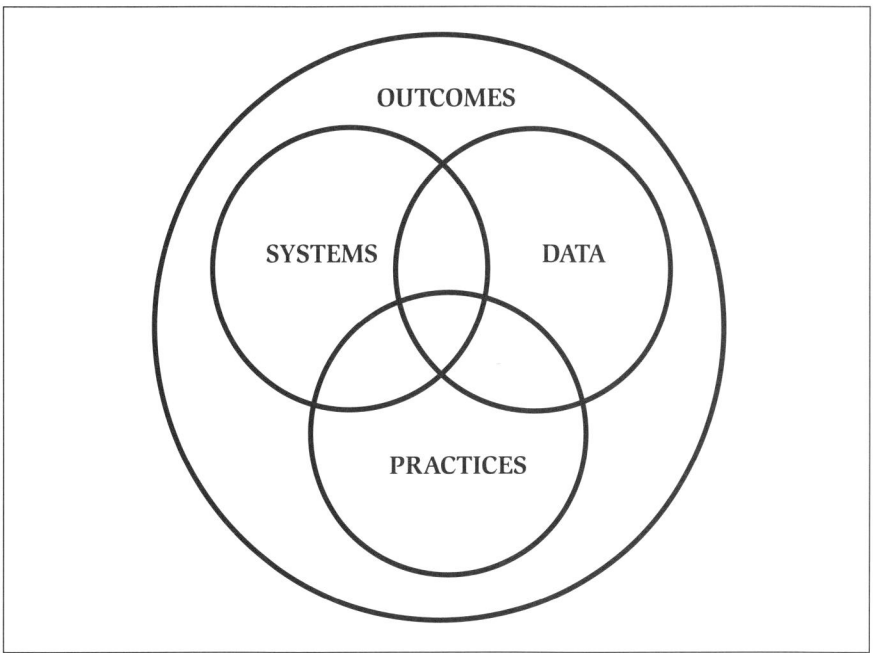

helpful for students who do not respond to primary/core instruction and are considered at risk for learning and behavioral difficulties (see Figure 4). Outcomes, data, practices, and systems focus on efficiently and effectively identifying and addressing the needs of the small group of identified students.

Individual Supports

Individual supports focus on the needs of students who require additional support to benefit from universal and targeted supports such as students who do not respond to either primary/core or secondary level interventions (see Figure 5). Outcomes, data, practices, and systems are student specific and highly individualized.

CONCLUSION

In this article, we suggest that educational initiatives that appear to have very different missions and goals can cooperate rather than compete when schools promote a comprehensive and coordinated approach to schoolwide improvement. By organizing efforts at the systems level, schools can effectively and efficiently leverage resources to ensure that multiple initiatives (e.g., academic and social-behavioral) work together to guarantee durable improvements in meaningful student outcomes.

Figure 3. Primary Tier Intervention Outcomes, Data, Practices, and Systems for Academic and Behavioral Domains

Outcomes	
Academic (Beginning Reading)	*Behavior*
• Meaningful increases in the percentage of students reading at or above grade level with the goal of all students becoming successful readers by Grade 3. • Clear, consistent, and measurable reading goals and expectations for all students at each grade. • Evidence-based standards or curriculum maps provide direction to teachers about what and when to teach.	• Meaningful increase in prosocial behaviors exhibited by the student body. • Meaningful decrease in the inappropriate behaviors exhibited by the student body. • A small number of positively stated schoolwide behavioral expectations.

Data	
Academic (Beginning Reading)	*Behavior*
• A common set of valid and reliable assessments linked to big ideas in beginning reading (e.g., comprehension, reading fluency, and decoding). • All students assessed three times per year. • Assessment data used to make school-level decisions about reading goals and practices.	• A common set of schoolwide indicators of student behavior (e.g., office discipline referrals, number of students suspended, and number of students referred or found eligible for special education). • Data used to make school-level decisions about behavioral goals and practices.

Practices	
Academic (Beginning Reading)	*Behavior*
• Consistent core reading instruction of validated efficacy implemented schoolwide with fidelity. • Core instruction designed to enable 80% or more of students to attain schoolwide reading goals. • Consistent, prioritized, and protected time allocated to core reading instruction.	• Consistent behavioral expectations posted and explicitly taught schoolwide. • Schoolwide behavior supports designed to enable 80% or more of students to meet behavioral goals. • A schoolwide system for acknowledging appropriate behavior (e.g., behavior tickets, positive office referrals, etc.).

Systems
• School-level leadership teams coordinate schoolwide initiatives. • Professional development designed to support the implementation of specific practices (e.g., core reading instruction and SWPBS). • Schoolwide assessment and data systems organized and managed at the school building level.

Figure 4. Secondary Tier Intervention Outcomes, Data, Practices, and Systems for Academic and Behavioral Domains

Outcomes	
Academic (Beginning Reading) • Accelerate the learning of at-risk students to meet grade level goals. • Determine individualized trajectories of acceleration needed for success.	*Behavior* • Increase the number of appropriate behaviors and decrease the number of inappropriate behaviors for at-risk students.
Data	
Academic (Beginning Reading) • Use schoolwide data to identify students at risk of not meeting reading goals. • Assess at-risk students more frequently to monitor progress (e.g., monthly). • Use progress monitoring data to make ongoing instructional decisions.	*Behavior* • Use schoolwide data to identify students at risk of negative behavioral outcomes (e.g., ratings of the students' prosocial behavior or number of office discipline referrals). • Use data to monitor student's behavior and adjust supports.
Practices	
Academic (Beginning Reading) • At-risk students receive additional instructional support in reading using research-validated supplemental and intervention programs and materials. • A continuum of programmatic, grouping, and scheduling options are available to at-risk students and coordinated at a schoolwide level. • Instruction for at-risk students is continually evaluated and adjusted based on data.	*Behavior* • At-risk students receive efficient intervention focused on increasing structure, self-management, opportunities for feedback, opportunities for reinforcement, and home–school connection. • A continuum of intervention options is available and coordinated at a schoolwide level. • Support for at-risk students is continually evaluated and adjusted based on data.
Systems	
• Teams meet weekly to evaluate progress of students currently participating in targeted intervention and make data-based decisions and instructional adjustments. • Feedback given to staff quarterly regarding number of students referred, participating, and making progress in targeted interventions.	

Figure 5. Tertiary Tier Intervention Outcomes, Data, Practices, and Systems for Academic and Behavioral Domains

Outcomes	
Academic (Beginning Reading)	*Behavior*
• Individualized student goals relate to the acquisition of specific beginning reading skills and strategies. • Individualized outcomes can align with individualized education program (IEP) goals and objectives.	• Individualized student behavior goals relate to the acquisition of appropriate social skills and decreases in specific problem behaviors. • Individualized outcomes align with IEP goals and objectives.

Data	
Academic (Beginning Reading)	*Behavior*
• Use individual student data to identify students most at risk of reading disability based on lack of response to core instruction and targeted intervention. • Collect specific diagnostic data on reading skills and strategies. • Assess most at-risk students more frequently to monitor progress (e.g., weekly). • Use individualized progress monitoring data to make ongoing instructional decisions.	• Use individual student data to identify students most at risk of negative behavioral outcomes based on lack of response to universal and targeted supports. • Collect specific diagnostic behavioral data (e.g., records review, functional behavioral assessment, and direct observation data). • Use individualized student data to make ongoing decisions about supports.

Practices	
Academic (Beginning Reading)	*Behavior*
• Students at high risk receive individualized intervention at higher levels of intensity (e.g., more time, smaller group size, with highly trained professionals) • Students may receive support through special education. • Instruction is continually evaluated and adjusted based on data.	• Students at high risk receive individualized positive behavior support strategies. • Students may receive support through special education, wrap-around process, and comprehensive person centered planning. • Supports continually evaluated and adjusted based on data.

Systems
• Individual student teams made up of professionals with specialized knowledge of a student's strengths and weaknesses (e.g., classroom teacher, parents, specialists, special educator, school psychologist, and consultants). • Supports and services are coordinated across general education, special education, etc. • Resources allocated to support implementation of individualized interventions.

REFERENCES

Adams, M. J. (1990). *Beginning to read: Thinking and learning about print*. Cambridge, MA: MIT Press.

Bambara, L., & Kern, L. (Eds.). (2005). *Individualized supports for students with problem behaviors: Designing positive behavior support plans*. New York: Guilford Press.

Carr, E. G., Dunlap, G., Horner, R. H., Koegel, R. L., Turnbull, A. P., & Sailor, W. (2002). Positive behavior support: Evolution of an applied science. *Journal of Positive Behavior Interventions, 4*, 4–16.

Fuchs, D., & Fuchs, L. (2006). Introduction to response to intervention: What, why, and how valid is it? *Reading Research Quarterly, 41*, 93–99.

Greenwood, C. R., Delquadri, J., & Bulgren, J. (1993). Current challenges to behavioral technology in the reform of schooling: Large-scale, high-quality implementation and sustained use of effective educational practices. *Education and Treatment of Children, 16*(4), 401–404.

Kame'enui, E. J. (2007). A new paradigm: Responsiveness to intervention. *TEACHING Exceptional Children, 39*(5), 6–7.

McCardle, P. & Chhabra, V. (2004). *The voice of evidence in reading research*. Baltimore: Brookes.

National Research Council. (1998). *Preventing reading difficulties in young children*. Washington, DC: National Academy Press.

National Reading Panel. (2000). *Teaching children to read: An evidence-based assessment of the scientific research literature on reading and its implications for reading instruction*. Washington, DC: National Institute of Child Health and Development.

OSEP Center on Positive Behavioral Interventions and Supports. (2004). *Schoolwide positive behavior support: Implementers' blueprint and self-assessment*. University of Oregon, Eugene: Author.

Peters, M. T., & Heron, T. E. (1993). When the best is not good enough: An examination of best practice. *Journal of Special Education, 26*, 371–385.

Safran, S. P., & Oswald, K. (2003). Positive behavior supports: Can schools reshape disciplinary practices? *Exceptional Children, 69*, 361–373.

Simeonsson, R. J. (1994). *Risk, resilience & prevention: Promoting the well-being of all children*. Baltimore: Brookes.

Sugai, G. (2001, June). *School climate and discipline: Schoolwide positive behavior support*. Invited keynote at the National Summit on Shared Implementation of Individuals With Disabilities Education Act (IDEA), Washington, DC.

Sugai, G., & Horner, R. H. (2002). The evolution of discipline practices: Schoolwide positive behavior supports. *Child and Family Behavior Therapy, 24*, 23–50.

Sugai, G., Horner, R. H., Dunlap, G. Hieneman, M., Lewis, T. J., Nelson, C. M., Scott, T., Liaupsin, C., Sailor, W., Turnbull, A. P., Turnbull, H. R., III, Wickham, D., Wilcox, B., & Ruef, M. (2000). Applying positive behavioral support and functional behavioral assessment in schools. *Journal of Positive Behavior Interventions, 2*, 131–143.

Sugai, G., Horner, R. H., & McIntosh, K. (2008). Best practices in developing a broad-scale system of support for schoolwide positive behavior support. In A. Thomas & J. P. Grimes (Eds.), *Best practices in school psychology V* (Vol. 3, pp. 765–780). Bethesda, MD: National Association of School Psychologists.

Vaughn, S., & Klingner, J. (2007). Overview of the three-tier model of reading intervention. In D. Haager, J. Klingner, & S. Vaughn (Eds). *Evidence-based reading practices for response to intervention* (pp. 3–9). Baltimore, MD: Brookes.

Walker, H. M., Horner, R. H., Sugai, G., Bullis, M., Sprague, J. R., Bricker, D., & Kaufman, M. J. (1996). Integrated approaches to preventing antisocial behavior patterns among schoolage children and youth. *Journal of Emotional and Behavioral Disorders, 4*, 194–209.

Originally published in *TEACHING Exceptional Children*, Vol. 40, No. 6, pp. 54–59.

Evaluating School Climate and School Culture

Andrew T. Roach and Thomas R. Kratochwill

When do trends in student behavior demand schoolwide policies and plans? How can we examine the school environment to see what positive changes we can make to a school's climate or culture? What tools are best suited to assessing how students and teachers view their school's climate or context for learning? This article takes a historical approach to evaluating school climate and offers practical guidance to modern measures of school culture.

SYSTEMIC SCHOOL IMPROVEMENT TO MEET CHANGING STUDENT NEEDS

To meet the needs of increasingly diverse student populations and the challenges of accountability-driven education systems, many mental health and education professionals have attempted to broaden the scope of their practice to include systemic prevention and intervention efforts. Ecological models have been proposed for the provision of educational services that embrace this systemic focus (e.g., Sheridan & Gutkin, 2000). Within an ecological framework, students' behavioral difficulties demand an awareness of contextual variables (e.g., learning environment, community resources, and home context), as well as students' intra-individual characteristics.

In their attempts to remediate and treat students' social-emotional and behavioral difficulties, practitioners are confronted with many extraneous factors that are difficult to address or rectify (e.g., families' socioeconomic standing, community safety and crime, and individual students' predisposition to disability and mental illness). School and classroom contexts, however, are factors that educators and communities can enhance or restructure to better meet students' needs (Lehr & Christenson, 2002).

Although researchers in school psychology and special education have created measures of classroom environment and interaction, researchers have generally given less attention to measures of school context. This is unfortunate because classrooms, nested within schools, have climates that are directly or indirectly influenced by wider school contexts (Anderson, 1982). By understanding and evaluating characteristics of the larger school context, educators can become aware of the following:

- Schoolwide protective or risk factors that may influence intervention outcomes.
- Resources within the larger school community to address students' needs.
- Pervasive trends in student or staff behavior and attitudes that demand systemic intervention efforts.

The data that researchers have collected in effectiveness studies of schoolwide behavior interventions have included the number and kinds of discipline referrals, school demographic information, school vandalism costs, and behavioral observations in classrooms (Sprague et al., 2001). Certainly, these data are essential for demonstrating the effectiveness of a school's implementation effort, but they may not provide a complete picture of the changes required and produced by schoolwide behavioral interventions.

Fullan and Steigelbauer (1991) suggested that educators need to attend to "the phenomenology of change—that is, how people actually experience change" (p. 4). The school climate and school culture measures described in this article are vehicles for achieving this goal, providing policymakers and practitioners with methods to collect information on stakeholders' perspectives and "sense-making" regarding schoolwide behavior interventions (Spillane et al., 2002; see box, "Theoretical Foundations for Evaluating School Context").

SCHOOL CLIMATE INSTRUMENTS

Most school climate measures are survey instruments completed by teachers, students, and school administrators. The Comprehensive Assessment of School Environments (CASE; National Association of Secondary School Principals, 1986), the Organization Health Inventory (OHI; Hoy & Sabo, 1998; Hoy et al., 1991), and the Organizational Climate Descriptive Questionnaire (OCDQ; Hoy & Sabo, 1998; Hoy et al., 1991) are three school climate instruments available to practitioners.

Theoretical Foundations for Evaluating School Context

In his seminal work, Brofenbrenner (1979) provided the following definition of the ecological orientation:

> The ecology of human development involves the scientific study of the progressive, mutual accommodation between an active, growing human being and the changing properties of the immediate settings in which the developing person lives, as this process is affected by the relations between these settings, and by the larger contexts in which the settings are embedded. (p. 21)

Using Apter and Conoley's (1984) framework, Sheridan and Gutkin (2000) modified the pivotal assumptions of ecological theory to address students within the contexts of classrooms, schools, and communities.

- *Assumption 1:* Each student is an inseparable part of a small social system.
- *Assumption 2:* Disturbance is not viewed as a disease located within the body of the student but, rather, as discordance (a lack of balance) in the system.
- *Assumption 3:* Discordance may be defined as a disparity between an individual's abilities and the demands or expectations of the environment—"failure to match" between child and system.
- *Assumption 4:* The goal of any intervention is to make the system work. (p. 489)

If we embrace these assumptions, then the need for techniques to measure and evaluate school context becomes apparent. Clearly, educators cannot "make the system work" without examining the influence of the school context on a particular student, the student's teachers, and his or her classmates.

Contrasting Constructs: Climate Versus Culture

Comprehensive reviews of school climate measures (Anderson, 1982; Lehr & Christenson, 2002) have addressed constructs and models used in school context research. The differences between the terms *setting, atmosphere, environment, culture,* and *climate* are both subtle and important. Creating a positive school context, however, is often a primary objective of school reform and restructuring efforts (e.g., Positive Behavior Support or the Yale Child Study Center School Development Program).

A survey of the school context research suggests that *climate* and *culture* are the generally preferred constructs for researchers' investigations of school context.

- *Definitions of School Climate.* Researchers have often described *climate* as a school's personality; some early conceptualizations of organizational climate were essentially adaptations of individual personality theory (Hoy & Sabo, 1998). Current measures of school climate grew out of a body of research on organizational climates in industry and university contexts. Early work by March and Simon (1958) and Argyris (1964) focused on the characteristics of business organizations that influenced employee morale, productivity, and commitment (Anderson, 1982). Stern's (1964) research in university settings concerning "press" (i.e., students' perceptions of environmental pressures on students exerted by a given school) suggested: (a) students' collective perceptions of school climate do reflect objective reality; (b) students' individual perceptions of school climate are not merely reflections of their personal characteristics; and (c) students' descriptions of the school climate can be separated from their attitudes (Anderson, 1982).

Thus, school climate can be defined as the pervasive quality of a school environment experienced by students and staff, which affects their behaviors (Hoy & Sabo, 1998). According to Haynes, Emmons, and Ben-Avie

continues

Theoretical Foundations for Evaluating School Context - *Continued*

(1997), school climate refers to "the quality and consistency of interpersonal interactions within the school community that influences children's cognitive, social, and psychological development" (p. 322).

To gather information on the "personality" of schools, measures of school climate tend to focus on individuals' behaviors and their perceptions of the patterns of communication and interactions within the school context.

- *Definitions of School Culture.* Reflecting the diversity of definitions for the term in the anthropological literature, definitions of school culture vary. (According to Berger, 1995, p. 136, "It has been estimated that anthropologists have advanced more than 100 definitions of culture.") Research on organizational culture dates back to studies of business and industry in the 1930s and 1940s. Barnard (1938) and Mayo (1945) originally conceptualized workplace culture as the "norms, sentiments, values, and emergent interactions" of an organization. School culture can be defined as "the way we do things around here" and consists of the organization's shared beliefs, rituals, and ceremonies, and patterns of communication (Deal & Kennedy, 1982).

School culture represents the underlying assumptions and beliefs developed through earlier problem solutions, which help to define reality within an organization (Angelides & Ainscow, 2000). In their definition, Hoy, Tarter, and Kottkamp (1991) attempted to synthesize the various definitions of school culture and suggest it is "a system of shared orientations (norms, core values, and tacit assumptions) held by members, which holds the unit together and gives it a distinct identity" (p. 5). School culture is generally more abstract than school climate, focusing less on individuals' behavior and more on the assumptions, interpretations, and expectations that drive individuals' behaviors within the school context.

Climate or Culture: Which Construct Is More Meaningful for Evaluating Schoolwide Behavior Interventions?

In their review of the research on school climate and school culture, Hoy and Sabo (1998) indicate their preference for using measures of school climate and suggest the following advantages: (a) an emphasis on survey technology and statistical analysis; (b) the utility of school climate as an independent variable for explaining student outcomes and staff performance; and (c) school climate measures' ability to produce a "snapshot" of organizational and individual behavior for the expressed purpose of managing and changing that behavior.

For professionals serving as outside consultants or those attempting to complete large-scale program evaluations with numerous variables, school climate measures are probably the more reasonable choice. However, when considering services within a particular school setting, the evaluation techniques typically used within investigations of school culture may provide more useful data for facilitating change. (Figure 1 provides a user-friendly overview of the advantages and disadvantages of each approach). As with any assessment, practitioners interested in assessing school context are advised to consider their "referral questions" to facilitate selection of an appropriate assessment technology.

Figure 1. Evaluating School Context: Advantages and Disadvantages of the Different Approaches

Evaluating School Climate

Comprehensive Assessment of School Environments (CASE)-School Climate Survey

Advantages
- Part of a larger information management system that includes 34 variables regarding school environment
- Computerized software available for scoring and data management.
- Includes student, parent, and teacher surveys.
- Adequate reliability information provided by developers.

Disadvantages
- Only available for secondary schools (Grades 6-12).
- No information on construct and consequential validity provided by developers.

Organization Health Inventory (OHI) and Organizational Climate Descriptive Questionnaire (OCDQ)

Advantages
- Time-efficient administration (i.e., approximately 10 minutes to complete).
- Adequate reliability and validity provided by developers.
- Research conducted by developers suggests the measure is related to school effectiveness.
- Separate measures for elementary, middle, and high schools.

Disadvantages
- Only includes measures of teacher and administrator—Student and parent questionnaires are unavailable.

Evaluating School Culture

Critical Incident Analysis

Advantages
- Provides an opportunity for reflection on the assumptions and beliefs that guide student, teacher, or administrator behavior.
- Utilizes the skills and knowledge of practitioners with training in conducting classroom observations (e.g., school psychologists, administrators, and special educators).

Disadvantages
- The definition of a "critical incident" is not well defined.
- The observation and evaluation process has the potential to damage collegial relationships—An outside evaluator may need to complete the process.

Quality Improvement Tools

Advantages
- Extensive professional literature on the use of Quality Improvement Tools is available.
- Provides a series of techniques for assessing and addressing "value gaps" (e.g., differences between a school's culture and the goals of the behavior intervention program).
- Process provides opportunities for evaluators to probe stakeholders' responses and for stakeholders to participate in evaluating the meaning of information produced.

Disadvantages
- Organizing and conducting focus groups can be time consuming.

The Comprehensive Assessment of School Environments (CASE)

The CASE is a product of the Task Force on School Climate, convened by the National Association of Secondary School Principals (NASSP) in 1982. Task force members conducted an extensive review of research and instrumentation concerning the construct of school climate. This review process led to the creation of an extensive model of the components of school environments, which subsequently formed the foundation for development of the Comprehensive Assessment of School Environments–Information Management System (CASE-IMS):

- Instruments for assessing 34 input, mediating, and output variables of a school environment.
- Computer software for scoring response sheets and for interpreting data.
- Procedures for predicting the effect of alternative paths of action on school outcomes.
- Suggested interventions for positively affecting selected variables.
- A step-by-step process for translating assessment information into significant school improvement projects (Howard & Keefe, 1991, p. vii).

The CASE School Climate Survey represents only one mediating variable within the larger CASE-IMS evaluation framework.

The CASE School Climate Survey consists of 55 items and is administered to students (Grades 6–12), teachers, and parents to assess their perceptions about 10 dimensions of school climate. You can administer the School Climate Survey alone or as part of the larger CASE evaluation package that includes three components:

- Satisfaction Surveys administered to parents, teachers, and students.
- Teacher Report Forms for collecting information about teachers' perceptions of school and district leadership.
- Student Report Forms for collecting information about students' academic self-concepts.

Evidence of the reliability of the School Climate Survey is adequate: Internal consistency coefficients for the surveys range from .63 to .92 and test-retest coefficients range from .63 to .92. Unfortunately, the technical manual provides no criterion-related evidence for the validity of the CASE School Climate Survey. Moreover, no evidence shows that the School Climate Scale differentiates between different school environments or reflects improvements in climate brought about by intervention efforts (Allen, 1992; Leong, 1992).

The CASE-IMS represents a promising method for measuring a variety of components that contribute to school effectiveness. Within the context of this system, inferences made from results on the CASE School Climate Surveys could provide important information for school reform efforts. Until additional evidence of construct and consequential validity is available, however, you should interpret CASE results with caution.

Organization Health Inventory (OHI) and Organizational Climate Descriptive Questionnaire (OCDQ)

Developed by Hoy and his colleagues, the OHI and OCDQ have several technical and practical features that enhance their appeal for educators and program evaluators. For example, both the OHI and the OCDQ have separate instruments for use in elementary, middle, and high schools. Although the instruments for each age group contain many of the same items and scales, they also have features that reflect the differences between school environments and organizations at the different grade levels.

The three OHI instruments consist of 37 to 45 items (depending on the version) that measure teachers' and administrators' perceptions about the organizational health of their school. The items are organized into five to seven distinct scales, each of which demonstrates an acceptable level of reliability (internal consistency coefficients ranged from .87 to .95). Administration of the *OHI* takes about 10 minutes and can be completed by each respondent independently. Moreover, an index of school health can be computed by summing the standardized scores for each of the individual scales (Hoy & Sabo, 1998).

Unfortunately, the OHI does not include instruments for measuring students' perceptions of school health. Hoy and his colleagues, however, have conducted extensive research to provide construct and criterion-related evidence for the validity of the OHI. Moreover, some studies have examined the contribution of organizational health to overall school functioning.

Similar to the OHI, three separate versions of OCDQ exist to measure teachers' and administrators' perceptions of school climate at the elementary, middle, and secondary school levels. The questionnaires consist of 34 to 50 items (depending on the version) that ask respondents to rate the extent to which statements (e.g., "Teachers help and support each other") are true of behavior in their school. Individual items contribute to five or six scales that describe teacher and administrator behavior. Potential users should note the relatively inadequate internal consistency for some of the scales on the middle and secondary school versions of the OCDQ (e.g., Disengaged-Elementary [internal consistency coefficient = .75]; Committed-Middle School [.60]; Disengaged-Middle [.46]; and Intimate-Secondary [.71].)

For the elementary and middle school versions of the OCDQ, factor analysis confirmed the existence of a second-order factor structure. For example, on the OCDQ for middle schools, one factor was comprised of measures of principal behavior (i.e., Supportive, Directive, and Restrictive), while the other factor consisted of measures of teacher behavior (i.e., Collegial, Committed, and Disengaged). The factor structure was similar for the elementary version of the OCDQ with the Intimate scale replacing the Committed scale in the factor that describes teacher behavior. These second-order factors contribute to the equation of Principal Openness and Teacher Openness Indices. The resulting standard scores for Teacher Openness and Principal Openness, which range from 200 to 800, are used to determine whether the school climate is best described as Open, Engaged, Disengaged, or Closed.

Because of the complex organization of most secondary school environments, the scales on the OCDQ for secondary schools do not conform to the same second-order factor structure as those on the versions for elementary and middle schools. Therefore, the Openness Index for secondary schools can be determined using the standard scores from four of the five subscales. The remaining scale standard score can be used as an index of Intimacy.

Similar to their work with the OHI, Hoy and colleagues have subsequently used the three versions of the OCDQ in numerous studies that provide construct- and criterion-related evidence of the OCDQ's validity. Additional studies have examined the contribution of organizational climate (i.e., openness) to overall school achievement. For example, Teacher Openness ($r = .52$) and Principal Openness ($r = .43$) Indexes were significantly correlated to a measure of academic press (i.e., the amount a school stressed academic performance and students respected other students who were academically successful; Hoy et al., 1991).

EVALUATING SCHOOL CULTURE

Investigators of school culture have typically used ethnographic and participant observation methods to gather information about school communities and their members. Although qualitative research methods may not attain the reliability and validity of the questionnaires used in School Climate Research, interviews and focus groups assessments may provide useful information that assists in analyzing school context. Climate questionnaires directly assess descriptions, indirectly assess patterns of relationship among these descriptions, and do not assess organizational members' interpretations of events. Investigation of school culture focuses on assessing the meaning individuals ascribe to interactions and events (Rentsch, 1990).

Unfortunately, many qualitative research methods demand extensive observation and participation within the school context. This level of commitment may be unreasonable for many practitioners.

Two approaches for data collection and analysis may represent less time-intensive methods for evaluating school culture: Critical Incident Analysis and Quality Improvement tools.

Critical Incident Analysis

The term *critical incident* was originally used by historians to describe turning points in the life of a person, an institution, or social movement (Tripp, 1993). Angelides and Ainscow (2000) proposed that by observing and analyzing critical incidents in classrooms, schoolyards, and teachers' lounges, researchers can "uncover" underlying assumptions and beliefs that guide behavior within a school. In a school context, critical incidents do not need to be monumental or "turning point" events. Instead, Angelides and Ainscow (2000) suggested that critical events can be relatively minor incidents—everyday events that happen in every school and in every classroom. Events attain "criticality" via the justification, the significance, and the meaning given to them by participants. Although this definition is appealing in its universality, without further elaboration the classroom observer would be at a loss to separate critical incidents from everyday occurrences. Therefore, Angelides and Ainscow (2000) recommended the following procedure for identifying and analyzing critical incidents.

When something occurs in the classroom that surprises or intrigues the observer, it should be recorded as a critical incident. The observer proceeds with an analysis, using the following "probing questions":

- Whose interests are served or denied by the actions of this critical incident?
- What conditions sustain and preserve these actions?
- What power relationships between principal, teachers, pupils, and parents are expressed in this incident?
- What structural, organizational, and cultural factors are likely to prevent teachers and pupils from engaging in alternative ways (Angelides & Ainscow, 2000, p. 158)?

Whenever possible, participants (e.g., teachers and pupils) should be interviewed about their perceptions and explanations of the critical incident. Following the interview, the observer synthesizes the information from the interviewees' multiple perspectives. This information is used to refine the observer's own analysis of the critical event.

When a collection of critical events have been recorded and analyzed, the observer should present his or her findings to the school staff and encourage reflection about the information. The staff can use the following questions to guide this discussion:

- What does this account tell us about ourselves?
- What can we learn from this analysis?
- What does this information point to about the nature of the way in which we work together?
- Does this information help us to see things that we could change (Angelides & Ainscow, 2000, p. 160)?

Angelides and Ainscow (2000) suggested that engaging in these reflective discussions could assist school staffs in identifying possible interventions for improving their school cultures. They caution, however, that presentations of critical incidents should be both sensitive and professional in tone to protect the feelings and reputations of involved parties.

Critical Incident Analysis is a potentially appealing technique for practitioners who have extensive training and experience with conducting classroom observations. Angelides and Ainscow (2000), however, recommended that schools hire an "outside" observer to complete the critical event observations. This approach seems wise because critical incidents have the potential to present teachers and their classrooms in a less-than-flattering light, leading to potentially strained professional relationships.

Quality Improvement Tools

Quality Improvement tools represent a more appropriate evaluation technique for practitioners who desire information about their own school's culture. Although many practitioners may not be familiar with the Quality Improvement tools, these procedures are not new. In fact, their development can be traced back to Deming's work with the Japanese Union of Scientists and Engineers (JUSE) in post-World War II Japan, and followed through the subsequent Total Quality Management (TQM) "revolution" in both Japanese and American businesses (Brassard, 1996).

The application of Quality Improvement processes to educational decision making has been prompted by the need for educators to become more cost efficient and solution oriented in their evaluation of schools' work environments and cultures. Snyder (1988) defined school culture as "the collective work patterns of a system (or school) . . . as perceived by its staff members" (Johnson, Snyder, Anderson, & Johnson, 1996, p. 140). The Quality Improvement evaluation process provides practitioners with tools to examine staff members' attitudes and beliefs about the school's work patterns and organizational structure.

Detert, Louis, and Schroeder (2001) offered a series of propositions that attest to the importance of considering a school's culture during implementation of the Quality Improvement process. School change facilitators need to address "value gaps" between a reform program and the underlying school culture. Moreover, school reformers should deal not only with the aggregate of stakeholder values in relation to an existing culture, but also to how individuals' values align with the dominant values of the school community, and how potential incongruities affect their well-being and productiveness (Detert et al., 2001). Therefore, one of the primary needs in most school improvement processes is the investigation of the school culture and its underlying values and the design of subsequent interventions to align individuals' values and needs with those of the change initiative.

Recruiting focus groups that represent each group of key stakeholders and completing a series of the Quality Improvement tools with each group is one method for gathering important information about current school culture and possible strategies for intervention. Unlike school climate questionnaires, the Quality Improvement process allows evaluators to probe participants' responses and engage in collectively drawing conclusions. A potential drawback to using the Quality Improvement tools is the time commitment required to recruit and organize representative focus groups.

FINAL CONSIDERATIONS: BEST PRACTICES FOR EVALUATING SCHOOL CONTEXT

Practitioners interested in evaluating school context are confronted with a plethora of options, including written questionnaires, ethnographic methods, and focus groups. The following guidelines are intended to assist the decision-making process when selecting a strategy for evaluating school climate or school culture.

Consider the Questions That Need to Be Answered. Within the domain of school climate, questionnaires are based on different theories and definitions of organizational climate. Therefore, practitioners should read user manuals and supplemental information to make certain that survey instruments measure the constructs of interest. Moreover, survey respondents, observation subjects, and interview participants should include members of the target group of the evaluation. For example, if the school climate's contribution to student behavior and connectedness are areas of interest, practitioners should use techniques that directly assess students' perceptions of the school climate.

Use Multiple Methods of Assessment. Information about school climate and school culture may be more meaningful within the context of data gathered from multiple sources. For example, results from school climate measures can be correlated with student achievement, attendance and discipline data, or measures of teacher satisfaction and sense of efficacy to provide a more meaningful picture of school functioning. Observations and interviews from school culture evaluations can be analyzed with behavior referrals and other artifacts that provide evidence of the themes and issues identified in the examination of school culture. When evaluating the effects of systemic interventions on school contexts, educators should attempt to follow the carpenter's rule: "Measure twice, cut once."

Consider Combining Measures of Climate and Culture. Information collected from school climate surveys can be enriched with interviews and observations. Surveys and questionnaires are useful for assessing descriptions of events, but they do not assess the personally relevant meanings attached to events. To understand meaning in schools, it is necessary to assess interpretations of students, staff, and other community members (Rentsch, 1990). The combination of quantitative and qualitative methods can provide more meaningful information about school contexts to guide systemic prevention and intervention efforts, resulting in improved outcomes for students.

REFERENCES

Allen, N. L. (1992). Review of the Comprehensive Assessment of School Environments. In J. J. Kramer & J. C. Conoley (Eds.), *The eleventh mental measurements yearbook*. Lincoln, NE: Buros Institute, University of Nebraska Press. Retrieved April 25, 2002 from http://webdbs.library.wisc.edu:8585/webspirs/start.ws?databases = s(YB).

Anderson, C. S. (1982). The search for school climate: A review of the research. *Review of Educational Research, 52,* 368-420.

Angelides, P., & Ainscow, M. (2000). Making sense of the role of culture in school improvement. *School Effectiveness and School Improvement, 11,* 145-163.

Apter, S. J., & Conoley, J. C. (1984). *Childhood behavior disorders and emotional disturbance: An introduction to teaching troubled children*. Englewood Cliffs, NJ: Prentice-Hall.

Argyris, C. (1964). *Integrating the individual and the organization*. New York: John Wiley.

Barnard, C. L. (1938). *Functions of the executive*. Cambridge, MA: Harvard University Press.

Berger, A. (1995). *Cultural criticism*. London: Rutledge.

Brassard, M. (1996). *The memory jogger plus: Featuring the seven management and planning tools*. Salem, NH: GOAL/QPC.

Bronfenbrenner, U. (1979). *The ecology of human development: Experiments in nature and design*. Cambridge, MA: Harvard University Press.

Deal, T., & Kennedy, A. (1982). *Corporate cultures*. Reading, MA: Addison-Wesley.

Detert, J. R., Louis, K. S., & Schroeder, R. G. (2001). A culture framework for education: Defining quality values and their impact in U.S. high schools. *School Effectiveness and School Improvement, 12,* 183-212.

Fullan, M. G., & Steigelbauer, S. (1991). *The new meaning of educational change*. New York: Teachers College Press.

Haynes, N. M., Emmons, C., & Ben-Avie, M. (1997). School climate as a factor in student adjustment and achievement. *The Journal of Educational and Psychological Consultation, 8,* 321-329.

Howard, E. R., & Keefe, J. W. (1991). *The CASE-IMS school improvement process*. Reston, VA: National Association of Secondary School Principals.

Hoy, W. K., & Sabo, D. J. (1998). *Quality middle schools: Open and healthy*. Thousand Oaks, CA: Sage.

Hoy, W. K., Tarter, C. J., & Kottkamp, R. B. (1991). *Open schools/healthy schools: Measuring organizational climate*. Newbury Park, CA: Sage.

Johnson, W. L., Snyder, K. J., Anderson, R. H., & Johnson, A. M. (1996). School work culture and productivity. *The Journal of Experimental Education, 64,* 139-156.

Lehr, C. A., & Christenson, S. L. (2002). Best practices in promoting a positive school climate. In A. Thomas & J. Grimes (Eds.), *Best practices in school psychology IV* (pp. 929-948). Bethesda, MD: National Association of School Psychologists.

Leong, F. T. (1992). Review of the Comprehensive Assessment of School Environments. In J. J. Kramer & J. C. Conoley (Eds.), *The eleventh mental measurements yearbook*. Lincoln, NE: Buros Institute - University of Nebraska Press. Retrieved April 25, 2002 from http://webdbs.library.wisc.edu:8585/webspirs/start.ws?databases = s(YB).

March, J., & Simon, H. (1958). *Organizations*. New York: John Wiley.

Mayo, E. (1945). *The social problems of industrial civilization*. Boston, MA: Graduate School of Business Administration, Harvard University.

National Association of Secondary School Principals. (1986). *Comprehensive assessment of school environments* (CASE). Reston, VA: Author.

Rentsch, J. R. (1990). Climate and culture: Interaction and qualitative differences in organizational meanings. *Journal of Applied Psychology, 75,* 668-681.

Sheridan, S. M., & Gutkin, T. B. (2000). The ecology of school psychology: Examining and changing our paradigm for the 21st century. *School Psychology Review, 29,* 485-502.

Snyder, K. J. (1988). *School work culture profile.* Tampa, FL: School Management Institute.

Spillane, J. P., Diamond, J. B., Burch, P., Hallett, T., Jita, L., & Zoltners, J. (2002). Managing in the middle: School leaders and the enactment of accountability policy. *Educational Policy, 16,* 731-762.

Sprague, J., Walker, H., Golly, A., White, K., Myers, D., & Shannon, T. (2001). Translating research into effective practice: The effects of a universal staff and student intervention on indicators of discipline and school safety. *Education and Treatment of Children, 24,* 495-511.

Stern, G. G. (1964). B = F(P,E). *Journal of Personality Assessment, 28,* 161-168.

Tripp, D. (1993). *Critical incidents in teaching.* London: Rutledge.

We express appreciation to Lois Triemstra and Katherine Streit for their assistance with this manuscript.

Originally published in *TEACHING Exceptional Children, Vol. 37, No. 1, pp. 10–17.*

8

High School Peer Mentoring That Works!

Judith Dopp and Tara Block

How can a general education classroom teacher effectively deal with the inclusion of students with disabilities who just do not "fit in"? What can that teacher do when his or her students with learning disabilities isolate themselves from the general student population by their inability to join in or by drawing attention to themselves through their inappropriate behavior? When such students are placed in cooperative settings, they often seem either to disrupt others or to do nothing, choosing to let other group members complete their work.

With the implementation of the Individuals with Disabilities Education Act (IDEA), schools have included students with disabilities in general education classrooms to learn positive social interactions as well as academics. Yet many teachers believe that the "included" students disrupt their classes, accomplish little or nothing, or reinforce inappropriate behavior. In fact, in a synthesis of 152 studies, Forness and Kavale (1996) reported that 75% of students with learning disabilities displayed inappropriate social skills that set them apart from other students. How can teachers help students improve their social skills and learn from classroom instruction if the students refuse to participate in the class or are rejected by their classmates?

Educators have identified many effective strategies for educating all students within the inclusive general education classroom. But to prevent certain students from isolating themselves, we must implement new ideas. Difficulties arise when students with poor social skills display behaviors that cause their peers to reject them, preventing the students from receiving the

Working cooperatively while one-handed stresses good communication.

positive benefits that peers can provide. Instead, some are faced with additional rejection and isolation in a classroom environment that should be supportive but that ends up lowering their self-esteem and negating any positive benefit from being part of it. Farmer, Pearl, and Van Acker (1996) suggested that, even if fully included, "students with disabilities have low social acceptance in general education classrooms," p. 232, so teachers need to foster positive interactions with peers. Students with social skill deficits need to learn appropriate classroom social skills that they can also apply to their future work environment. According to Cartledge and Johnson (1996), in many inclusion programs, teachers witness the positive influence general education students have on the social skills of students with disabilities. Many teachers have found an effective way to teach communication and problem-solving skills: peer leadership. Researchers have shown that peer tutoring can help classmates learn (Elbaum, Moody, Vaughn, Schumm, & Hughes, 1999), but can peers actually teach social skills to their classmates?

   This article presents a program that was implemented in a Midwest high school that educators could easily adapt for other schools. We describe how peer leaders planned and systematically taught positive communication skills and problem-solving techniques to their classmates (see box, "Implementing a Peer-Mentoring Program"). We also show how the students who exhibited undesirable classroom behavior became class leaders, modeling positive skills when they had to teach those skills themselves.

> **Implementing a Peer-Mentoring Program**
>
> - **Emphasize ongoing training of the peer leaders.** An initial training session and weekly reviews reinforce the necessary skills and provide a supportive atmosphere.
> - **Use hands-on activities to foster creativity.** Because the student leaders enjoy the activities, they try to "think outside the box" as they find or devise activities that will be appealing to their classmates.
> - **Practice problem-solving skills universally throughout the school.** If a specific problem-solving model is used universally throughout the school, students will frequently practice that problem-solving skill, as well as observe it being used by others.
> - **Incorporate discussion and review of previous lessons.** As students adjust to creative freedom in the peer-mentoring environment, they want to share more ideas.
> - **Ask students to help create their own program.** Students take pride and feel important when their ideas are implemented.
> - **Encourage students with weak skills to become peer leaders.** Teachers should encourage participation by students who have social skills deficits that alienate them from their classmates. Students should be given leadership roles in planning and teaching the interactive group activities.
> - **Include volunteer groups to help support appropriate social interaction.** Groups such as the National Honor Society, "Best Buddies," Future Teachers Association, can help specific students teach skills to their own classes, as well as serve as good role models.

PREPARING PEER LEADERS

Finding Out What Teachers Need

We distributed a teacher-made survey, Communication Needs Assessment for Classroom Teachers, to 60 teachers at a Midwest high school with an enrollment of about 1,000 students. The survey asked teachers to rate their student's use of nine different social skills. A team then prioritized the top three skills that teachers believed were most crucial to school success: cooperation, problem-solving, and preventing aggression.

Freshman and Sophomore Student Participants

The program targeted 114 students in average and remedial freshman English classes, as well as two sophomore instructional classes for those with learning disabilities and mild to moderate mental retardation. Class schedules and teachers' willingness to cooperate were the determining factors in choosing the classes for participation. Because of the time constraints

Peer leaders are introducing the CLASP method of problem-solving.

that many teachers and administrators faced, the faculty emphasized the need for "quick/short" activities that left time to carry out academic agendas.

Setting Goals

The training team, which consisted of the school social worker and special education teacher, created a general plan of action to teach specific social skills designed to encourage cooperation, prevent aggression, and solve problems. Because interactive groups are often asked to work together to solve the problems assigned to them, the team believed that students needed training in resolving disagreements logically, voicing opinions appropriately, and brainstorming ideas creatively. Who better to model these social skills than their peers? The team selected a group of students and trained them to conduct social skills lessons in front of their peers under the guidance of trained staff. The team

- Used peers to facilitate learning.
- Structured the classroom activities.
- Expected students to be successful.
- Gave leaders valued roles.
- Used the existing expertise of trained staff members.

The program incorporated five natural supports for collaboration recommended by Gilberts, Agran, and Hughes (2001). The overall goal of the pro-

By closing their eyes to visualize their calming places, students are asked to de-stress and relax by enjoying their favorite scents, and listening to sounds of dolphins frolicking in the water.

gram was for students to resolve conflict by developing better communication, cooperation, and problem-solving skills (see box, "Benefits of Peer Support").

Training in a Day

A teacher and the school social worker conducted a daylong training session for 25 sophomore, junior, and senior volunteers. The trainers were selected on the basis of teacher recommendations and availability. Six were members of the National Honor Society, 7 were future teachers, 2 had behavior problems, and the remaining 10 had learning disabilities. The materials used for the training activities came from social-skills training curriculums, such as those found in Tom Jackson's *Activities That Teach* series (1993). In these activities, students participate in their own learning by physically taking part in the lesson. Each lesson was then followed up with a discussion topic centered on the goal of the activity.

The teacher and the school social worker conducted get-acquainted activities with the students and led discussions in which feelings were shared, goals were restated, and some of the students' anxieties were allayed. After the get-acquainted activities, the students and instructors practiced their own problem-solving skills, experimenting with some of the social skills activities that the students themselves would subsequently be teaching.

Next they brainstormed ideas to create lessons that emphasized the skills of conflict resolution and cooperative problem-solving, selecting their favorite activities that could be taught in about 10 to 20 minutes. Later in the day, the

Benefits of Peer Support

- Prater, Serna, and Nakamura, (1999) evaluated the effectiveness of teacher-directed social skill instruction on students with disabilities, and the students, in turn, taught the same social skill to other students with disabilities. After receiving training themselves and then teaching others, the **peer teachers had improved their social skills** in giving positive feedback, contributing to discussions, and accepting negative feedback.

- Schools known to use peers for mentoring have been shown to create **a more favorable school climate.** Some schools have even shown a decline in the dropout rate and an increase in the average daily attendance rate (Stader & Gagnepain, 2000).

- Peer-mediated instruction and interventions (PMII) **facilitated learning in various groups** of students with different abilities, interests, and backgrounds (Utley & Mortweet, 1997).

- Most students in peer-mediated programs have **demonstrated improvements in self-concept; growth in social skills; increased understanding of human differences; increased tolerance for others; and development of personal values, interpersonal acceptance, and friendship** (Kamps, Kravits, Stolze & Swaggart, 1998).

- Peer reinforcement, another type of peer assistance, provides **immediate reinforcement by peers.** "Students with disabilities often have difficulties in determining socially appropriate and academically correct behaviors, therefore, receiving appropriate feedback from their peers can provide essential information concerning behavioral expectations" (Gartin & Murdick, 1992, p. 241).

- Prater, Bruhl, and Serna (1999) found that **students teaching other students is frequently more effective than teachers teaching students.**

- Researchers have consistently found **clear benefits to tutoring, both to those being tutored and to those doing the tutoring.** Many peer tutors actually improve their own skills, simply because they are practicing them regularly and are consciously thinking about them (Elbaum, Moody, Vaughn, Schumm, & Hughes, 1999).

- Cooperative learning has also been shown to be effective in facilitating interactive education, increasing academic capabilities, and increasing self-esteem for students at all levels (Goodwin, 1999).

- Students with disabilities have **inappropriate social skills that isolate them** from those without disabilities (Prater, Bruhl, & Serna, 1998).

students were given time to role-play some of the beginning activities so that they felt prepared and comfortable to present the information to their peers.

When the training session ended, the students were eager to begin and excited about leading their peers in some of the activities they had created.

Peer Leader Support

The new peer leaders met for a half-hour weekly to review the week's activity. They were free to supply props, substitute different activities, and vary ways to "present" their skill for maximum enjoyment by their classmates, as long as their approach was reviewed with the teacher or the social worker. The new peer leaders again practiced their problem-solving methodology to help them accomplish their own group goals. Those activities and the review were strong contributors to the effectiveness of the program.

Peer Leaders on the Job

The trained peer leaders began conducting the 10- to 20-minute activities with their classmates in nine different classes, supported by classroom teachers and the school social worker. At first, the peer leaders were extremely nervous and required frequent support and guidance, but the students quickly became more comfortable in front of their peers and relied on the teacher and social worker less often. The students in their classes responded enthusiastically to the peer trainers, and the peer trainers became increasingly more adept in leading activities as the 12 weeks progressed.

Various activities taught specific skills (see box, "Student-Designed Activities That Encourage Skill Development"). For example, peer leaders started their first class lesson by creating an acronym that cued the step of active listening. One group chose the acronym STAR—**S**it up in your desk, **T**urn toward the speaker, **A**ctively listen, and **R**espect the speaker by not interrupting. This acronym served as a reminder for the class. The leaders brought in their favorite candles for an aromatherapy session accompanied by "dolphin" music (Hanneman, 1994) or "angel" music (Fink, 1994) and centered on reducing stress and "focusing on positives." Other leaders guided students through relaxation techniques like taking deep breaths and visualizing happy moments in their lives.

Many activities revolved around problem-solving and communication strategies. One problem-solving strategy introduced was the CLASP method—**C**larify the problem, **L**ook for factors causing the problem, **A**ctively brainstorm, **S**elect the best idea/plan, **P**ut the plan into action (Voltz, Elliot, & Harris, 1995). This approach provided a simple format for addressing complex problems. The students easily implemented the strategy, concentrating particularly on brainstorming ideas when attempting to resolve problems. Within several weeks, the peer leaders truly took ownership of their groups and increased their autonomy, accepting the trainers' offer of assistance only when necessary.

Student-Designed Activities That Encourage Skill Development

Social interaction skills address the skills of communicating appropriately and listening actively to one another. Some of the following team-building activities were suggested by the students from activities in which they had participated in other social situations, such as youth groups and camps.

Human Scavenger Hunt—Students must mingle appropriately, asking questions of one another to find students who (a) were born on _____, (b) have two initials the same, (c) have the same hobbies, or the like (Jones, 1999).

Star Search—Leaders assign the names of popular personalities to students by putting the stars' names on students' backs without letting the students see the names. Then students must interact with one another to ask questions of their classmates for the purpose of identifying their assigned persona. This game teaches students to interact with others and listen to responses.

♪ *Gossip (often called Telephone)*—One student creates "gossip" to tell to one person, then each in turn gossips to another until the last person tells the class what he or she thought was said.

Blind Walk—After creating a maze out of the desks, students direct their blindfolded partners through the maze, asking students to trust the instructions of their partners (Jackson, 1993).

Conflict-resolving skills address the skills of expressing feelings effectively, calming stress levels, and focusing on positives.

"I" Message Scenarios—In defusing inflammatory situations, partners must practice expressing their feelings with "I" messages when given a role to act out (Goldstein, 1997).

Carrying Garbage—Partners role-play daily teenage problem scenarios, then all write down their own personal problems and literally throw them into garbage cans. This activity demonstrates the physical release of the "emotional baggage" that people often carry around.

Aromatherapy—Students listen to dolphin or angel music while closing their eyes, visualizing happy positive scenes in their minds. Then the leaders share various aromas and exercises designed to induce relaxation.

Problem-solving skills address the skills of setting priorities, brainstorming problems, and using a problem-solving strategy to help resolve situations by thinking first before acting.

Chain Gang—The object of this activity is to work as a team to create the longest paper chain while each group member has one hand tied behind his or her back (Jackson, 1995).

Auction Block—This activity focuses on establishing personal goals and values that are important to each of the students. Each participant is given $2,000 to bid on items from a list. Throughout the auction, the leader holds up a "secret box" that can be purchased at the end of the auction. Follow-up discussion focuses on the choices that individuals make and why they make them. (Jackson, 1993).

Eskimo Survival Gear—Teams prioritize a list of items they need to survive when their airplane crashes, working together to decide what items they need and could carry to safety.

Marshmallow-Spaghetti Tower Competition—Teams compete to build the strongest and tallest tower out of marshmallows and spaghetti, implementing their problem-solving strategies and cooperative work skills (Jackson, 1993).

Vignettes—Teams use problem-solving strategies to solve typical high school problems, for example, school cheating, boyfriend-girlfriend infidelity, parental conflicts, and alcohol or drug abuse (Goldstein, 1997).

Literally throwing their problems (their mental "garbage") into the trash demonstrates to students how they can free their minds temporarily.

The Teachers Speak

A final survey of the nine participating classroom teachers indicated that during the 12 weeks of peer training, they observed their students making progress toward the identified goals of

- Using socially appropriate skills.
- Controlling themselves to prevent aggression.
- Cooperating with one another to solve problems.

Because the activities were fun but challenging, the students brainstormed creatively and used the skills, as one teacher said, "at least while the peer leaders were in the class." One especially dramatic change was observed in a particular group; the peer leaders themselves became very positive role models, showing tremendous progress in their own development, particularly in the areas of self-esteem, self-control, and problem-solving.

Student Results

Seven of the nine classroom teachers surveyed agreed that most of their students seemed to develop in the ability to stand up for themselves in appropriate ways. This skill was addressed with the "I messages" activity that focused on teaching students how to change negative statements into positive statements by simply rewording a phrase to precede it with "I." For example, changing "You make me so angry!" to "I get angry when you borrow my clothes without asking" softens the accusation, helps the other person understand and identify with the speaker's feelings rather than become defensive, and keeps the disagreement from escalating into an argument (Goldstein, 1997).

Twenty of the students in the classrooms reported to their peer leaders that they had implemented previously taught strategies outside of class with positive results. We hope that learning a strategy to defuse hostile situations will help students grow in their own self-confidence, giving them needed tools to handle conflict. Although the survey of classroom teachers suggested that their students actively practiced the social skills, no evidence is available to suggest that they were able to carry over these skills beyond the 12 weeks of peer training. To encourage further skill generalization, classroom teachers could employ one or more of the following tactics:

- Assign writing reflections.
- Display visual prompts throughout the classroom.
- Create further role-playing.
- Give extra credit for reporting outside practice of a skill.

What About the Peer Trainers?

All classroom teachers surveyed reported that they witnessed very positive changes in the self-esteem of the peer trainers. This outcome, however, was not the original focus of this study, and we collected no qualitative data to substantiate these claims. Teachers reported that they observed peer leaders becoming more independent in researching activities and bringing in their own props for a lesson.

By the end of the 12 weeks, all peer leaders were conducting the social skills lessons in the classrooms with minimal guidance from the school social worker or special education teacher. The peer leaders referred to the classes as "their groups" and were visibly animated when they were able to help others solve problems. As a result of the program, all the peer leaders (100%) agreed that in training their peers, they themselves had learned skills that they could use in building relationships in later life! The following are some examples of peer leaders:

- Tom, a student with physical disabilities, played an integral role in planning the program. As soon as he became involved, his mother mentioned that Tom seemed to become more motivated about everything at school, finding a sense of purpose. His growth in self-confidence was evident when he took the initiative to mentor a class with another peer helper without the presence of an adult trainer (because of difficulty with scheduling). He soon found that he enjoyed helping others and "performing" for others, so he joined the speech team, demonstrating new confidence in his own abilities.
- Eve, a student with learning disabilities, was conscientious and had probably "volunteered" to participate as a peer mentor because she simply did not possess sufficient assertiveness to say, "No, thank you!" Although she

The problem-solving activity of building the tallest spaghetti tower helped students work together as a team.

did not become more vocal by the end of the program, she evidently learned from the "I" messages activity that taught constructive criticism. One day in another class, she diplomatically pointed out to the teacher that a study guide created by that teacher was only half completed! Even though Eve was very hesitant to criticize, she began her question with an "I" statement: "I think you may have missed part of the study guide. Do you have more questions that have not been run off?" She had spoken out on her own behalf, using a skill that she had been taught. Even though she remained extremely quiet, Eve had clearly become more assertive.

- In the final evaluation three of the leaders who had significant behavior problems declared that focusing on positives had helped them work through their issues and acquire more patience. Their classroom teachers observed that these students had demonstrated much more appropriate social skills during that time period. Because they had been taught specific skills that they in turn had to "teach" to others, the peer leaders with behavioral issues had to practice those skills that they had been lacking. Acting as a role model had exacted much improved self-control from those students, demonstrating that they could respond in positive ways instead of "getting mad," as one of the students reported. They had learned the possibility of thinking through their problems and brainstorming ideas rather than simply reacting negatively to situations.

- Sandy, who had previously received detentions for insubordination, had volunteered to help in a class of students with severe disabilities. With her past history, the team was concerned that she might be a negative influence, but the classroom special education teacher was eager to have her help. Sandy thrived on the attention of "her kids"! During the time period when she worked with the students, she was much more cheerful and positive in her overall demeanor, and she had no referrals for insubordination. The classroom teacher thought that she had been a tremendous example for her students and requested her return.

- William, a student with a behavior disorder, also showed dramatic improvement in his behavior during the peer-mentoring program. Prior to the program, he had usually refused to do any homework, choosing to fail classes simply because he would not do any of the work. However, during the mentoring program, his case manager and he devised a contract that would make his participation contingent on class behavior and work completion. Not only did he meet those requirements 10 out of 12 weeks, he came to school a half-hour early just to offer his ideas for the weekly review and training. His case manager and several teachers believed he had made noticeable progress in changing his behavior.

CLASSROOM IMPLICATIONS

The success of this peer-training program demonstrates that students can teach peers effectively. In this program older peers were successful in teaching social skills to younger peers, but the more dramatic results were observed in the peer leaders themselves. By helping create their own program, the student leaders demonstrated pride in their own creativity, sharing excitement in reaching out to peers with imaginative activities that could be enjoyed by all.

Peer leaders were very creative in developing activities that would appeal to their classmates. They seemed to know which ones would stimulate interaction and which ones would not, corroborating the recommendation of Giangreco, Cloniger, Dennis, and Eldelman (2000) that students need to be involved in developing their own programs. The students with special needs who acted as peer leaders demonstrated the most signficant positive increases in their own social skills.

With increasing numbers of special needs students being included in general education, the implementation of a peer-training program may help such students learn the techniques to benefit from inclusion. To be effective, peer helpers need to be trained in methodology that encourages and supports all students. Instructors need to "teach the students about the rationale and purpose of the model, emphasize collaboration rather than competition" (Fulk & King, 2001, p. 50), and must involve students in planning their own programs.

FINAL THOUGHTS

This high school peer program clearly demonstrates that students with disabilities and other at-risk students can be taught to work cooperatively within groups and that they can problem solve—if they are shown ways to interact appropriately. It also illustrates that students who are weak in specific skills can improve while teaching appropriate social skills to others. Our program is positive proof that all students can become positive role models for others to emulate!

REFERENCES

Cartledge, G., & Johnson, C. T. (1996). Inclusive classrooms for students with emotional and behavioral disorders: Critical variables. *Theory into Practice, 35,* 51–57.

Elbaum, B., Moody, S., Vaughn, S., Schumm, J., & Hughes, M. (1999). *The effect of instructional grouping format on the reading outcomes of students with disabilities: A meta-analytic review. Keys to Successful Learning.* Washington, DC: National Center for Learning Disabilities.

Farmer, T., Pearl, R., & Van Acker, R. (1996). Expanding the social skills deficit framework: A developmental synthesis perspective, classrooms social networks, and implications for the social growth of students with disabilities. *The Journal of Special Education, 30,* 232–256.

Fink, M. (1994). *Music of the angels.* (Cassette Recording No. 2 7-99007-7501-4). Minneapolis: Orchard Lane Music.

Forness, S. R., & Kavale, K, A. (1996). Treating social skill deficits in children with learning disabilities: A meta-analysis of the research. *Learning Disability Quarterly, 19,* 2–13.

Fulk, B. M., & King, K. (2001). Classwide peer tutoring at work. *TEACHING Exceptional Children, 34*(2), 49–53.

Gartin, B. C. & Murdick, N. L. (1992). Cooperative activities to assist in the integration of students with disabilities. *Journal of Instructional Psychology, 19,* 241–246.

Giangreco, M., Cloniger, C., Dennis, R. & Eldelman, S. (2000). Problem solving methods to facilitate inclusive education. In R. A. Villa & J. S. Thousand (Eds.). *Restructuring for caring and effective education* (pp. 293–329). Baltimore, MD: Paul Brookes.

Gilberts, G. H., Agran, M., & Hughes, C. (2001). The effects of peer delivered self-monitoring strategies on the participation of students with severe disabilities in general education classrooms. *The Journal of the Association for Persons With Severe Handicaps, 26,* 25–36.

Goldstein, A. P. (1997). *The Peace Curriculum: Expanded aggression replacement training.* Florissant, MO: The National Peace Institute.

Goodwin, M. (1999). Cooperative learning and social skills: What skills to teach and how to teach them. *Intervention in School and Clinic, 35*(1), 29–33.

Hanneman, R. (1994). *Dance of the dolphins. Eco-voyage nature's relaxing sounds with music.* (Cassette recording No. EV-48907.) St. Laurent, Quebec: Madacy Music Group.

Jackson, T. (1993). *Activities that teach.* Shepherdsville, KY: Publisher's Press.

Jackson, T. (1995). *More activities that teach.* Shepherdsville, KY: Publisher's Press.

Jones, A. (1999). *Team building activities for every group.* Richland, WA: Rec Room.

Kamps, D., Kravits, T., & Lopez, A. (1998). What do the peers think? Social validity of peer-mediated programs. *Education and Treatment of Children, 21*(2), 107–134.

Kamps, D., Kravits, T., Stolze, J., & Swaggart, B. (1999). Prevention strategies for at-risk students and students with EBD in urban elementary school. *Journal of Emotional & Behavioral Disorders, 7,* 178–189.

Kavale, K. A. & Forness, S. R. (1996). Social skill deficits and learning disabilities: A meta-analysis. *Journal of Learning Disabilities, 29,* 226–237.

Prater, M., Serna, L., & Nakamura, K. (1999). Impact of peer teaching on the acquisition of social skills by adolescents with learning disabilities. *Education and Treatment of Children, 22*(1), 19–35.

Prater, M. A., Bruhl, S., & Serna, L. A. (1998). Acquiring social skills through cooperative learning and teacher-directed instruction. *Remedial and Special Education, 19,* 160–172.

Stader, D., & Gagnepain, F. G. (2000). Mentoring: The power of peers. *American Secondary Education, 28*(3), 28–32.

Utley, C., & Mortweet, S. (1997). Peer-mediated instruction and interventions. *Focus of Exceptional Children, 29,* 5.

Voltz, D. L., Elliott, R. N., & Harris, W. B. (1995). Promising practices in facilitation collaboration between resource room teachers and general education teachers. *Learning Disabilities Research & Practice, 10,* 126–136.

Originally published in *TEACHING Exceptional Children,* Vol. 37, No. 1, pp. 58–62.

Classroom Strategies

9

Making It Work: Differentiating Tier Two Self-Regulated Strategies Development in Writing in Tandem With Schoolwide Positive Behavioral Support

Karin N. Sandmel, Mary Brindle, Karen R. Harris, Kathleen Lynne Lane, Steve Graham, Jessica Nackel, Rachel Mathias, and Annette Little

Ms. Berger teaches in a second grade inclusive classroom. Her school has been implementing a positive behavioral support (PBS) model for 3 years, and she has seen meaningful improvements in student behavior and the school environment. Many of her students, however, are struggling with writing, and she has noticed some behavioral issues become more challenging during her writing instruction. She recently learned about Self-Regulated Strategies Development (SRSD) for writing, an evidence-based approach for teaching writing and self-regulation strategies. She wonders if SRSD can be differentiated to meet the various writing needs of all her students—those who struggle, the typically developing writers, and the students who excel. What types of modifications or accommodations can Ms. Berger, or others who work with her students, make to facilitate learning to write for all of her students?

Many teachers face similar concerns in their classrooms. Differentiating instruction to meet the varying needs of their students is challenging. We conducted two studies as part of a federally funded project to improve the writing performance of students identified as at risk for behavioral difficulties and struggling with writing (Lane, et al., 2008; Lane et al., in press). One study focused on improving persuasive writing abilities, whereas the second study focused on improving story writing abilities. Many of the students we worked with needed accommodations or modifications to the SRSD approach. As Tomlinson (1999) noted, instruction can be differentiated or modified for students in three different areas: content, process, or products. Content can be differentiated two ways, by adjusting the materials the teacher uses with the student or by amending what the teacher wants the student to learn. Process involves meeting the learning needs of the student through different activities. Product involves students demonstrating their learning in ways that reflect their abilities.

Ben was a 7½-year-old Caucasian male who struggled with writing and whose teacher found it difficult to keep him on task. Both content and process were modified to help him master the writing and self-regulation strategies. Cory was a 9-year-old Caucasian male who had difficulties with memory; his teacher found that he had great difficulty expressing his wonderful ideas in writing. His needs were addressed by modifying the process and the product. Mara was a 7-year-old Caucasian female who initially struggled with writing, but quickly acquired the writing and self-regulation strategies and was able to implement them independently in just a few lessons. To challenge Mara, content, process, and product were modified. These students presented unique challenges that needed to be addressed in order for them to develop powerful writing and self-regulation strategies that made a real difference in their writing.

SCHOOLWIDE POSITIVE BEHAVIORAL SUPPORT

Ben, Cory, and Mara attended an elementary school in the Southeast that implemented schoolwide Positive Behavioral Support (PBS; Lane, Kalberg, & Menzies, 2009). The intent of PBS is to prevent and respond to problem behaviors by instituting a three-tiered model of prevention that begins with an instructional approach to behavior (Hendley, 2007). The PBS model implemented in this school included the following three tiers of support:

1. Tier one—primary prevention supports in which students are taught the desired behavioral expectations and then given opportunities to practice and receive reinforcement for demonstrating the behaviors.

2. Tier two—secondary prevention supports designed for students who were nonresponsive or not adequately responsive to primary prevention efforts and who needed more intense support.

3. Tier three—tertiary prevention supports developed for students with multiple risk factors requiring more intensive intervention such as special education services (Walker et. al., 1996).

The first tier, or primary prevention program, developed at this school involved faculty and staff generating schoolwide behavioral expectations for students in all areas of the school (e.g., cafeteria, library, classrooms, hallways). Expectations (respect, best effort, and responsibility) were explicitly taught to all students, and students had multiple opportunities to practice and receive reinforcement for meeting these expectations. Students received school-designed PBS tickets for displaying appropriate behavior, and positive behavior was supported and recognized schoolwide.

Students identified as needing additional academic and behavioral support received tier two services. In this tier, students received direct and intensive instruction and behavioral support individually or in small groups. As part of the schoolwide PBS plan to identify students needing second tier interventions, teachers routinely identified students in their classrooms exhibiting high levels of internalizing or externalizing behaviors through the use of the Systematic Screening for Behavior Disorders (SSBD; Walker & Severson, 1992) and the Student Risks Screening Scale (SRSS; Drummond, 1994). Participating schools completed these two behavior screening tools as part of regular school practices.

Students who were identified as having behavioral concerns according to one of these two measures, and who struggled with writing, were invited to participate in the larger study. Writing performance was measured using the Test of Written Language–3 (TOWL–3; Hammill & Larsen, 1996). In order for students to participate in our study and work with us, they had to write at least one complete sentence and score below the 25th percentile on this assessment. The students we worked with, including Ben, Cory, and Mara, were considered candidates for our tier two intervention because of behavioral concerns indicated by the SSBD (exceeded stage 2 criteria) or SRSS (moderate or high risk categories) and they met criteria on the TOWL–3. The third tier of the PBS model was an intensive support system for students who were not responsive to tier one or tier two interventions. The students we worked with did not require tier three support at this time.

SELF-REGULATED STRATEGIES DEVELOPMENT

Research on SRSD for writing has been conducted for more than 25 years with students from second grade through high school. SRSD is designed to improve students' strategic behavior, knowledge, self-efficacy, and motivation. Students learn to carry out specific writing strategies and self-regulation strategies (e.g., goal setting, self-monitoring, self-instruction, and self-reinforcement). Students are also taught concepts, vocabulary, and skills needed to use both genre specific and general writing strategies, such as using good word choice, creating interesting openings and conclusions, and considering the reader (Graham & Harris, 2005; Harris & Graham, 1996). SRSD enhances motivation by developing self-efficacy while promoting effort and attributions for success to strategy use. Research shows SRSD improves students' attitudes about writing as it increases the quality of written compositions, knowledge about writing, amount of time spent planning, and length of written compositions for students with learning disabilities, attention deficit hyperactivity disorder (ADHD), struggling writers without an identified disability, and regularly achieving writers (e.g., De La Paz & Graham, 2002; Graham & Harris, 1989; Harris, Graham, & Mason, 2006; Reid & Lienemann, 2006).

As we prepared to work with the students in our two studies, we were faced with the challenge of modifying the instructional process and components of SRSD to make it more responsive to the needs of second-grade students who demonstrated behavioral challenges and struggled with writing. Before these two studies, little work had been done with students with these characteristics (cf., Adkins, 2005; Lane et al., 2008, Lane et al., in press).

An essential characteristic of SRSD, however, is responsiveness to students' individual needs. Writing and self-regulation strategies are taught as explicitly as needed for each student. If students need more time to master the strategies and their use, teachers can adapt instruction and provide as much assistance and support as necessary. Motivational support is also tailored to individual students (see Harris, Graham, Mason, & Friedlander, 2008, for more examples).

A second characteristic of SRSD is students and teachers initially plan, write, and self-regulate collaboratively. Teachers gradually withdraw assistance as the students take ownership of the writing and self-regulation strategies.

Another characteristic of SRSD is the development of explicit goals, using guidance from teachers, that are tailored to the needs of individual students. The goals are designed so that they are achievable, but challenging. For students who excel, more advanced goals are developed to keep them engaged and challenged. Teachers may also determine that some students do not need SRSD or may determine that some stages of instruction are not needed with all students.

A fourth, and critical, characteristic of SRSD is that instruction is criterion-based rather than time-based. Students are allowed the time and support needed to master the critical writing and self-regulation strategies. For our studies, students met our basic criteria when they could independently write essays or stories that included all of the genre-specific elements. Thus, some students moved through the lessons at a quick pace and worked toward additional goals, whereas other students needed more time to reach the basic criteria.

Finally, SRSD is a flexible and recursive process; any of the six stages of instruction may be revisited, deleted, or combined as needed. Thus, we carefully reviewed the previous work with students at risk for behavioral and writing difficulties and continuously made adaptations for our students.

Based on the limited work done before our studies, students received higher rates of verbal reinforcement and greater opportunities to respond than in previous studies as needed to keep these students engaged and actively participating. Additional positive reinforcement was provided in conjunction with the school's PBS plan, which included a ticket system. At the beginning of each lesson, the teacher and student discussed the behavioral expectations for that lesson. Each student had the opportunity to earn one PBS ticket at the end of each session for meeting one of the schoolwide expectations delineated on the ticket. At the end of each lesson, the teacher and student discussed whether or not the student had earned the ticket and, if so, which social competency the student displayed.

Next, we carefully describe the six stages of SRSD instruction. Further support for implementing SRSD is available. Detailed lesson plans and support materials for instruction are provided in Harris et al. (2008), and detailed discussion of classroom implementation is provided by Harris, Graham, & Mason (2006). All of the stages of instruction can be seen in both elementary and middle school classrooms in the video, "Teaching Students With Learning Disabilities: Using Learning Strategies" (Association for Supervision and Curriculum Development, 2002). Finally, online interactive tutorials on SRSD are available at http://iris.peabody.vanderbilt.edu/pow/chalcycle.htm and the lesson plans used in our studies can be found at http://hobbs.vanderbilt.edu/projectwrite/

SRSD: Stages of Instruction

Six recursive, flexible stages of instruction are used to introduce and develop writing and self-regulation knowledge and strategies: *Develop Background Knowledge, Discuss It, Model It, Memorize It, Support It, and Independent Performance*. These stages provide a general format and guidelines for teachers and students as they acquire, implement, evaluate, and modify the strategies. One or more days of instruction occurs in each stage, with some stages expected to take longer than others, depending on student needs and rate of progress.

In our two studies, all of the students first learned POW (**P**ick an idea, **O**rganize notes, **W**rite and say more). This mnemonic guides students through the writing process and makes them a POWerful writer. First, the students **P**ick an initial idea. Next, the students learn a strategy for **O**rganizing their notes. To make and organize notes for persuasive writing, they learned the TREE strategy (see Figure 1):

- **T**opic sentence—tell what I believe.
- **R**easons (3 or more)—why do I believe this? Will my readers believe this?
- **E**nding—wrap it up right!
- **E**xamine—do I have all my parts?

For story writing, they learned the W-W-W, What = 2, How = 2 strategy (**Wh**o is the main character? **Wh**en does the story take place? **Wh**ere does the story take place? **What** does the main character do or want to do; what do other characters do? **What** happens then? **How** does the story end? **How** does the main character feel; how do the other characters feel?). Finally, the students

Figure 1. POW + TREE Strategy

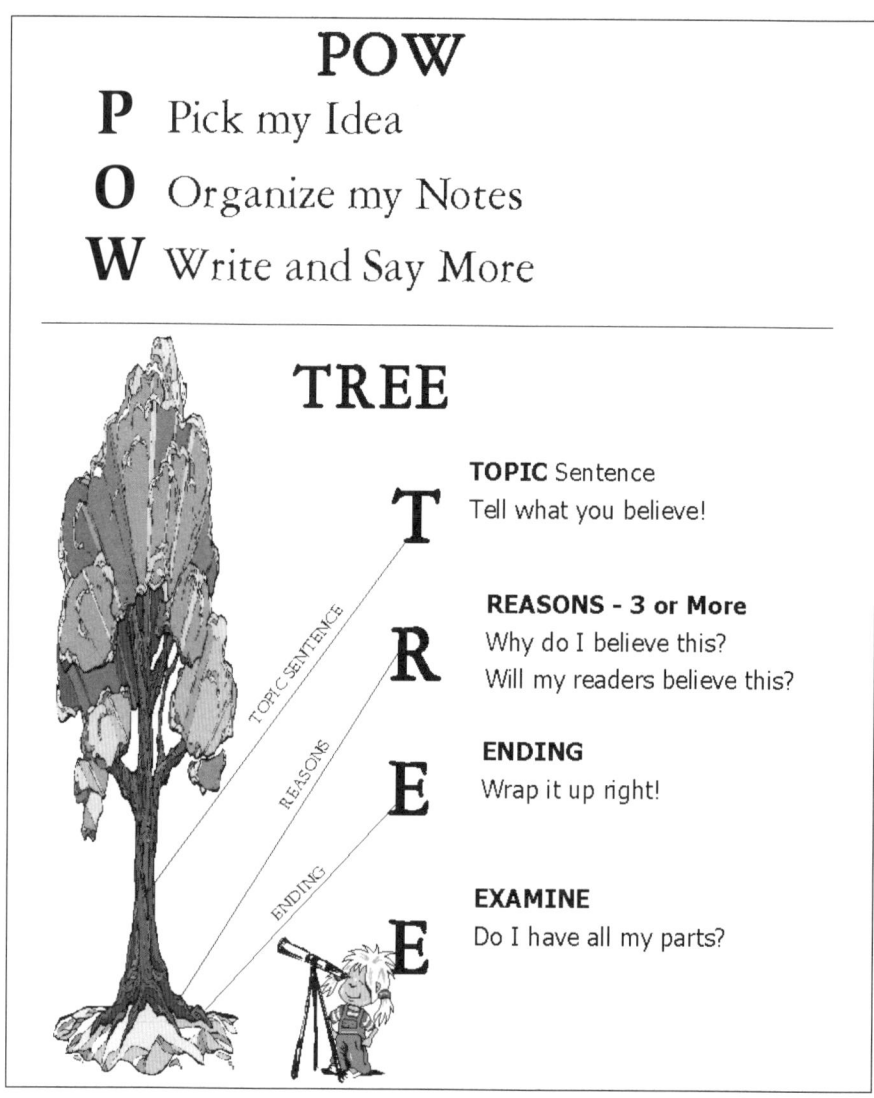

learned to use their notes to **Write** and **Say More** about their topic (see Figure 2).

Develop and Activate Background Knowledge. During this stage of instruction students acquire the vocabulary, knowledge, and concepts needed to apply POW and the strategy for story or persuasive writing. Teachers begin by talking with students about writing to assess what they already know about good writing and help foster new ideas and ways of thinking about writing. The characteristics of good writing (e.g., fun to read and write,

Figure 2. POW + WWW Strategy

P ick my Idea

O rganize my Notes

W rite and Say More

W-W-W What=2 How=2

W ho is the main character?

W hen does the story take place?

W here does the story take place?

W hat does the main character do or want to do; what do other characters do?

W hat happens then? What happens with other characters?

H ow does the story end?

H ow does the main character feel; how do other characters feel?

makes sense, has several parts, includes exciting colorful descriptive words, or includes transition words) are discussed. Vocabulary specific to the genre they are learning is also introduced. For example, for persuasive writing, students need to know what it means to persuade, the difference between a fact and an opinion, and when this type of writing might be used (e.g., writing a letter to convince your parents to let a friend sleep over). We also talk about techniques that help capture and maintain the reader's attention (e.g., a catchy opening and transition words).

POW and its corresponding steps are introduced, and the teacher and students discuss what each letter stands for and why each step is important. POW is revisited each lesson, as is the genre specific strategy (TREE or W-W-W) until the student can explain each step and its importance. Students'

Figure 3. POW + TREE Graphic Organizer

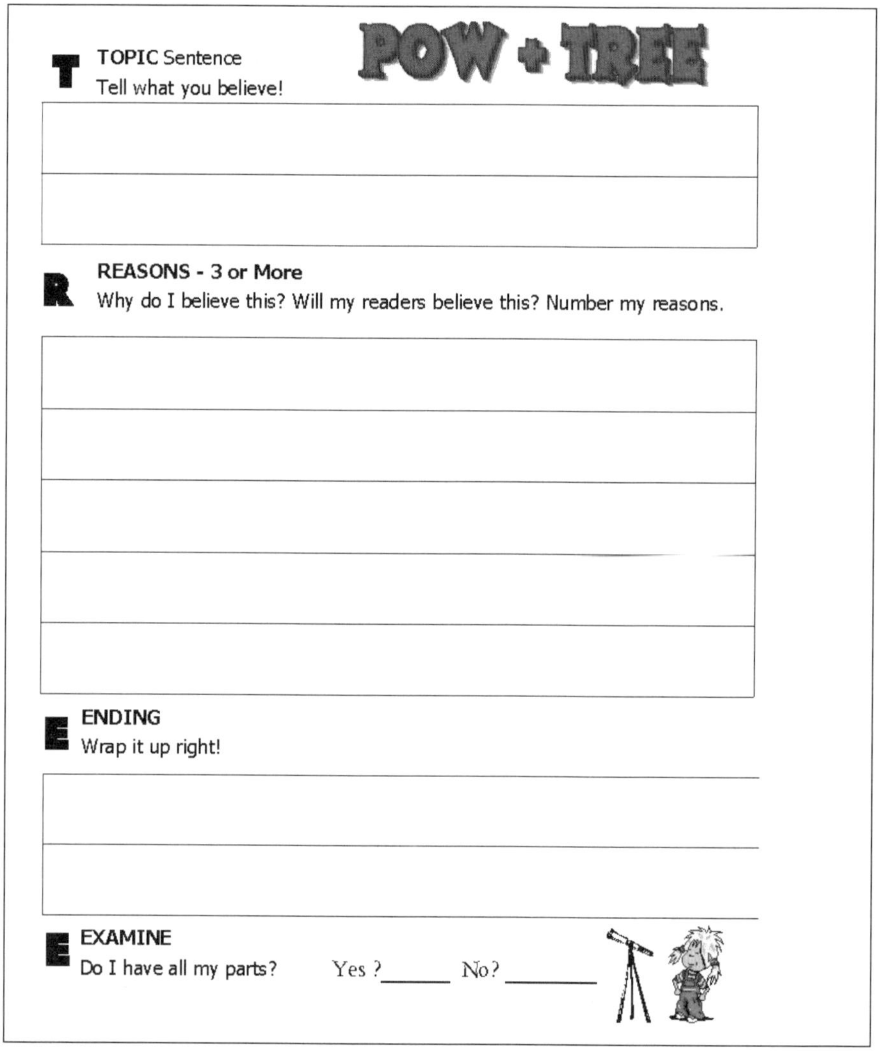

T TOPIC Sentence
Tell what you believe!

R REASONS - 3 or More
Why do I believe this? Will my readers believe this? Number my reasons.

E ENDING
Wrap it up right!

E EXAMINE
Do I have all my parts?   Yes ?_____   No?_____

knowledge is extended by teaching them mnemonics, or "tricks," (POW and W-W-W, What = 2, How = 2 for stories or TREE for persuasive essays) to help them remember the writing process and parts of a good story or essay. Teachers and students discuss each part and brainstorm examples of the parts (e.g., a character could be a cat, dog, teacher, etc.). Students find the parts in a story or essay that the teacher reads out loud. As students identify the parts, teachers model taking notes by writing each element in the graphic organizer (see Figure 3), explaining that notes are short phrases, not complete sentences, to help the writer remember thoughts and ideas. One student we worked with described notes as "caveman talk," and this was helpful for many of our students in understanding how to make notes. This process is repeated in successive lessons until students accurately identify all of the parts from a story or essay with ease and can identify the characteristics of good writing that are present. In addition, a few minutes during each subsequent lesson is spent reviewing POW, the genre-specific mnemonic, and the characteristics of good writing. This process continues throughout the instructional sessions until students memorize the mnemonics.

Discuss It. In this stage of instruction, teachers continue to help students memorize POW, the genre-specific mnemonic, their meanings, and their importance. Students continue to practice finding the genre-specific elements as teachers read a story or essay out loud and write notes for each part of the composition on the graphic organizer. Gradually, students begin to write the notes on their own organizers. Teachers and students discuss how the writing tricks can help improve the students' writing. Teachers and students then discuss the importance of using the new strategies in different contexts and for different purposes and brainstorm where the strategies can be used (e.g., other classes or home), setting the stage for maintenance and generalization. Teachers stress that these tricks cannot work unless the student puts forth the effort to use them, and the student is asked to commit to making that effort.

Model It. Teachers model by "talking out loud" how to *P*lan, *O*rganize, and *W*rite a story or essay using POW and the genre-specific mnemonic. Teachers begin by setting a goal to include all of the parts and emphasize the importance of using the POW and the writing strategies. Students can observe or help teachers during the modeling process. Students may generate ideas for the parts of the composition as well as "million dollar" (exciting and descriptive) words for stories or transition words for essays. Teachers record their ideas on a graphic organizer in note form. While applying the strategies, teachers use a variety of self-statements to assist with problem definition (e.g., What do I have do here?); planning (e.g., What comes next?); self-evaluation (e.g., Do I have all my parts?); self-reinforcement (e.g., I really like that part!); and coping (e.g., I can do this if I use my strategy and take my time.). Students can help with additional planning while the composition is written (i.e., "Write and say more"), by suggesting new words and ideas or modifying ideas initially recorded on the graphic organizer.

Once the story or essay is written, the importance of what we say to ourselves while writing is discussed and the self-statements teachers used are identified. Students identify two to three self-statements that they can use while planning an essay or story, while writing, and while checking their work when the essay or story is complete. These statements are recorded on a small chart to be used in future lessons as a reference for students when they are struggling or when they write something of which they are proud. It is emphasized that these statements can be said out loud or thought to yourself. Students are not forced to use these statements, but encouraged to do so until they can write independently.

Figure 4. TREE Rockets

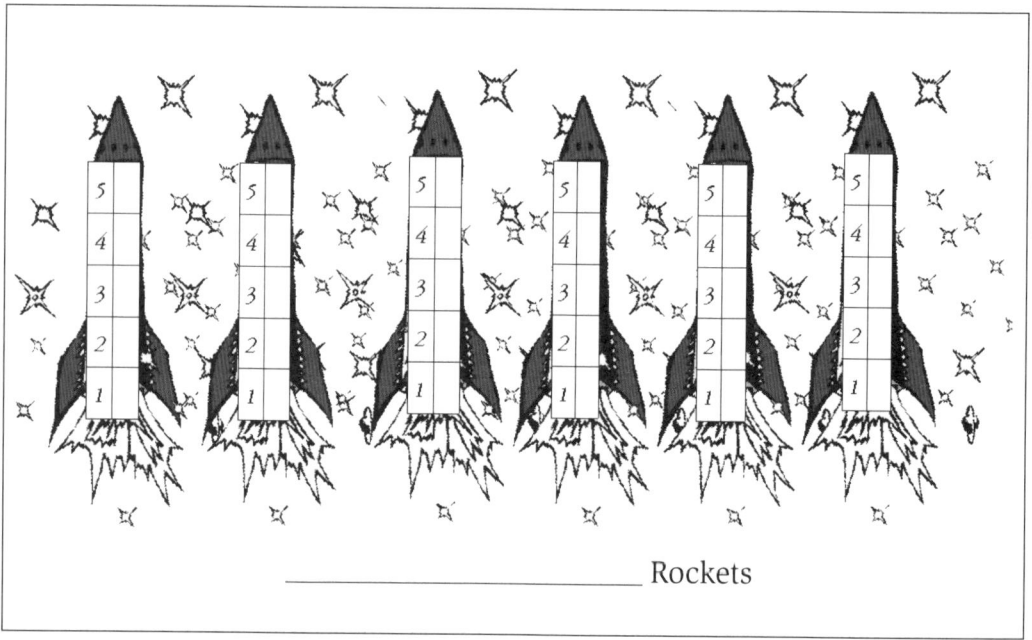

_____ Rockets

Next, self-monitoring and graphing are introduced. Teachers and students examine the composition to check for all parts and to determine if their goal was met (e.g., the composition was fun to write, is fun to read, makes sense, or is persuasive). They graph the results by coloring in a rocket that is divided into parts that equal the number of genre elements expected in the composition (seven parts for story or five parts for essays, see Figure 4). If all genre elements are included, the student then colors all of the rocket which causes it to "blast off." Students color in a star next to the rocket for each million dollar word or transition word used in that story or essay. Each student has a chart containing several of these rockets with stars around them, in order to track their progress. Teachers then model self-reinforcement for a job well done.

Memorize It. During each lesson, students practice recalling the POW and WWW, What = 2, How = 2 or POW and TREE mnemonics and their meanings. Practice includes writing the mnemonic on a sheet of paper, explaining the mnemonics, as well as playing fun activities using flash cards. At this point, most students have the mnemonics memorized. For students who need it, further practice is provided. It is important for students to have the mnemonics memorized before moving into the _Independent Performance_ stage.

Support It. During this stage, teachers and students examine students' writing before SRSD began and discuss how the writing tricks have helped improve their writing. (In some cases, this has been done earlier in the instruction, but we moved this to the *Support It* stage to allow these students to successfully use the tricks before examining their pretest writing abilities.) This stage is characterized by collaborative writing experiences. Teachers and students begin by setting goals for their composition: (a) it includes all the parts, (b) it makes sense, and (c) it is fun to read and write. Then they plan, organize their notes, and write the story or essay together using the genre-specific-mnemonic, graphic organizer, and self-statements. Teachers scaffold the students' strategy use, while encouraging students to work independently, and providing prompts and guidance as needed to ensure students achieve their goals. Students respond differently during this stage. Some students need a lot of assistance and guidance through the writing process for some time, whereas other students more quickly pick up and apply the tricks independently. During this stage, when each composition is complete, students identify and graph the included parts, and use self-statements to positively reinforce themselves for meeting their goals. They also look for and graph any "million dollar" or transition words used. Teachers and students discuss how the strategies help them make each part of a story or essay better and more fun to read and write.

Another component of the *Support It* stage is weaning students off the graphic organizer. Teachers explain that even though students may not always have the graphic organizer available, they can create their own on any paper. Teachers model this process by writing POW at the top of notebook paper and writing either the story or persuasive writing strategy mnemonic down the side, which is then used for making notes. When students complete writing the story or essay, they graph the parts present on the rockets chart.

Independent Performance. During this stage of instruction, students use POW and the genre-specific writing strategy without props (e.g., chart with strategy steps, graphic organizer, self-statement chart) or assistance from teachers. Graphing the compositions may be faded out as well. For the purpose of our studies, we considered instruction to be complete when students were able to independently include all necessary elements (e.g., seven parts for story or five parts for essays) in their compositions.

DIFFERENTIATING INSTRUCTION FOR OUR STUDENTS

After securing teacher and parental consent and student assent to participate in the study, the students completed two subtests of the WISC-III, the block design and writing subtests (WISC-III; Wechsler, 1991) and teachers completed the Social Skills Rating System (SSRS; Gresham & Elliott, 1990) to obtain additional information on students' social, behavioral, and academic performance.

Ben, an active student with average cognitive ability, often needed to be redirected to finish his writing task. He resisted making notes, but learned their value. Cory, a student with low-cognitive abilities, struggled with memorization and putting ideas into writing. Mara, a shy student with low-average cognitive abilities, quickly adopted the writing strategies and implemented them independently. Accommodations and modifications for these students were made based on their individual academic, behavioral, and/or social needs.

The students in our studies worked individually with a "writing teacher" trained in SRSD. Most of the writing teachers were graduate students who were former teachers with several years of classroom experience. Teachers met with students for 8 to 15 sessions for 20 to 30 minutes over a 4- to 6-week period. (Because instruction is criterion based, as noted earlier, the amount of time in instruction varied.)

Ben

Ben had an average cognitive abilities score (102.9 on the WISC-III; Wechsler, 1991) and no documented disabilities. His teacher rated him on the SSRS as having below average social skills, problems with cooperation, and high hyperactive behaviors. Ben was a creative and active student. During the instructional sessions, Ben often looked around the hallway or wiggled in his chair. Prior to the intervention, Ben's average score for story elements was 0; his average quality score was 0; and his average length was 33.14 words. (He wrote a description of the story starter picture rather than a story.) Ben did not make notes prior to writing his stories. He was easily distracted, and the teacher redirected him often to complete his story. This is one of Ben's stories prior to SRSD instruction:

> The aliens are bad. The door is open. The alien ship has a ladder. The door has windows.

During the first instructional session, Ben quickly learned the POW and W-W-W strategies. He created his own strategy to remember the parts by relating it to a story about Spiderman. He easily found the different story parts in example stories the teacher read out loud, although he often became distracted. In the *Develop and Activate Background Knowledge* stage, when the teacher modeled taking notes, Ben shared unrelated stories about his family, eating bugs, or Spiderman. The teacher, therefore, had Ben begin taking notes on the graphic organizer in the early lessons to help him keep focused and attentive.

Ben continued to perform well throughout the next few instructional sessions. During the *Model It* stage he suggested the characters in the story, what the characters wanted, how they felt, where the story took place, when the story happened, and how the story ended. He was eager to write. When the teacher asked Ben what he might want to say to himself while writing, he paused for a moment and stated, "This doesn't stink! I have all my parts." During the *Support It* stage, Ben collaboratively wrote exciting and funny stories that were usually about Spiderman.

Unfortunately, the only available workspace for Ben and his teacher was in the hallway. Because Ben was easily distracted, the teacher developed a plan to help regulate the learning environment. One strategy the teacher tried was to limit Ben's view by having him face the wall at the end of the hallway, and she sat perpendicular to him. This strategy helped, but was not sufficient. Another strategy the teacher used was putting more emphasis on the PBS ticket Ben could receive. At the beginning of each lesson, the teacher asked Ben what he wanted to work on, and Ben selected respect, best effort, or responsibility. The behavioral ticket stayed on the top of the table while Ben worked. If Ben strayed off task, the teacher pointed to the ticket and reminded him which component he selected. If Ben remained off task throughout the lesson, the teacher would not give him the ticket. This happened only once, and the teacher and Ben set a goal to work harder during the next session.

Another component of SRSD that helped keep Ben focused during the lessons was the opportunity to color the rockets. Ben enjoyed coloring the rockets, and at the beginning of every lesson he asked if he would get to color a rocket. The teacher explained that if he worked hard, finished his story, and stayed focused, he would have time to color a rocket. Ben suggested another self-statement to add to his list when he worked, "Try to bust the rocket!" The teacher thought this was a great goal setting and self-reinforcement statement that would help keep Ben focused, and she encouraged him to use the statement often. Thus, the rocket chart was an important motivational component for Ben and helped to keep him focused on the writing task.

During the *Support It* stage, as he began to work more independently, Ben resisted making notes before writing his stories. Ben believed he could speed through the writing process, skip making notes, and still write a good story. During one instructional session, Ben refused to write notes and then became confused as he wrote his story. When Ben finished the story, he checked to see if he had included all the story parts. He had only included the main character, where the story took place, and when the story happened. The teacher used this opportunity to show Ben the importance of taking notes. She explained that notes help you to remember your ideas and to include all of your parts when you write. She also emphasized rereading the story to make sure all the story parts are included. The teacher was able to accommodate for Ben's learning style and abilities by re-teaching him about the importance of organizing notes. Following this experience, Ben began using notes more frequently.

After instruction ended, Ben was administered posttest story writing prompts when instruction ended. In the postinstruction writing samples, Ben included an average of six story elements, the average length of his stories was 32.33 words, and his average quality score was 4.67. Ben did not increase the length of his stories, however, his stories were now more substantive rather than descriptive. The following is an example of Ben's stories after instruction:

> One year ago, Bill and his friends were at home. It was Bill's birthday. They ate cake together and had lots of fun. When the party was over, they went home. Bill was sad because they went home.

Ben quickly learned and used the writing and self-regulation strategies. In the beginning, the teacher had Ben take notes as they read stories to help keep him focused on the writing task. As the sessions progressed, the teacher implemented different behavioral strategies to keep Ben focused. When Ben became resistant to using the graphic organizer or making notes before writing his essays, the teacher used the opportunity to show him the value of writing notes and how they helped improve his stories. After instruction ended, for each story Ben wrote down the story strategy mnemonic, made notes for each of the story elements, and checked them off as he included them while writing his story.

Although our SRSD goals for Ben were met, story writing instruction is obviously not finished for him! Ben has a lot more to learn about effective story writing, but he is now "on the playing field" and ready to progress from here. Were Ben's writing teacher to continue working with him, she would work with him to move on to new, personalized goals for both process and product.

Cory

Cory had a low cognitive abilities score (62.3 on the WISC-III) and an individualized education program (IEP). His teacher and parents reported on the SSRS that he exhibited greater than average behavior problems. Cory was a polite student who struggled to learn new ideas and socialized with only a few peers. Prior to intervention, Cory's average score for both persuasive essay elements and quality was 0 and the average number of words was 9.43. Cory did not make notes; rather, he quickly scribbled his thoughts on paper and announced he was done. The following is a sample of Cory's essays prior to intervention in response to an essay prompt:

> I think so.

During the *Develop and Activate Background Knowledge* stage, Cory struggled. He had difficulty remembering the mnemonics, understanding the purpose of notes, identifying transition words, and finding the parts in example essays. Cory told his teacher that he had never heard the words *persuade* or *persuasive*. The teacher gave examples of when it might be necessary to persuade someone and asked Cory to think of instances when he would need to persuade someone. Cory was unable, at that point, to think of any ideas. The teacher told Cory they would read more essays to help him understand.

The teacher explained each part of the mnemonic, asking Cory to repeat what she said. The teacher stated, "T, this means the topic sentence. What does T mean?" Cory was unable to answer. The teacher used flash cards to help Cory with the mnemonic. She placed P-O-W and TREE cards on the table. Cory looked down at the cards and exclaimed, "I'm going to learn ALL of these!" The teacher assured Cory that she would help him learn the parts, and they would work on learning them each time they met. At the end of the lesson, as the teacher escorted Cory back to his class, he commented, "I hope these tricks help me because I am a terrible writer." The teacher, at this point, began to have some concerns about whether SRSD was appropriate for Cory. She brought these concerns to our weekly team meetings. We determined that she should slow the pace of instruction to meet Cory's needs, and that we would continue to monitor whether or not the initial goals we had set for Cory were appropriate for him.

During the *Discuss It* stage, Cory could not find the parts of essays in exemplars. The teacher was concerned with Cory's understanding of the purpose of essays and the relationship between TREE and the parts in example essays. The teacher decided to color code the different parts of the essay; she underlined the topic sentence in blue, the reasons in red, and the ending sentence in purple. As the teacher and Cory searched for transition words, Cory circled them in green. This visual prompt helped Cory see all of the parts within the context of written text. When the teacher wrote notes from the sample essay on the graphic organizer, Cory showed no interest and looked bored. His teacher worried that Cory might have been bored because of having difficulty understanding the purpose of notes.

Also during the *Discuss It* stage, the teacher and Cory discussed other places where the tricks could be used. The teacher provided different examples (a letter to persuade a parent, an article for a class newspaper) and asked Cory for his ideas of other places to use the "tricks." He replied that he could use it on his dirt bike. Although his teacher felt progress was being made as Cory increased his understanding about the parts of the essay and was able to find the elements in examples, she was concerned about Cory's understanding about the purpose of the tricks and was uncertain he would be able to implement them. At our team meeting, his teacher noted that once the tricks were modeled for Cory, he might develop a better understanding of how to use the "tricks." We decided to continue with our initial goals for Cory, but began to discuss modifying these goals if needed.

The *Memorize It* stage was visited at the beginning of each lesson. The teacher spent extra time helping Cory memorize and understand the writing strategies. In each successive session, Cory began to remember more of the parts. In the second session, Cory remembered P—pick my idea and E—ending. In the next session, he remembered P—pick my idea, E—ending, O—organize my notes, and T—topic sentence. The teacher used several strategies to help Cory remember the mnemonics and their meaning. She had Cory repeat the parts after her, played games with flash cards repeatedly, and had Cory write the mnemonic on scratch paper and recite the meanings of each of the letters. Cory eventually was able to state the mnemonics and explain the meaning of each letter.

During the *Model It* stage, Cory's teacher felt he began to gain a better understanding of the writing process and how to implement the strategies, but there were moments when Cory was distracted or sleepy. The teacher increased the level of collaborative writing during modeling to help him stay engaged. After modeling, the teacher discussed self-statements with Cory. She asked if he could recall any of the statements she said to help her as she wrote. When Cory answered, "No," she repeated some of the self-statements she used. Cory interrupted her and volunteered, "I can do it even if I get tired." The teacher complimented Cory on a great self-statement and they recorded it on his sheet.

The *Support It* stage was extended and modified to meet Cory's needs. In addition, the writing team agreed the goals for Cory should continue to be considered. The teacher continued to modify the pace of instruction to allow additional time for Cory to take ownership of the strategies. During the first few sessions, the teacher and Cory collaboratively wrote essays. Cory applied the tricks by telling the teacher the different steps to take to write the essay and to generate the parts of the essay. Because Cory continued to struggle with transition words, the teacher allowed him to list reasons for the essay by putting a 1, 2, and 3 before each reason rather than using transition words.

As the teacher observed that Cory had made progress in understanding the writing and self-regulation strategies, she asked him to write notes and lead the writing process. Cory became unsure of himself and told the teacher he had bad handwriting, was a bad speller, and asked the teacher to take the notes. The teacher agreed to write the notes, but then asked Cory to write the essay. She reassured him that she was not worried about his handwriting or spelling at this point in the writing process, and encouraged him to try his best. Cory struggled using his notes to make complete sentences for his essay and simply rewrote the notes from the graphic organizers. When the teacher asked Cory to read the "essay," he simply read the notes. However, when the teacher asked him to verbalize the essay, Cory stated full sentences for each of the parts of the essay. His teacher knew that Cory had good ideas and was able to generate reasons, but she felt the mechanics of writing were inhibiting his ability to express himself. The teacher decided to try dictation with Cory.

With a lot of prompting, scaffolding, and reinforcement, Cory was able to dictate an essay. However, because he struggled with stating a topic and ending sentence, his teacher decided to focus on further developing these elements. She provided multiple examples of topic and ending sentences. She continued to encourage Cory to restate the writing prompt question in the form of a statement (e.g., *Should children have to go to school in the summer?*

could become *Children should not have to go to school in the summer.*). The teacher also tried making the ending sentence more standard (e.g., *These are the reasons I believe children should not go to school in the summer.*) and encouraged him to use this format for each ending. This helped Cory better understand how to verbalize topic and ending sentences, but he continued to struggle.

At this point, the writing team decided that Cory's goals should be modified. We believed that Cory needed further development of prerequisite writing abilities to profit from further POW + TREE instruction. We felt, however, that Cory had made important progress in understanding the concept of persuasion through writing and in expressing his ideas both through dictation and in writing. After 15 lessons, we felt that Cory had met reasonable goals, and instruction was ended.

Cory was administered posttest writing prompts in two ways: writing independently and dictating his essay to the teacher. Cory did show increases in the number of essay elements, length, and quality of his essays. He included an average of five essay elements, average length was 30 words, and his average quality score was 1.5. Two examples of Cory's postinstruction essays follow.

- Independently written essay:

  I think so. You need to. Because I think they have to. I think they need to take them to Blockbuster. Those are the reasons.

- Independently dictated essay:

  No, because they don't need pets. They need somebody to play with. Because they need to go outside. Because they need milk. That's the reasons why kids don't need pets.

Cory needed extra support, encouragement, and time during SRSD instruction. Cory memorized the mnemonics, found essay components in examples, gained an understanding of the purpose of persuasive essays, and generated persuasive essays with support. At this point we decided to end instruction in POW + TREE with Cory. In hindsight, we believe that Cory did not yet have the prerequisite abilities to continue with the goals we had set, although he had met our criteria for inclusion in instruction, and we felt that what he had accomplished was appropriate at this time. For future instruction with Cory, we recommended breaking down persuasive essay writing into smaller parts and more proximal goals. We would have continued using dictation, while at the same time continued working with Cory on his handwriting (or keyboarding) and spelling. Cory was a determined student; during one session, using a self-statement, Cory yelled, "Come on Cory! You can do this!" Cory's teacher believed his beliefs in his abilities and his self-confidence had increased. Because the writing team believed that Cory's level of cognitive ability may have been a factor in his response to SRSD as planned for these second graders, and we had not previously worked with a second grader scoring this low on cognitive ability, we also determined that level of cognitive ability and responsiveness to PBS plus SRSD should be investigated in future research. It may well be that further revisions to the SRSD approach are needed for students with lower cognitive ability levels.

Mara

Mara had a low average cognitive abilities score (86 on the WISC-III; Wechsler, 1991) and no documented disabilities. Her teacher and parents reported that she exhibited lower than average social skills and greater than average problem behaviors. Mara was a shy student and rarely interacted with her teachers and peers. Prior to intervention, Mara's average score for essay elements was 4, her average quality score was 5, and her average length was 63 words. Mara did not make notes prior to writing, but waited an average of 30 seconds before beginning. Her essays, prior to intervention, included one, two, or three reasons, and some included an ending sentence. The following is an example of one of Mara's essays prior to SRSD instruction:

> Children should not be allowed to choose their bedtime because of school and you stay there a long time. You should go to bed at least 8:00 or 9:00 because you have to be at school at 8:00.

In the *Develop and Activate Background Knowledge* stage, Mara quickly learned the mnemonics, accurately stated the meanings of the parts, easily found the parts in sample essays, and suggested notes the teacher could write in the graphic organizer. Mara understood the meaning of persuade and was eager to use the tricks. During the *Discuss It* stage, the teacher and Mara brainstormed ideas of other places to use the tricks. When Mara arrived for the next session, she told her teacher how she tried to persuade her Mom to let a friend sleep over the previous evening. She told her Mom what she believed, gave four reasons, and repeated what she believed. Mara said it wasn't successful and thought it was because she didn't have time to give a fifth reason because it was her bedtime! Later, as the teacher walked Mara back to her classroom, Mara commented, "I had fun. I want to come back tomorrow."

During the *Model It* stage, the teacher modeled the writing process and self-statements. While the teacher was working through the essay, Mara excitedly contributed her own ideas, which she felt were better than the teacher's. The teacher complimented Mara on her great ideas and used her reasons to write the essay. Mara quickly grasped the concept of making notes and then using the notes to *Write and Say More*. Mara needed little assistance during the *Support It* stage and chose mostly to work independently. She sometimes hid her notes from the teacher because she wanted the essay to be a surprise. In her practice essays, she usually included more than three reasons and began to elaborate on these reasons.

Mara used the tricks outside of class a few more times. Mara presented the teacher with an essay she wrote at home to persuade her Mom to let a friend sleep over, as she hadn't given up on that goal. Her essay included a topic sentence, five reasons, and an ending. She exclaimed to her teacher, "It worked!" She believed it worked this time because she had five reasons and had written the essay rather than verbalizing her argument. Our team thought that perhaps it also worked because she didn't ask at bedtime on a school night, but we were delighted that her attempt at using persuasive writing for her own goals had succeeded! In a second instance, Mara used her "trick" in her classroom. She wrote an essay during free time to convince her teacher to give the class a longer recess. After reading the essay, the classroom teacher was persuaded and gave the whole class an extra 5 minutes, crediting Mara for the longer recess.

On the persuasive writing prompts after instruction, Mara spent an average of 8 minutes, 20 seconds planning her essays and used the mnemonic to organize her notes. On her postinstruction essays, the average number of essay elements was 8.67, the average quality score was 5.33, and the average number of words was 80. Following is an example of Mara's essays after instruction:

> I believe children should have their own pet. First, your friend won't have to come over a lot. You can play with your pet. Another reason is you can see what it's like to have a pet. Next, you will have another family member in your family. Another reason, if you have another pet, it will have a friend to play with. Next, pets are fun. Pets need food and water. Another reason you have to be responsible to your pet. That's why I believe children should have their own pet.

There were several important outcomes for Mara. Although a shy, introverted student, she had interacted more with her teachers and peers and independently implemented the strategies to meet her social needs in appropriate, acceptable ways. She quickly learned the POW + TREE strategies, and independently produced essays that included all the parts after seven instructional sessions. Like Ben, if Mara's writing teacher were to continue working with her, she would collaboratively set new, personalized goals for both process and product. Future lessons with Mara could focus on creating catchy openings, making sure the reasons are coherent and make sense, adding additional elaboration, using exciting and expressive language, and adding counterarguments to help gain the readers' interest and improve the persuasive nature of the essay. Although our initial SRSD goals for Mara were met, writing instruction is not "done."

Classwide SRSD

During the time the writing teachers worked with Ben, Cory, and Mara, they were in close communication with their classroom teacher, as well as the teachers of other students we were working with. As the teachers saw the progress their students were making with SRSD as a tier two intervention, they indicated a desire to try SRSD classwide. Thus, we met with these teachers and worked together to modify the one-on-one approach we used for use with entire classes. We are now working with these teachers to study the outcomes of this instruction with their new second graders. We believe that this will result in meaningful improvements in writing for their students, but that some students may still need the one-on-one instructional support possible at the tier two level. We plan to continue research to test this, and plan to collaborate with teachers in making PBS and SRSD work for their students.

CONCLUSION

We were able to modify instruction and accommodate for the differing academic, social, and behavioral needs of our students. The SRSD approach for writing, used within schoolwide PBS, helped our students improve the quality, length, and use of genre-specific elements in their essays and stories. We believe that embedding SRSD within schoolwide PBS made instruction more powerful and efficient for our students, a belief that will need to be tested in future research. We would like to note, however, several caveats regarding SRSD. First, SRSD is not a panacea. Academic, behavioral, and social competences are complex. Although students may display similar characteristics, what works for one student will not necessarily work for another student. Further, writing is a complex ability that cannot be developed with SRSD alone. Thus, SRSD is not a complete writing program. The SRSD approach and the writing strategies can be used to enhance curricular materials and facilitate the learning of students who struggle with writing.

Finally, in order for students to maintain the writing and self-regulation strategies they have learned, these strategies need to be revisited on a regular basis. We administered maintenance writing prompts to our students a month after instruction ended. Some students easily remembered the prompts and wrote high-quality essays and stories that included all of the parts. A few students, however, needed booster sessions (one to two sessions to review the strategies and to allow the students to practice). With the booster sessions, students quickly recalled the strategies and were able to implement them and write high-quality essays or stories. In the classroom, teachers can create differing opportunities for students to maintain and generalize the strategies.

We have presented how instruction in the SRSD approach and writing strategies can be differentiated within a PBS approach for second-grade students in need of additional supports. Although we worked with students individually, we believe teachers can also differentiate instruction in whole group or small group settings, and this will be the focus of our future research. Writing is an important ability for students to develop, and we must learn how to best meet their diverse needs.

REFERENCES

Adkins, M. H. (2005). *Self-regulated strategy development and generalization instruction: Effects on story writing among second and third grade students with emotional and behavioral disorders.* Unpublished doctoral dissertation, University of Maryland, College Park.

Association for Supervision and Curriculum Development (Producer). (2002). *Teaching students with learning disabilities: Using learning strategies* [Video]. (Available from the Association for Supervision and Curriculum Development, 1703 North Beauregard Street, Alexandria, VA 22311-1714)

De La Paz, S., & Graham, S. (2002). Explicitly teaching strategies, skills, and knowledge: Writing instruction in middle school classrooms. *Journal of Educational Psychology, 94,* 291–304.

Drummond, T. (1994). *The Student Risk Screening Scale (SRSS).* Grants Pass, OR: Josephine County Mental Health Program.

Graham, S., & Harris, K. R. (1989). A components analysis of cognitive strategy instruction: Effects on learning disabled students' compositions and self-efficacy. *Journal of Educational Psychology, 81,* 353–361.

Graham, S., & Harris, K. R. (2005). *Writing better: Effective strategies for teaching students with learning difficulties.* Baltimore: Brookes.

Gresham, F. M., & Elliott, S. N. (1990). *Social Skills Rating System.* Circle Pines, MN: American Guidance Service.

Hammill, D., & Larsen, S. (1996). *Test of Written Language–3.* Austin, TX: Pro-ED.

Harris, K., Graham, S., Mason, L., & Friedlander, B. (2008). *Powerful writing strategies for all students.* Baltimore: Brookes.

Harris, K. R., & Graham. S. (1996). *Making the writing process work: Strategies for composition and self-regulation* (2nd ed.). Cambridge, UK: Brookline Books.

Harris, K. R., Graham, S., & Mason, L. (2006). Improving the writing, knowledge, and motivation of struggling young writers: Effects of Self-Regulated Strategy Development with and without peer support. *American Educational Research Journal, 43,* 295–340.

Hendley, S. L. (2007). Use positive behavior support for inclusion in the general education classroom. *Intervention in School and Clinic, 42,* 225–228.

Lane, K., Graham, S., Harris, K. R., Little, L., Sandmel, K., & Brindle, M. (in press). Story writing: The effects of Self-Regulated Strategy Development for second grade students with writing and behavioral difficulties. *Journal of Special Education.*

Lane, K., Harris, K. R., Graham, S., Weisenbach, J., Brindle, M., & Murphy, P. (2008). The effects of self-regulated strategy development on the writing performance of second grade students with behavioral and writing difficulties. *Journal of Special Education, 41,* 234–253.

Lane, K. L., Kalberg, J. R., & Menzies, H. M. (2009). *Developing schoolwide programs to prevent and manage problem behaviors: A step-by-step approach..* New York: Guilford.

Reid, R., & Lienemann, T. (2006). Self-regulated strategy development for written expression with students with attention deficit/hyperactivity disorder. *Exceptional Children, 73,* 53–68.

Tomlinson, C. A. (1999). *The differentiated classroom: Responding to the needs of all learners.* Alexandria, VA: Association for Supervision and Curriculum Development.

Walker, H. M., Horner, R. H., Sugai, G., Bullis, M., Sprague, J. R., Bricker, D., et al. (1996). Integrated approaches to preventing antisocial behavior patterns among school-age children and youth. *Journal of Emotional and Behavioral Disorders, 4,* 194–209.

Walker, H. M., & Severson, H. (1992). *Systematic screening for behavior disorders: Technical manual.* Longmont, CO: Sopris West.

Wechsler, D. (1991). *Wechsler Intelligence Scale for Children–Third Edition.* San Antonio, TX: Harcourt Brace Jovanovich.

Originally published in *TEACHING Exceptional Children,* Vol. 42, No. 2, pp. 22–33.

10

Classwide Interventions: Effective Instruction Makes a Difference

Maureen A. Conroy, Kevin S. Sutherland, Angela L. Snyder, and Samantha Marsh

Whether teaching in a general education classroom or in a specialized program for students with special needs, teachers face a variety of classroom behaviors that can detract from the learning process. At times, they may spend so much time with a few students who exhibit disruptive and off-task behaviors that they are less available for academic instruction with all students.

The research literature provides numerous examples of effective teaching strategies that can help teachers address problem behavior in their classrooms. These strategies include manipulating *antecedents* (i.e., environmental factors that are likely to increase a behavior), such as increasing opportunities to respond to academic requests (OTRs), and manipulating *consequences* (i.e., environmental factors that maintain behaviors), such as providing contingent praise. Unfortunately, some teachers are not skilled at employing these effective teaching tools in their classrooms. Consider the case scenarios "A Classroom That Works" and "A Classroom With Challenges."

CREATING A POSITIVE CLIMATE THROUGH CLASSWIDE INTERVENTIONS

Classrooms are dynamic environments in which teachers and students engage in ongoing reciprocal interactions throughout the school day. As indicated in both case scenarios, classes that include classwide effective intervention practices are likely to have positive teacher–student interactions and to promote

> **Case Scenario: A Classroom That Works**
>
> Collaboration between special and general education teachers in the classroom can be beneficial to students with and without special needs, especially when the collaboration works seamlessly. Ms. Harman and Ms. Easley teach in an urban elementary school. At the beginning of the school year, they worked collaboratively with their students to develop classroom rules that both special and general education students could follow and to identify specific procedures, such as turning in homework and lining up to go to lunch, for regular classroom activities. In addition, they spent a significant amount of time praising their students not just for work done correctly but also for good attempts.
>
> Ms. Harman and Ms. Easley, who continuously sought ways to improve their teaching and help their students learn, took part in an applied research project that facilitated positive changes in their instructional language and methods. They incorporated a group behavior management system called *the good behavior game (GBG;* Barrish, Saunders, & Wolfe, 1969) into their instructional time.
>
> Ms. Hammond and Ms. Easley audiotaped an instructional lesson and graphed the numbers of opportunities to respond (OTRs) that they provided, as well as the number of times that they praised their students during the lesson. Through this self-evaluation of their instructional language, they developed a greater awareness of the frequency with which they provided their students with OTRs to instructional requests and of the frequency of their praise statements. Using these self-management procedures enabled Ms. Harman and Ms. Easley to increase the number of OTRs from only 10 per 15 minutes to almost 6 per minute, approximating the recommendations of the Council for Exceptional Children (1987). This change in the OTR rate encouraged student engagement and led to decreased undesirable behavior. In addition, the teachers increased their rate of praise from only 2 per 15 minutes to almost 1 per minute, resulting in further improvements in the behavior of the students. Making small changes in the ways that they instructed their students and rewarding their students more often for work attempted resulted in an improved positive classroom atmosphere and an increase in students' effort.

student learning and engagement while minimizing problem behaviors. However, when classwide interventions are missing from a classroom, teacher–student interactions are likely to become reactively negative (and perhaps even coercive). Such interactions interfere with learning and create a chaotic and aversive classroom atmosphere.

Classwide interventions are a group of research-based effective teaching strategies used positively and preventively to promote and reinforce social and behavioral competence in students while minimizing problem behaviors (Farmer et al., 2006). Classwide interventions do not represent a single type

> **Case Scenario: A Classroom With Challenges**
>
> Ms. Walters taught 12 students, whose grade levels ranged from second grade to fifth grade, in an urban elementary school. The students had a variety of disabilities—for example, emotional disorders (ED), learning disabilities (LD), and attention deficit hyperactivity disorder (ADHD).
>
> As a group, these students presented many classroom challenges. Each day, Ms. Walters greeted her students by saying "Good morning, class," only to be confronted by disruptive student talk, papers flying at her, and students who were not in their assigned seats. Along with her paraprofessional, Ms. Johnson, Ms. Walters spent the first 45 minutes of every day just trying to get her students to sit down, hand in their homework, and attend to language arts, the first lesson of the day. She had very few doable procedures in place for daily tasks, and most of the students regularly ignored classroom rules. Ms. Walters had assigned students to small groups on the basis of their skill levels; however, she spent a tremendous amount of time correcting disruptive students, who would provoke others. Needless to say, she was frustrated and often raised her voice at her students in an effort to persuade them to pay attention to her. She knew that what she was doing was not working, but she and her students were caught in a negative, coercive interaction cycle.
>
> Discouraged and ready to quit before she had even finished her first year, Ms. Walters agreed to have a behavioral consultant come into her classroom to help her with classroom management. The consultant worked with Ms. Walters to arrange her classroom so that all students could see her and the blackboard. The consultant and Ms. Walters developed procedures for entering the classroom in the morning (e.g., routines for putting away backpacks and homework), and Ms. Walters distributed students with disruptive behavior across the small groups in the classroom. As a reward for good behavior, she assigned a "daily leader" to each group for the next day.
>
> The consultant also trained the paraprofessional to step in when Ms. Walters was having difficulty with a particular student and engage other students in small-group or individualized work so that Ms. Walters was not responsible for the whole class. After Ms. Walters received this support, her teaching strategies improved, and she felt and looked more competent and effective in her ability to manage her students' behavior and promote their learning. Students responded to her effective teaching practices; and as a result, they were more engaged. Although more growth was necessary, the classwide atmosphere improved, and everyone had hope for a better school year.

of intervention; instead, they include a combination of effective behavior management practices that have a long history in our field, such as using contingent and frequent *praise*, providing *OTRs*, and applying *classroom rules*.

CLASSWIDE INTERVENTIONS: UNIVERSAL CLASSROOM TOOLS FOR EFFECTIVE INSTRUCTION

Teachers should consider the following classwide interventions when implementing positive behavior supports:

- Using close supervision and monitoring.
- Establishing and teaching classroom rules.
- Increasing OTRs.
- Increasing contingent praise.
- Providing feedback and error correction and monitoring progress.
- Implementing the good behavior game (GBG).

Close Supervision and Monitoring

Close supervision and monitoring generally means that the teacher has active, frequent, and regular engagement with students. These engagements may include placing students close to the teacher, scanning and moving frequently, initiating and reciprocating purposeful interactions, and providing opportunities for direct instruction and feedback (Colvin, Sugai, & Patching, 1993). When teachers are in proximity to students and monitor students' learning and behavior, they can prevent problem behaviors before they occur and can redirect them before they escalate. For example, when a teacher is near a student who is becoming frustrated and is struggling with a task, the teacher can intervene quickly and provide academic and behavior supports before a problem behavior occurs.

Implementing close supervision and monitoring may require developing a plan in collaboration with other adults or paraprofessionals in the classroom. For example, a classroom teacher may implement a zone-monitoring and supervision plan during an instructional time when many students need assistance and engage in problem behaviors. With a zone-monitoring plan, adults in the classroom are at strategic locations throughout the classroom, and each of them monitors a small number of students. This system enables adults to closely supervise and monitor students and facilitates students' access to teacher assistance.

Considerable evidence supports the use of close supervision and monitoring as a classwide intervention. For example, research has documented that close supervision and monitoring result in decreases in disruptive behavior across various educational settings, including classroom instruction (DePry & Sugai, 2002); recess (Lewis, Powers, Kelk, & Newcomer, 2002); and transition time (Colvin, Sugai, Good, & Lee, 1997).

Classroom Rules

The development and implementation of classroom rules is another universal classwide intervention that influences the learning environment for all students. Classroom rules serve as behavioral expectations that create an organized and productive learning environment for students and teachers by promoting appropriate classroom behaviors. Without classroom rules, such problem behaviors as aggression and disruption are more likely (Walker, Colvin, & Ramsey, 1995). Research has indicated that effective teachers do the following:

- Establish rules for expected behavior at the beginning of the year.
- Systematically teach the rules to the students.
- Monitor and reward students' compliance with the rules.
- Consistently apply consequences to rule violations (Anderson, Evertson, & Emmer, 1980; Evertson & Emmer, 1982).

Opportunities to Respond (OTRs)

Increasing instructional pacing through OTRs is a questioning, prompting, or cueing technique that begins a learning trial (e.g., "What number comes after 10?"). This technique helps increase the number of active child responses, which in turn can result in increases in correct responses and engagement of all students in the classroom (Greenwood, Delquadri, & Hall, 1984). Although OTRs vary in type and characteristics (e.g., choral responses, individual responses, and visual or auditory cuing), all types of OTRs generally include the following components:

- Increasing rates of teacher instructional talk that includes repeated verbal, visual, or verbal and visual types of prompts for responding.
- Presenting information in a manner that increases student correct responding (e.g., "This is an *A*. What letter is this?").
- Implementing individualized instructional modifications appropriate for the students' level of functioning, along with frequent checks for understanding and accuracy.
- Using repeated instructional prompting that incorporates wait time to allow students to respond.
- Providing corrective feedback, error correction, and progress monitoring (Stichter & Lewis, 2006).

When researchers increase rates of OTR, they have found increases in on-task student behavior and in correct responses, as well as fewer disruptive behaviors by students (Brophy & Good, 1986; Carnine, 1976; Greenwood et al., 1984; Sutherland, Gunter, & Alder, 2003). Students who are engaged in learning are less likely to demonstrate problem behaviors (Sutherland et al.)

and more likely to engage in active and correct responses (Sutherland & Snyder, 2007).

Contingent Praise

"Catch 'em being good" is a familiar strategy to most teachers. Although many teachers are aware of the powerful effects of praise, they often underuse it. Fortunately, training can help teachers learn to use praise as a reinforcer. Praise is a generalized reinforcer and has a rich research base that demonstrates its effectiveness in increasing social and behavioral competence in students (Alber, Heward, & Hippler, 1999; Sutherland, 2000). *Effective* praise is specific and contingent (Sutherland). *Specific* praise occurs when the teacher specifies the target behavior reinforced within the praise statement (e.g., "Good, you stayed in your seat during the entire reading session"). Praise is *contingent* when it is a consequence for a specific expected behavior, such as completing an assigned task, following a teacher's instruction, or engaging in appropriate social behavior.

Researchers have found that when teachers increase their use of specific and contingent praise, improvement occurs in the number of correct responses by students, task engagement, words read correctly per minute, problems completed, and student engagement (Kirby & Shields, 1972; Luiselli & Downing, 1980; Sutherland, Wehby, & Copeland, 2000). In general, teachers should offer praise statements more often than corrective statements. For example, Good and Grouws (1977) recommend that teachers strive to achieve and maintain a ratio of 4 or 5 positive statements to 1 corrective statement.

Feedback, Error Correction, and Progress Monitoring

Providing students with feedback relative to their behavior and performance level is another important classwide intervention. When used effectively, feedback should

- Help students learn the correct response in a timely way.
- Be specific to students' skill and knowledge levels.
- Occur following a student error (i.e., error correction).

Error correction procedures begin with the teacher's providing a corrective model (e.g., "Remember that to determine the area of a square or rectangle, multiply length times width"). This corrective model precedes the student's correct response, which the student should base on the teacher's model (e.g., "If the length of a rectangle is 5 feet and its width is 4 feet, I multiply length by width to obtain a result of 20 square feet."). Corrective feedback should accompany continuous monitoring of the student's academic and/or social behavior performance (e.g., curriculum-based measurement), as well as accurate and consistently presented instruction and interventions (i.e., fidelity of implementation).

Effective feedback can take many forms (e.g., answering questions, checking seatwork, and responding directly), and researchers have linked it positively to student engagement and achievement (Fisher et al., 1980). Similarly, when teachers use error correction, increases occur in academic performance (Barbetta, Heron, & Heward, 1993; Barbetta & Heward, 1993) and correct responses (Bangert-Downs, Kulik, Kulik, & Morgan, 1991).

Good Behavior Game (GBG)

The GBG is a group contingency designed to

- Improve the teacher's ability to define tasks, set rules, and discipline students.

- Reduce disruptive, aggressive, off-task, and shy behaviors in elementary-age children.

- Promote good behavior by rewarding teams that do not exceed maladaptive behavior standards.

The teacher begins the GBG by assigning each student in the class to a team and selecting team leaders. The teacher and students read and review the classroom rules, and the teacher informs students that each rule violation results immediately in a check mark on the blackboard next to the team's name. In addition, the teacher tells the students that he or she will state the rule that a student has violated, identify the student who has violated the rule, and praise the other teams for adhering to the rules. At the end of an instructional session, the teacher and students review the number of check marks per team, repeat the preset criteria for winning the game, and announce the winning team or teams. Team leaders then hand out rewards to winning team members (e.g., stamps, stickers, or "I did it" badges), and the nonwinning teams must stay in their seats and continue to engage in their lesson. Because teams try to beat the preset limit, more than one—or even all—teams can win.

Researchers initially associated the GBG with reduced rates of out-of-seat and talking-out behaviors of fourth-grade students (Barrish et al., 1969). Over the next 35 years, this finding led to a line of research that has documented the effectiveness of the GBG with students of varying ages and disabilities across many different settings. For example, Dolan and colleagues (1993) examined the effect of the GBG on first graders' disruptive classroom behaviors and found that teacher ratings of aggressive and shy behavior were significantly lower in the spring of the first grade than in the fall. In sum, the GBG is a good example of a classwide intervention that can have an effect on the behavior—and ultimately, on the learning—of many students.

WHERE DO YOU BEGIN? STEPS FOR CREATING A POSITIVE CLASSROOM ATMOSPHERE

Creating a positive classroom environment through implementing classwide interventions does not solve all classroom problem behaviors overnight. As illustrated in the classroom of Ms. Harman and Ms. Easley in "Case Scenario: A Classroom That Works," implementing these effective teaching practices requires up-front planning and ongoing problem solving. In addition, teachers must implement these practices efficiently and correctly (i.e., with fidelity) and individualize the practices to make them appropriate for unique aspects of their classrooms. For example, classroom rules may vary from classroom to classroom, depending on the expectations and ability levels of the students. Similarly, the teacher may implement close supervision and monitoring differently depending on the classroom size and layout. Like other behavior support strategies, implementing classwide interventions requires ongoing monitoring and evaluation of the use and effectiveness of these strategies. Thus, teachers will want to monitor their implementation of targeted classwide strategies and student outcomes. Ms. Harman and Ms. Easley demonstrated that collecting data on their own teaching behaviors helped them improve their skills. Additionally, by collecting data on their students' behavior, they obtained enough evidence to know that the practices were working.

Finally, as illustrated by the example of Ms. Walters in "Case Scenario: A Classroom With Challenges," teachers sometimes need a person outside their classroom to teach them classwide interventions and help them discover how to implement these strategies in their classrooms. Teachers may want to begin by assessing their current use of classwide interventions (see Table 1) and systematically identifying and targeting specific classwide interventions for classroom application.

FINAL THOUGHTS

When teachers systematically implement classwide interventions, teacher–student interactions become more positive, students are more engaged, and teachers are able to focus on teaching appropriate behaviors—all these result in a positive classroom environment that promotes student learning and engagement.

REFERENCES

Alber, S. R., Heward, W. L., & Hippler, B. J. (1999). Teaching middle school students with learning disabilities to recruit positive teacher attention. *Exceptional Children, 65*, 253–270.

Table 1. Universal Classwide Interventions

Classwide Interventions	What Are You Currently Doing?	What Do You Want to Change to Improve Your Instruction?
Close supervision and monitoring	Are students in proximity to you? Can you visually monitor all the students in your classroom? Do you actively engage with your students? Do students in your classroom have quick and efficient access to teacher assistance? Is the adult–student ratio sufficient to provide close supervision and monitoring?	During which instructional time will you implement closer supervision and monitoring? What staff will you involve in close supervision and monitoring? How will you implement close supervision and monitoring? How will you monitor the effectiveness of close supervision and monitoring?
Classroom rules	Do you have classroom rules? Did you develop your classroom rules in collaboration with your students? Do your students know the classroom rules, and are they able to perform them? Do you communicate classroom rules to your students in an effective and efficient manner? Do adults in the classroom contingently and regularly provide reinforcement to students for adhering to the rules? Do you apply consequences consistently when students break classroom rules?	Do you and your students implement the classroom rules effectively? Do you need to rewrite or adapt your classroom rules? How will you communicate your classroom rules to your students? How will you monitor whether the rules are working? How will you provide positive reinforcement to students for complying with the rules? What will you do if students do not comply?
Opportunities to respond (OTRs)	Do you use various types of OTRs in your classroom (e.g., choral, individual)? Do you provide students with an adequate rate of OTRs? What type of instructional delivery model do you use (direct, whole group, small group, etc.)?	Can you increase the number of OTRs for your students? Can you "switch up" the delivery method you use to offer more OTRs? How can you use more direct instruction?
Contingent praise	Do you regularly praise students for answering correctly? Do you praise students for an attempt to answer, even if it is not correct? Are you specific about what you are praising a student for (rather than simply "good girl" or "good boy")? Do you praise students for desirable social behavior?	Can you increase your positive interactions with your students? Can you increase your use of specific praise statements? Can you increase your use of contingent praise? Can you find reasons to praise all students in your class more frequently than you reprimand them?

Anderson, L., Evertson, C., & Emmer, E. (1980). Dimensions in classroom management derived from recent research. *Journal of Curriculum Studies, 12,* 343–356.

Bangert-Downs, R. L., Kulik, C. C., Kulik, J. A., & Morgan, M. (1991). The instructional effects of feedback in test-like events. *Review of Educational Research, 61,* 213–238.

Barbetta, P. M., Heron, T. E., & Heward, W. L. (1993). Effects of active student response during error correction on the acquisition, maintenance, and generalization of sight words by students with developmental disabilities. *Journal of Applied Behavior Analysis, 26,* 111–119.

Barbetta, P. M., & Heward, W. L. (1993). Effects of active student response during error correction on the acquisition and maintenance of geography facts by elementary students with learning disabilities. *Journal of Behavioral Education, 3,* 217–233.

Barrish, H., Saunders, M., & Wolfe, M. (1969). Good behavior game: Effects of individual contingencies for group consequences on disruptive behavior in a classroom. *Journal of Applied Behavior Analysis, 2,* 119–124.

Brophy, J. H., & Good, T. (1986). Teacher behavior and student achievement. In M. C. Wittrock (Ed.), *Handbook of research in teaching* (3rd ed.; pp. 328–375). New York: Macmillan.

Carnine, D. W. (1976). Effects of two teacher-presentation rates on off-task behavior, answering correctly, and participation. *Journal of Applied Behavior Analysis, 9,* 199–206.

Colvin, G., Sugai, G., Good, R. H., & Lee, Y. (1997). Using active supervision and precorrection to improve transition behaviors in an elementary school. *School Psychology Quarterly, 12,* 344–363.

Colvin, G. Sugai, G., & Patching, W. (1993). Precorrection: An instructional approach for managing predictable problem behaviors. *Intervention in School and Clinic, 28,* 143–150.

Council for Exceptional Children. (1987). *Academy for effective instruction: Working with mildly handicapped students.* Reston, VA: Author.

DePry, R. L., & Sugai, G. (2002). The effect of active supervision and pre-correction on minor behavioral incidents in a sixth grade general education classroom. *Journal of Behavioral Education, 11,* 255–267.

Dolan, L. J., Kellam, S. G., Brown, C. H., Werthamer-Larson, L., Rebok, G. W., Mayer, L. S., et al. (1993). The short-term impact of two classroom-based preventive interventions on aggressive and shy behaviors and poor achievement. *Journal of Applied Developmental Psychology, 14,* 317–345.

Evertson, C., & Emmer, E. (1982). Effective management at the beginning of the year in junior high classes. *Journal of Educational Psychology, 74,* 485-498.

Farmer, T. W., Goforth, J., Hives, J., Aaron, A., Hunter, F., & Sgmatto, A. (2006). Competence enhancement behavior management. *Preventing School Failure, 50,* 39–44.

Fisher, C. W., Berliner, D. C., Filby, N. N., Marliave, R., Cahen, L. S., & Dishaw, M. M. (1980). Teaching behaviors, academic learning time, and student achievement: An overview. In C. Denham & A. Lieberman (Eds.), *Time to learn* (pp. 7–32). Washington, DC: U.S. Department of Education, National Institute of Education.

Good, T., & Grouws, D. (1977). Teaching effects: A process-product study in fourth grade mathematics classrooms. *Journal of Teacher Education, 28,* 49–54.

Greenwood, C. R., Delquadri, J. C., & Hall, R. V. (1984). Opportunity to respond and student academic performance. In W. L. Heward, T. E. Heron, D. S. Hill, & J. Trap-

Porter (Eds.), *Focus on behavior analysis in education* (pp. 58–88). Columbus, OH: Charles E. Merrill.

Kirby, F. D., & Shields, F. (1972). Modification of arithmetic response rate and attending behavior in a seventh-grade student. *Journal of Applied Behavior Analysis, 5*, 79–84.

Lewis, T. J., Powers, L. J., Kelk, M. J., & Newcomer, L. L. (2002). Reducing problem behaviors on the playground: An investigation of the application of school-wide positive behavior and supports. *Psychology in the Schools, 39*, 181–190.

Luiselli, J. K., & Downing, J. N. (1980). Improving a student's arithmetic performance using feedback and reinforcement procedures. *Education and Treatment of Children, 3*, 45–49.

Stichter, J., & Lewis, T. J. (2006). Classroom assessment: Targeting variables to improve instruction through a multi-level eco-behavioral model. In M. Hersen (Ed.), *Clinician's handbook of child behavioral assessment* (pp. 569–586). Burlington, MA: Elsevier.

Sutherland, K. S. (2000). Promoting positive interactions between teachers and students with emotional/behavioral disorders. *Preventing School Failure, 44*, 110–115.

Sutherland, K. S., Gunter, P. L., & Alder, N. (2003). The effect of varying rates of OTR on the classroom behavior of students with EBD. *Journal of Emotional and Behavioral Disorders, 11*, 239–248.

Sutherland, K. S., & Snyder, A. (2007). Effects of reciprocal peer tutoring and self-graphing on reading fluency and classroom behavior of middle school students with emotional or behavioral disorders. *Journal of Emotional and Behavioral Disorders, 15*, 103–118.

Sutherland, K. S., Wehby, J. H., & Copeland, S. R. (2000). Effect of varying rates of behavior-specific praise on the on-task behavior of students with emotional and behavioral disorders. *Journal of Emotional and Behavioral Disorders, 8*, 2–8, 26.

Walker, H., Colvin, G., & Ramsey, E. (1995). *Antisocial behavior in school: Strategies and best practices.* New York: Brooks/Cole.

Originally published in *TEACHING Exceptional Children*, Vol. 40, No. 6, pp. 24–30.

11

Classwide Secondary and Tertiary Tier Practices and Systems

Sarah Fairbanks, Brandi Simonsen, and George Sugai

Ms. Green let out a sigh of relief after her last student left for the day and muttered, "I didn't know that my first year of teaching would be this hard." Ms. Green sat down and drafted an e-mail to her principal explaining that she has eight students with extremely disruptive behavior, five of whom have identified disabilities, and she needs a behavior specialist to develop individualized plans for each student. She further elaborated that with all of her focus on preparing her class for the upcoming statewide high-stakes test, she has no time or energy to work with these students, worries that they are interfering with the learning of their peers, and has tried everything with these students and nothing seems to work.

Like Ms. Green, many present day classroom teachers face greater challenges than perhaps during any time in the past. Teachers are expected to (a) provide evidence-based instruction to ensure that students make adequate yearly progress under the No Child Left Behind Act of 2001, Public Law No. 107-110 (NCLB); (b) serve an increasingly diverse group of students including students with disabilities within general education settings; and (c) manage classrooms while creating a safe and effective learning environment. Fortunately, there is support for teachers through ongoing educational research on the latest teaching strategies. Teachers can access a variety of validated instructional and classroom management practices such as empirically supported classroom management practices (Conroy, Sutherland, Snyder, & Marsh, 2008). When implemented effectively, evidence-based classroom management can greatly reduce problem behavior in classroom settings (Lohrmann, Talerico, & Dunlap, 2004).

When teaching in classroom settings, working from a three-tiered intervention framework for academics is helpful. For example, classroom management practices are considered primary or universal tier classroom interventions. Unfortunately, even with high quality implementation of evidence-based practices, some students are not successful with only primary intervention. Many teachers are equipped with skills to differentiate or modify instructional strategies to meet the needs of a diverse group of students. Thus, they have a strategy for working with students who do not respond to primary tier academic intervention. If needed, teachers implement or refer students to targeted groups (secondary tier intervention) or individualized academic supports (tertiary tier intervention). In a social setting, a similar approach is needed to prevent and correct inappropriate social behavior. Schoolwide positive behavior support (SWPBS; Sugai et al., 2000) provides a primary level of behavior support for students in and out of the classroom. Secondary and tertiary behavior interventions are layered onto primary interventions and are designed to support a range of students with behavioral needs in classroom settings (Crone, Horner, & Hawken, 2004).

In order to implement secondary and tertiary tier interventions in the context of SWPBS, evidence must be available to support the recommendation. In SWPBS, secondary tier interventions are introduced to targeted groups of students whose behaviors do not respond to primary tier intervention (Hawken & Horner, 2003). Tertiary interventions provide support for students (a) whose behaviors do not respond to secondary intervention or (b) whose behaviors are sufficiently intensive to warrant individualized support. Although secondary and tertiary tier interventions fit best within the context of SWPBS, they can be implemented in the classroom in schools where SWPBS is not in place. This article describes typical features, steps required to implement, and intervention prerequisites for secondary and tertiary intervention systems within classroom settings. Also included is an applied example of incorporating primary, secondary, and tertiary interventions in the classroom.

SECONDARY TIER INTERVENTIONS

Typical Features

Secondary tier interventions require minimal time to implement, incorporate similar features across various students, and typically provide extra doses of primary interventions. For example, a secondary intervention would include strategies and features to increase daily structure, provide more frequent behavioral prompts, and deliver additional praise for appropriate behavior. Although a variety of interventions can be used at the secondary tier (e.g., check in and check out [CICO], targeted social skills instruction, and peer/adult mentoring), most secondary interventions share some of the following key features: (a) instruction on targeted skills (Gureasko-Moore, DuPaul, & White, 2006; Hawken & Horner, 2003; Lane et al., 2003); (b) self-monitoring strategies (Gureasko-Moore et al.); (c) acknowledgements for appropriate behavior (Hawken & Horner; Hawken, MacLeod, & Rawlings, 2007); (d) regular performance feedback concerning target behaviors (Hawken & Horner; Hawken et al.); and (e) peer tutoring (Mitchem, Young, & West, 2001). Implementation of secondary tier interventions typically results in problem behavior reduction for participants (Hawken et al.; Hawken & Horner; Lane et al.).

A common example of a secondary intervention is CICO, also known as the Behavior Education Program (BEP; Hawken & Horner, 2003). The CICO intervention is a schoolwide intervention that all staff is aware of and potentially any student in the school can utilize. For example, teachers may use CICO for students who receive between two to five office discipline referrals (assuming that consistent referral and data systems are in place) and engage in relatively low-level disruptive problem behaviors such as talk-outs, irregular work completion, or tardiness.

Steps to Implement

When implementing CICO interventions within a classroom, develop and run the intervention by (a) creating the materials required to implement the intervention (e.g., the CICO point card with classroom expectations listed and prompts to rate the student throughout the day; see Figure 1); (b) identifying students whose behaviors are not responsive to the universal classroom management system as evidenced by available behavioral data (e.g., office discipline referrals); (c) inviting parents or guardians of identified students to participate in home check-ins; and (d) orienting and training students on the CICO process (Crone et al., 2004). Also develop a system to continuously track and monitor student data (i.e., points earned, office discipline referrals received, and daily behavioral ratings) to make informed decisions about the program's effectiveness for each student over time.

While using CICO, follow a standard implementation routine each day. In the morning check in with each student by reviewing expectations, providing a CICO point card, setting a daily goal for points to be earned, and ensuring that the student has the required materials. At regular time intervals throughout the day, give the student points and specific performance feedback (e.g., praise or correction) based on how well the student follows classroom rules. At the end of the day, check out with the student by reviewing the point sheet, determining if the student met his or her goal, providing acknowledgement if the goal was met (e.g., a token reinforcement), and making a copy of the point card for the student to take home for a parent's review and signature.

On a weekly basis, review classroom data to determine if additional students might require secondary intervention. Also review the data for students

Figure 1. Sample Check-In and Check-Out Card

<table>
<tr><td colspan="8" align="center">**Check In & Check Out Card**</td></tr>
</table>

Name _____

Date _____

Rating Scale	Points Possible	_____
2 = Great	Points Received	_____
1 = OK	Percentage of Points	_____
0 = Goal not met	Goal Met?	Y N

GOALS	8:30–9:30	9:30–10:30	10:30–11:30	11:30–12:30	12:30–1:30	1:30–2:30
1. Respect Others	2 1 0	2 1 0	2 1 0	2 1 0	2 1 0	2 1 0
2. Manage Self	2 1 0	2 1 0	2 1 0	2 1 0	2 1 0	2 1 0
3. Solve Problems Responsibly	2 1 0	2 1 0	2 1 0	2 1 0	2 1 0	2 1 0

currently receiving secondary intervention and determine if each student is benefiting. As students' behaviors improve, fade the system by (a) systematically increasing the time intervals on the point card (i.e., decrease the number of times the student receives points and feedback); (b) gradually increase the amount of points required for a student to meet a goal and receive a reward; or (c) explicitly transition the student to a self-managed program versus a teacher-managed program.

Intervention Prerequisites

Because secondary tier interventions are layered within the three-tiered continuum, classwide primary intervention is an important prerequisite for secondary and tertiary supports. In fact, fewer students are likely to require more intensive support when primary intervention is in place first (Fairbanks, 2007). Classwide primary interventions typically include (a) identifying and teaching expectations, (b) implementing continuum of strategies to acknowledge appropriate behavior, and (c) using evidence-based instructional practices (Simonsen, Fairbanks, Briesch, Myers, & Sugai, in press).

TERTIARY TIER INTERVENTIONS

Typical Features

Tertiary tier interventions involve an individualized assessment followed by the development of an individualized, function-based intervention plan. Most function-based interventions include (a) providing teacher attention (e.g., praise and points; Kamps, Wendland, & Culpepper, 2006); (b) self-monitoring (Kamps et al.); (c) teaching social skills (e.g., asking for help; Kamps et al.); (d) reducing task duration and breaking down task steps (Moore, Anderson, & Kumar, 2005); (e) receiving breaks and working with adults or peers (Peterson, Caniglia, & Royster, 2001); and (f) interspersing instruction between preferred activities (Blair, Liaupsin, Umbreit, & Kweon, 2006). More intensive tertiary supports are described in another article in this issue (Eber, Breen, Rose, Unizycki, & London, 2008).

Students whose problem behavior is not reduced by secondary intervention or who engage in severe and dangerous behavior (e.g., regular physical aggression) are candidates for tertiary tier intervention. An example of tertiary tier intervention is the development of a function-based behavior support plan (BSP; Horner, 1994) in which information about the function or purpose of behavior is obtained through a functional behavior assessment (FBA). The information is used to enhance the effectiveness, efficiency, and relevance of elements of the behavior intervention plan. FBA is a process to determine the events that reliably predict (i.e., setting events and antecedents) and follow/reinforce (i.e., consequences) problem behaviors. The individualized function-based plan also documents environmental changes that staff members make to (a) minimize the events that predict problem behavior; (b) teach an appropriate replacement behavior that is as easy and efficient in accessing reinforcement as the problem behavior (e.g., if talking out is a concern, explicitly teach hand-raising and provide immediate adult attention when the child does so, instead of when the child talks-out); (c) increase reinforcement for the appropriate behavior; and (d) eliminate or reduce reinforcement for the problem behavior. An individualized behavior support team develops and supports implementation of tertiary tier interventions, which are generally more expensive in terms of time and resources compared to primary and secondary interventions.

Steps to Implement

When a student requires individualized support, the first step is to organize a team of relevant people to begin planning the intervention. Administration and behavior specialists are typically core members of tertiary intervention teams. Dynamic members of tertiary intervention teams are family representatives, a student's teachers, and other relevant specialists (e.g., Title 1 teacher). All teams should include someone with behavioral expertise and someone familiar with the context in which problem behaviors occur

(Benazzi, Horner, & Good, 2006). In addition, the student and his or her family need to be actively involved in the formation of this team (Eber et al., 2008). Other individuals such as siblings, friends, or community members may provide support and play advocacy roles in the process.

When the team meets, discuss student strengths and concerns as well as routines in which problem behaviors are likely to occur as well as events and conditions that reliably precede and follow problem behaviors. For example, double-digit addition may be an antecedent to making loud noises, jokes, and getting out of one's seat, which is typically followed by peer attention (e.g., laughter). The goal of meeting as a team is to develop hypothesis statements that best describe conditions under which problem behaviors are likely to occur. If the team fails to develop a reasonable statement or fails to agree, team members may collect more information through interviews, observations, or archival record reviews.

Once one or more testable hypothesis statements are confirmed, the information is used to draft a behavior intervention plan that typically includes (a) student strengths, (b) behaviors of interest, (c) setting events and antecedents, (d) consequences, (e) acceptable alternative behaviors, and (f) desired behaviors. The selection of alternative behaviors, based on what is acceptable in a teacher's classroom, allows the participant access to the same consequence that maintains the problem behavior and is comparable to the problem behavior with respect to effort and efficiency. The desired behavior is what teachers view as acceptable behavior from all students.

BSPs also include intervention and instructional strategies designed to minimize the influence of setting events, antecedents, and maintaining consequences (Fairbanks, Sugai, Guardino, & Lathrop, 2007). Strategies for teaching (social skills instruction) and strengthening alternative and desired behaviors through positive reinforcement are also important to include and should serve as the basis for developing lesson plans and implementation scripts and schedules. Additionally, the behavior plan should outline implementation tasks, data collection methods, measurable goals, and criteria for intervention decision making.

Initial team meetings focus on developing and scheduling supports for the implementation of the behavior plan (e.g., review the plan with the student and determine how and who will monitor progress). Then, as the plan is implemented, the team meets frequently to ensure that implementation occurs as planned and to make adjustments to enhance outcomes.

Intervention Prerequisites

Unless student behavior is highly severe and ongoing (e.g., regular property destruction or physical aggression), implement primary and secondary tier interventions before developing tertiary tier supports. Evaluate the accuracy with which primary and secondary tier interventions are implemented and consider the impact of the interventions. For example, a student on a CICO plan may have a daily goal that is too high, receive incentives that do not reinforce, or may receive inconsistent teacher feedback and points. If this occurs, make minor adjustments such as changing incentive options and monitor the effect of these changes before considering tertiary tier intervention.

Applied Example

Ms. Green was relieved when her principal explained in response to her e-mail that a systematic approach existed for addressing her students' behaviors. Specifically, the principal explained that a continuum of supports could be implemented in her classroom. The principal elaborated that she should implement primary tier intervention (i.e., evidence-based classroom management) for all students, implement secondary tier interventions for some students requiring additional support, and implement tertiary tier interventions for individual students with the most intensive behavioral needs who did not respond to secondary tier interventions or who have an ongoing or serious problem behavior.

"Simple as that?" Ms. Green asked.

"Of course, simple as that." the principal replied.

However, as simple as it may seem, implementing a continuum of support in the classroom requires training, coaching, and ongoing support. To demonstrate the effectiveness of implementing the three tiers of intervention in a classroom setting, researchers recruited teachers to participate in a research study (Fairbanks et al., in preparation). Four classroom teachers in two schools in the Northeast agreed to participate, and they received support to implement tiered intervention systems in their classrooms. The teachers work in first, second, fourth, and fifth grade classrooms and have students engaging in disruptive and problematic behavior.

Before implementing any intervention, teachers received information about each intervention tier. Teachers and principals selected target students to participate in the study and, following consent procedures, 12 participants were selected. Teachers and researchers completed prestudy information about each participant including a rating scale, a teacher interview, and two observations of each student. This information was used to predict the intervention level to which students were likely to respond. For example, clinically significant ratings indicated the need to use tertiary tier interventions.

Primary Tier Intervention

Although teachers were eager to use secondary and tertiary tier support, the researchers first implemented primary tier interventions across each classroom. Teachers developed their own primary intervention, but the interventions were all comprised of the same key features and components: (a) identifying expectations; (b) defining expectations; (c) explicitly and directly teaching expectations; (d) posting expectations; and (e) designing a system to encourage, reinforce, and acknowledge appropriate behavior.

All teachers identified and posted three to five positively stated expectations for all students in the classroom such as be responsible, respectful, and safe. Teachers then completed a matrix that outlined concrete examples of those expectations across classroom routines and settings (see Figure 2). Each box in the matrix then became part of a lesson plan that was developed and later delivered by the teacher. Lesson plans included an introduction and rationale for teaching the target behavior, adult-modeled examples and nonexamples of the target behavior, and opportunities for students to practice the behavior with and without an adult. Finally, each teacher created a classwide acknowledgment or reward system. Teachers used tokens such as smiley faces on a poster board to (a) acknowledge students' behaviors that followed expectations and (b) track students' progress. When students earned a certain number of tokens or on a random basis, the teacher awarded a classwide incentive such as a popcorn and movie party or pajama day.

Primary interventions were implemented and observers watched target and peer students to monitor changes in problem behaviors. Students whose problem behaviors did not improve (e.g., problem behavior occurring during 25% or more of intervals as measured by observational data), participated in secondary tier intervention.

Secondary Tier Intervention

Four of the 12 student participants required additional behavior support. The researcher explained the CICO intervention to the teachers, and parents were given information about the intervention via phone calls with the teachers as well as through a letter.

The schools did not have a schoolwide CICO system. Therefore each teacher became the CICO coordinator and developed a CICO card for his or her classroom with expectations on one side and corresponding time intervals on the other. In the morning, each teacher checked in with target students, set daily goals, and reviewed expectations. The teachers also checked in with students throughout the day providing specific praise and corrective feedback while assigning points. At the end of the day, the teacher checked out with each student and offered an incentive if the student met the goal.

Progress monitoring occurred through observation data, daily points, and teacher feedback. Again, when students did not respond to the secondary intervention (e.g., problem behavior occurring during 25% or more of intervals) over a minimum of a week long period, tertiary tier intervention was considered.

Tertiary Tier Intervention

Following secondary intervention, two participants required support at the tertiary level. A group of relevant personnel (e.g., researcher, classroom teacher,

Figure 2. Sample Classroom Matrix

Rules Within Routines Matrix

Routines ➡ Rules ⬇	Transitions	Independent Seat Work	Small Group Activity	Teacher-Led Instruction
Respectful	• Hands to self • Keep 8 inches between yourself and others in line	• Raise hand before talking • Stay on task	• Listen to each other • Accept each other's answers • Give eye contact	• Give eye contact to teacher • Raise hand before talking
Responsible	• Admit mistakes • Ignore your neighbor • Put materials away	• Complete your own work • Keep materials in folders	• Help with the group work • Use time wisely	• Follow along/be in the right place • Listen to teacher instructions • Take notes
Safe	• Follow adult directions • Remain quiet	• Sit with 6 legs on the floor • Stay in your space	• Keep objects out of hands • Use materials carefully	• Keep objects out of hands • Sit with 6 legs on the floor

and resource teacher) discussed next steps. Each student, teacher, and another relevant adult (e.g., instructional assistant) was interviewed. The student interview included questions about the times of day at school that were difficult or positive for the student and what typically happened in those situations. The interviews of the teacher and other adult were compared for consistency in terms of environmental predictors and consequences of disruptive behavior. In this research, interview summaries were the same and therefore confidence about the accuracy of observations was high. As a result, the team developed an individualized plan with guidance from the researcher using input from the student interview. If confidence is not high because the interview summaries vary, additional information sources (e.g., additional interviews and observations) are identified and assessments conducted. Each intervention plan includes elements to (a) minimize problem behavior (e.g., shorten tasks or teach peers to ignore problem behavior), (b) maximize appropriate behavior (e.g., receive praise and incentives more frequently), and (c) provide goals and tools to measure and monitor progress.

Results

Eight of 12 participants required primary tier intervention; two participants required primary plus secondary tier intervention; and two participants required primary, secondary, and tertiary tier intervention. The level of problem behavior was reduced overall for each student in response to at least one intervention. All students responded to the three-tiered continuum of support that was implemented in the classroom.

Before beginning intervention, teachers predicted that most participants required at least secondary intervention. Like Ms. Green, teachers in this study were eager to implement more intensive interventions than was necessary. A comparison of the predictions made, using information collected before the study for each participant with actual results, were less than 20% accurate: prestudy predictions were too high in terms of intervention level. In other words, teachers consistently believed that students needed more support than was actually required in a three-tiered model.

Overall, teachers considered the three interventions to be useful and practical according to poststudy questionnaires. Teachers found the primary intervention most acceptable and valuable. From qualitative observations, teachers also increased their use of specific classroom management strategies (e.g., active supervision).

IMPLICATIONS AND CONCLUSIONS

Classroom teachers face multiple challenges when managing student behavior. A multi-tiered approach to behavior support in the classroom is a data and needs-based approach to serve all students. When a classwide primary tier intervention can be implemented, the number of students requiring more intensive support is often reduced. Primary tier intervention may be the most efficient and accepted level of support and, therefore, a substantial investment of time at the primary tier could be a wise use of resources. Secondary and tertiary tier supports require greater behavioral expertise and resources and may require collaboration with other professionals. However, secondary and tertiary tier interventions such as CICO and individualized behavior interventions are effective means to reduce problem behavior of students with challenging behavioral concerns. Classrooms are a place where all three tiers of intervention can be implemented.

When considering the implementation of a three-tiered approach to behavior support and behavior management in the classroom, teachers should take into account the elements summarized in the self-assessment (see Figure 3). Programmatic action plans can be developed based on the missing or partially missing elements. In addition, teachers should consult the resources included in Figure 4 for secondary and tertiary tier interventions and system ideas.

Figure 3. Self-Assessment for Classroomwide Secondary and Tertiary Tier Interventions and Systems

	Classroom Element	**Self-Rating**
Getting Ready	Accurate, positive, and comprehensive schoolwide PBS system, including a schoolwide data-management and monitoring system.	IP PP NP
	Accurate, positive, and comprehensive classroomwide PBS system, including behavioral expectations, lesson plans for teaching routines, positive reinforcement, etc.	IP PP NP
	Knowledgeable and fluent support staff (e.g., school psychologists, counselor, special educator) to assist in classroom implementation.	IP PP NP
	Secondary and tertiary tier intervention materials (e.g., point cards, social skill lesson plans, data recording forms, parent letters, functional behavior assessments [FBA] and behavior support plan [BSP] forms).	IP PP NP
	Menu of daily and weekly positive reinforcers.	IP PP NP
	Decision rules and routines for regular universal screening.	IP PP NP
	Behavior function considered in intervention selection and development.	IP PP NP
Implementation	Distribution of written explanations and information for staff, family members, etc.	IP PP NP
	Daily morning check-in and afternoon check-out.	IP PP NP
	Four to five daily self/other assessments.	IP PP NP
	Daily time for progress monitoring, summarizing, and feedback.	IP PP NP
	Parents and staff informed of student progress.	IP PP NP
Monitoring Implementation	Weekly team meeting scheduled to review student progress and enhance implementation accuracy.	IP PP NP
	Data-decision rules for determining responsiveness to intervention and transitions between intervention tiers.	IP PP NP
	Procedures for assessing fidelity of implementation.	IP PP NP

Note. IP = In Place, PP = Partially In Place, NP = Not In Place.

Figure 4. Resources for Classroom Implementation of Secondary and Tertiary Tier Interventions

The Office of Special Education Programs National Technical Assistance Center on Positive Behavior Interventions and Supports
- **Web site:** http://pbis.org
- **Details:** This Web site contains links to presentations, forms (e.g., Functional Assessment Checklist for Teachers and Staff), and other resources critical to implementing secondary and tertiary tier interventions.

Schoolwide Information Systems
- **Web site:** www.swis.org
- **Details:** This Web site facilitates data input and output for office discipline referral and other behavioral data (e.g., points earned) used to monitor progress of students supported by primary and secondary tier interventions

Additional user-friendly texts
- Secondary Tier Interventions:
  - Crone, D. A., Horner, R. H., & Hawken, L. S. (2004). *Responding to problem behavior in schools: The behavior education program.* New York: Guilford Press
- Tertiary Tier Interventions:
  - O'Neill, R. E., Horner, R. H., Albin, R. W., Storey, K., & Sprague, J. R. (1997). *Functional analysis of problem behavior: A practical assessment guide* (2nd ed.). Pacific Grove, CA: Brookes/Cole.
  - Crone, D. A., & Horner, R. H. (2003). *Building positive behavior support systems in schools.* New York: Guilford Press.

REFERENCES

Benazzi, L., Horner, R. H., & Good, R. H. (2006). Effects of behavior support team composition on the technical adequacy and contextual fit of behavior support plans. *Journal of Special Education, 40*(3), p 160–170.

Blair, K. C., Liaupsin, C. J., Umbreit, J., & Kweon, G. (2006). Function-based intervention to support the inclusive placements of young children in Korea. *Education and Training in Developmental Disabilities, 41*(1), 48–57.

Conroy, M., Sutherland, K., Snyder, A., & Marsh, S. (2008). Classwide interventions: Effective instruction makes a difference. *TEACHING Exceptional Children, 40*(6), 24–30.

Crone, D. A., Horner, R. H., & Hawken, L. S. (2004). *Responding to problem behavior in schools: The behavior education program.* New York: Guilford Press.

Eber, L., Breen, K., Rose, J., Unizycki, R., & London, T. (2008). Wraparound as a tertiary level intervention for students with emotional/behavioral needs. *TEACHING Exceptional Children, 40*(6), 16–22.

Fairbanks, S. (2007). *Integrating levels of behavior support in the classroom.* Unpublished dissertation, University of Connecticut, Storrs.

Fairbanks, S., Sugai, G., Guardino, D., & Lathrop, M. (2007). Response to intervention: Examining classroom behavior support in second grade. *Exceptional Children, 73*, 288–310.

Gureasko-Moore, S., DuPaul, G. J., & White, G. P. (2006). The effects of self-management in general education classrooms on the organizational skills of adolescents with ADHD. *Behavior Modification, 30*(2), 159–183.

Hawken, L., & Horner, R. (2003). Evaluation of a targeted group intervention within a schoolwide system of behavior support, *Journal of Behavioral Education, 12*, 225–240.

Hawken, L. S., MacLeod, K. S., & Rawlings, L. (2007). Effects of the behavior education program on office discipline referrals of elementary school students. *Journal of Positive Behavior Interventions, 9*(2), 94–101.

Horner, R. H. (1994). Functional assessment: Contributions and future directions. *Journal of Applied Behavior Analysis, 27*, 401–404.

Kamps, D., Wendland, M., & Culpepper, M. (2006). Active teacher participation in functional behavior assessment for students with emotional and behavioral disorders risks in general education classrooms. *Behavioral Disorders, 31*(2), 128–146.

Lane, K. L., Wehby, J., Menzies, H. M., Doukas, G. L., Munton, S. M., & Gregg, R. M. (2003). Social skills instruction for students at risk for antisocial behavior: The effects of small-group instruction. *Behavioral Disorders, 28*(3), 229–248.

Lohrmann, S., Talerico, J., & Dunlap, G. (2004). Anchor the boat: A classwide intervention to reduce problem behavior. *Journal of Positive Behavior Interventions, 6*, 113–120.

Mitchem, K. J., Young, K. R., & West, R. P. (2001). CWPASM: A classwide peer-assisted self-management program for general education classrooms. *Education & Treatment of Children, 24*(2), 111–140.

Moore, D. W., Anderson, A., & Kumar, K. (2005). Instructional adaptation in the management of escape-maintained behavior in a classroom. *Journal of Positive Behavior Interventions, 7*(4), 216–223.

No Child Left Behind Act of 2001, Pub. L. No. 107–110. Retrieved October 15, 2006, from http://www.ed.gov/policy/elsec/leg/esea02/index.html

Peterson, S. M. P., Caniglia, C., & Royster, A. (2001). Application of choice-making intervention for a student with multiply maintained problem behavior. *Focus on Autism and Other Developmental Disabilities, 16*(4), 240–246.

Simonsen, B., Fairbanks, S., Briesch, A., Myers, D., & Sugai, G. (in press). Evidence-based practices in classroom management. *Education and Treatment of Children.*

Sugai, G., Horner, R. H., Dunlap, G., Hieneman, M., Lewis, T. J., Nelson, C. M., Scott, T., Liaupsin, C., Sailor, W., Turnbull, A. P., Turnbull, H. R., III, Wickham, D. Reuf, M., & Wilcox, B. (2000). Applying positive behavior support and functional assessment in schools. *Journal of Positive Behavior Interventions, 2*, 131–143.

Originally published in *TEACHING Exceptional Children*, Vol. 40, No. 6, pp. 44–52.

12

Using Positive Behavioral Support to Manage Avoidance of Academic Tasks

Nina Zuna and Dennis McDougall

One of the most frequent concerns expressed by teachers and administrators is how to manage behavioral problems in the classroom (Langdon, 1999). Behavior that disrupts instruction is problematic for teachers and students, in part, because we have known for quite some time that the amount of time students engage actively in academic tasks is positively correlated to how much they learn (Black, 2004). Functional assessment and positive behavioral support (PBS) are two management approaches that are extensions of applied behavior analysis (Repp & Horner, 1999). Unlike some classroom management practices that rely heavily on aversive consequences, these approaches use more proactive techniques to manage challenging behavior and increase students' active engagement in learning. These approaches

- Use research-validated procedures to address causes or functions, of a behavior in the environmental context in which the behavior operates.
- Teach students more efficient and desirable ways to achieve the same outcome that a problematic behavior serves.
- Emphasize simple antecedent changes to the environment that often lead to substantial improvements in behavior.

As this article shows, "simple antecedent changes" often included accommodating a student's interests, even to the extent of bringing Barbie doll accessories into the curriculum or allowing short social breaks during academic tasks. Such changes had great effects on a young girl's disruptive behavior.

Beyond addressing educators' concerns about how to manage challenging behaviors, use of these two procedures is mandated, in certain cases, by federal law (Gartin & Murdick, 2001).

FUNCTIONAL ASSESSMENT AND POSITIVE BEHAVIORAL SUPPORT

The reauthorization of the Individuals with Disabilities Education Act of 1997 (IDEA) introduced *functional assessment* to federal legislation and directed school personnel to use this research-validated procedure. In addition, IDEA mandated that educators use PBS strategies to address behaviors that impede a student's learning or interfere with the learning environment. Long before these legal mandates, research indicated that functional assessment and PBS were effective tools for managing undesirable behaviors, especially behaviors that serve functions of seeking attention, communicating one's needs, and escaping or avoiding academic tasks. For example, Carr, Newsom, and Binkoff (1976) used PBS to reduce escape-motivated behavior during instruction. Carr, Newsom et al. identified features of the instructional environment that had promoted a student's self-destructive behavior—behavior that had served the function of escaping or avoiding instruction. Carr, Newsom et al. then altered key features of the instructional environment; that is, he embedded instruction within a more positive context. This change reduced the student's escape-motivated self-destructive responses during instruction.

The Carr, Newsom et al. (1976) study is important because it is one of the first studies that applied a positive behavioral approach to ameliorate problem behavior after numerous contingency programs had failed to help the student. Carr, Newsom et al. suggested, "The failure of treatment using consequence approaches underlines our imperfect understanding of self-destructive behavior and provides us with an incentive to seek out new interventions" (p. 140).

The Carr, Newsom et al. (1976) study and many subsequent PBS studies demonstrate that simple antecedent changes to the academic environment, such as incorporating students' interests into curricular tasks (Clarke et al., 1995), permitting students' choice in the sequence of assigned tasks (Kern, Mantegna, Vorndran, Bailin, & Hilt, 2001), and modifying instructional antecedents (Wheeler & Wheeler, 1995) can lead to dramatic improvements.

Not surprisingly, students with disabilities often struggle with learning, and they often display their most disruptive behavior during academic instruction. So, how can educators use PBS to minimize students' resistance to academic instruction without disrupting classroom routines? The case study of Callie may offer some answers.

> **Tip 1: Seek Assistance**
>
> Identifying conditions and events in the classroom that are related to a student's disruptive behavior can be very challenging, especially when you are the student's teacher. As teachers, often we are too close to the situation, or too busy with other students and teaching tasks, to effectively identify the classroom variables that trigger and maintain disruptive behavior. Therefore, seek assistance from a capable and trusted colleague.

CALLIE—A CASE STUDY IN POSITIVE BEHAVIORAL SUPPORT

We conducted this study within and mindful of the ongoing routine of a classroom because naturalistic assessment examines the actual settings where challenging behaviors occur, not in isolated or contrived settings. We wanted our assessment to be relatively unobtrusive. In addition, interventions based on our assessment had to be practical, flexible, and suitable to the needs of the teacher, students, and classroom, while using effective, research-supported methods.

Callie was a 6-year-old female with attention deficit/hyperactivity disorder (ADHD), seizure disorder, and developmental coordination disorder. She received no medications to treat symptoms associated with ADHD. Two weeks before this study, her physician discontinued her seizure medication due to lack of seizure activity. We observed zero seizures from 1 month before the study through the end of the study. Callie did not receive any physical therapy intervention for developmental coordination disorder, although she did display some of its characteristics (e.g., clumsiness in motor movements; delays in achieving developmental motor milestones, such as crawling, walking, buttoning, zipping; and, in older children, difficulties in writing, ball-playing, biking, and skating; Fox, 1998).

Callie, one of four students in a self-contained classroom, often behaved in ways that disrupted her own and peers' work, as well as the teacher's

> **Tip 2: Get a Different View**
>
> - Take 15 minutes to sit back and view your students and classroom environment while your educational assistant or a colleague teaches.
> - When is the last time you saw yourself and your students in action in your classroom? View some videotape of yourself.
> - Visit a colleague's classroom and observe.
> - Visit the cafeteria or playground to practice identifying things that "predict" and precede disruptive behavior (e.g., overcrowding, elevated noise levels, inadequate equipment, age-inappropriate games, or peer-buddy mismatches).

> **Tip 3: Watch for Behavioral Red Flags**
>
> "He always acts that way. I tried everything."
> "He misbehaves for NO REASON at all."
> "She is just doing that to get back at me."
>
> These "within-the-skin" statements signal frustration. Understanding that behavior occurs for a reason and is linked to antecedent and consequence events is the foundation of behavior analytic research.
>
> Recall Tip 1, "Seek Assistance." Using a colleague's input is often helpful during times of frustration because their unbiased observations can provide objective data that are free from emotion.

routine, during academic tasks. She also displayed challenging behavior during lunch, snack, recess, and free time. A classwide token reinforcement system, which the teacher used before this study began, failed to improve Callie's behavior. Her challenging behavior was so frequent that we conducted a two-phase case study. Our purpose was to improve Callie's behavior through the use of PBS strategies acceptable to the teacher and Callie.

EXPERIMENTAL DESIGN AND ANALYSIS—PHASE 1 AND PHASE 2

During Phase 1, assessment, we used a multi-element design (Kazdin, 1982) to conduct a functional analysis. We examined and compared Callie's behavior in five normally occurring school contexts: academic work, snack, recess, lunch, and free-time. For Phase 2, intervention, we used a changing conditions design (Alberto & Troutman, 1999) to accommodate teacher preferences. The classroom teacher requested no "return to baseline" due to ethical considerations about withdrawing interventions. The changing conditions design was a design that permitted implementation of multiple interventions across time, for a single student, with no return to baseline (Alberto & Troutman).

PHASE 1: ASSESSMENT

Functional Assessment-Hypothesis Development

Interviews. First, the special education teacher and Callie's parents completed a single functional assessment interview form (O'Neill et al., 1997).

Direct Observations. Next, to better utilize information provided via the functional assessment interview, the first author conducted six, 10-minute observations, in several school settings, over the course of one full school day, using an A-B-C recording format, as outlined by Repp and Horner (1999). These observations—written objectively in narrative, anecdotal style—

Figure 1. Frequency of Problem Behavior Across Sessions (Escape and Attention Combined)

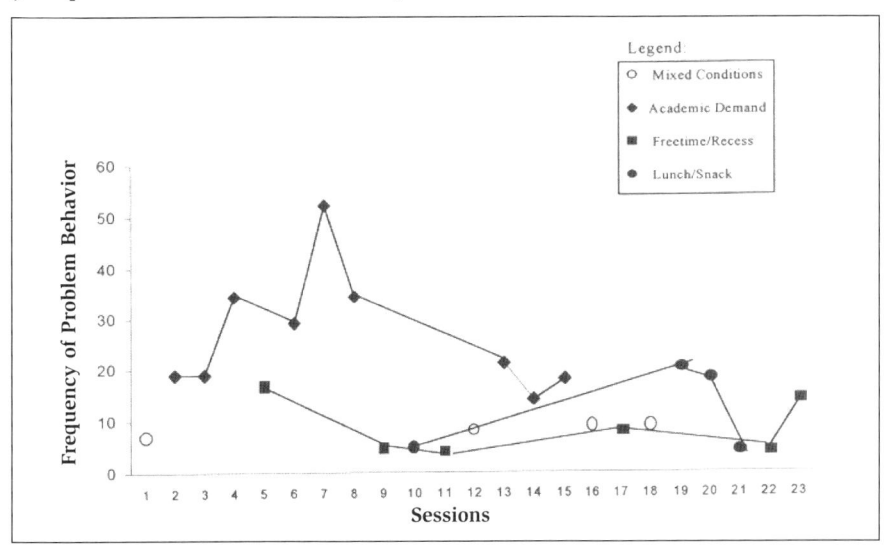

provided insights about the times and conditions under which Callie did and did not exhibit various types of challenging behavior.

Functional Analysis. The first author conducted a functional analysis to validate information obtained from both the interview form and direct observations. The functional analysis was conducted during a 4-hour period, on 1 day, beginning at 8 a.m. and ending at about noon.

The functional analysis occurred on a separate day from other data-collection events (i.e., after the interviews and direct observations, and prior to intervention). We conducted a total of 23, 10-minute observations of five regularly occurring routines—academic work (9 sessions), snack (1 session), recess (1 session), lunch (3 sessions), free-time (5 sessions), plus four "mixed" sessions in which routines overlapped (see Figure 1). We counted the frequency of Callie's escape-motivated and attention-seeking behaviors during each 10-minute observation session. In Figure 1, we have grouped data from similar routines (i.e., lunch and snack; recess and free time) to promote presentation clarity.

Functional Assessment Results

Interviews. Information gleaned from the teacher interview suggested tentatively two possible types (i.e., functions) of challenging behavior—escape and attention. The teacher (a) reported that Callie's behavior was "very unpredictable," (b) was unaware of specific classroom settings that contributed to Callie's problem behavior, and (c) did not identify specific reinforcers that had maintained such behavior.

> **Tip 4: Who Changes What First?**
>
> Recall Abbott and Costello's famous skit, "Who's on First?" Well, consider our PBS sequel, "Who Changes What First?" As professionals, we must acknowledge that by changing our own actions, or by modifying how we arrange classroom settings and tasks, we can mitigate students' disruptive behavior. Habitually challenging behavior is often a sign that the current environment does not meet the needs of a particular student. Who's more likely to change what first—the student or teacher?

Direct Observations. Direct observations suggested further that Callie engaged in two distinctive types of problem behaviors. The first type, escape-motivated behavior, included

- Refusing to begin academic tasks.
- Hurrying to complete academic tasks.
- Asking unrelated questions and voicing unrelated comments during academic tasks (e.g., "Why do I have to do this work?" and "My chair is too short").
- Fidgeting during academic tasks (e.g., handling materials in and on her desk unrelated to task, excessive erasing, repositioning body in seat, and twirling hair).

The second type, attention-seeking behavior, included

- Tattling on peers.
- Asking personal questions (e.g., "Do you have any sisters?").
- Soliciting adults' attention (e.g., asking an adult to watch her).

Direct observations also suggested that Callie's problematic behavior, during academic tasks, was maintained and reinforced inadvertently via specific consequences. That is, the teacher often sent Callie to a timeout corner, or directed Callie to place her head on her desk, after Callie exhibited disruptive behavior during academic tasks.

These consequence-based procedures allowed Callie to escape from what was, for her, an aversive situation (i.e., academic tasks or demands) by engaging in disruptive behaviors. Direct observations, combined with interview data, also revealed minimal behavior problems from 12:00–2:30 p.m., a period that included group activities, free time, snack, recess, and dismissal—*but not academic tasks or demands*.

Functional Analysis. Functional analysis results confirmed that Callie displayed the highest frequencies of problematic behaviors during instructional periods that included academic demands, as opposed to free time-recess and snack-lunch (see Figure 1). During the nine academic demand sessions

> **Tip 5: Consider the Alternatives**
>
> Functional behavior assessment (FBA) and positive behavioral support (PBS) interventions range from informal and simple to formal and comprehensive. You can apply PBS to individual students, classrooms, and school systems. Simple changes within a classroom teacher's control include
>
> - Making task or instructional modifications.
> - Incorporating student interests.
> - Chunking or reducing assignments.
> - Providing advance organizers.
> - Using peer tutors or models.
> - Allowing student choice.
> - Teaching alternative forms of communication.
> - Limiting homework assignments to tasks that the student has clearly mastered previously.

observed, total problem behaviors averaged 26.6 occurrences per session and ranged from 14 to 52.

Escape-motivated behaviors constituted 26.2 of this total, whereas attention-seeking behaviors constituted only 0.4. The "spike" in Figure 1 during session 7 (n = 52 problematic behaviors) occurred during Callie's least favorite subject, math. According to the teacher, high frequencies of problem behavior during math assignments were typical responses from Callie. While this data point might be a statistical outlier, it is consistent with the teacher's description and interview data about Callie's day-to-day performance.

Figure 1 also indicates that Callie tended to exhibit attention-seeking behavior during the snack-lunch and free time-recess contexts. Average occurrence of all problem behavior during the snack-lunch context was 11.75 and ranged from 4 to 20, with a mean of 3.5 for escape-only and 8.25 for attention-seeking behavior. Average occurrence of problem behavior during the free time-recess context was 8.7, with a range from 3 to 17. Escape-only behaviors during this context averaged 1.0, while attention-seeking behaviors averaged 7.7.

The assessment results indicated clearly that, from the standpoint of frequency, escape-motivated behavior during academic demands constituted our greatest concern. The assessment results also identified the academic context as the antecedent *setting* most likely associated with this behavior. Therefore, in conjunction with the teacher, we (a) selected escape-motivated behavior as the dependent variable worthy of immediate intervention, and (b) used functional analysis results from the academic-demand context as our baseline data.

We developed several hypotheses and interventions based on our assessment data. We did not develop or implement specific interventions to manage

Figure 2. Hypotheses

1. Callie's escape-motivated behavior will be reduced during academic work when
    a. Her escape behavior is no longer followed by timeout or other escape-allowing strategies.
    b. She is given praise for appropriate academic behavior, and inappropriate behavior is ignored.
    c. Her tasks are modified to reduce escape behavior by incorporating her interests.
    d. Verbal attention is provided as a reward for task completion.
    e. Choice is provided during instructional periods.
2. Callie's attention-seeking behavior will be reduced when
    a. The staff ignores instances of tattling.
    b. The staff ignores inappropriate attempts to gain attention.
    c. She is taught appropriate methods for soliciting attention.
    d. The staff provides praise for polite and appropriate social interactions.

Callie's attention-seeking behavior because of our aforementioned decision to prioritize and immediately address escape-motivated behavior. Figure 2, however, includes some approaches that, if needed, might help Callie and her teacher address both escape-motivated and attention-seeking behaviors.

PHASE 2: INTERVENTION

We based our interventions on assessment results. Because escape-motivated behavior occurred almost entirely in the presence of academic demands, we chose to modify curricular activities and reinforcement contingencies that the teacher used during academic periods.

Four Interventions

We implemented four interventions (see Table 1) in the following order: differential reinforcement of alternative behavior (DRA) = 6 sessions during 1 morning; DRA and task modification = 6 sessions during the next morning; DRA and social breaks = 5 sessions during the next morning; and DRA and choice = 14 sessions during the next 2 mornings, with 5 sessions 1 morning and 9 sessions the next morning.

We collected data for the final intervention for 2 days, rather than 1 day, because the teacher expressed a strong interest in this intervention. Finally, 19 days after Intervention 4, we collected data for three sessions, during 1 morning, to assess maintenance of intervention results. Intervention 4 conditions were in effect during these last three sessions.

Table 1. Interventions We Used to Help Callie Do Academic Work

Name of Intervention	Description
DRA (Miltenberger, 2001)	Positive verbal reinforcement for on-task behavior, plus extinction/no response for inappropriate behavior.
DRA and task modification	DRA plus modification of academic tasks to include student's interests (Barbie doll accessories, pink rather than standard paper/pencil, and stencils).
DRA and social breaks	DRA plus a short social break consisting of 2-3 minute conversations with the Educational Assistant (EA). The social break was provided contingent on assignment completion.
DRA and choice of task and break activity	DRA plus choice of task and choice of break activity. Choice of tasks was allowed for all academic seatwork. After completing 3 tasks, a 5-minute break was provided. To ease transitions from break back to work, Callie was asked what she would like to do for her next break. This was written on her assignment as a visual reminder.

Intervention Results

Figure 3 shows that occurrences of Callie's escape behavior slightly decreased from baseline ($M = 26.2$) to the initial DRA intervention ($M = 22.5$). Escape behavior was considerably less frequent during subsequent interventions including: DRA plus task modification ($M = 12.3$); DRA plus social breaks ($M = 16.0$); DRA plus choice of task or break ($M = 13.0$); and follow-up ($M = 12.0$).

BEGINNING AND EXPANDING USE OF PBS—A MATTER OF PROFESSIONALISM

Our experiences with Callie and her teacher, our own students, and the research literature suggested that teachers can use PBS effectively to manage disruptive behaviors, within the context of ongoing classroom routines, when they have sufficient assistance and expertise. Callie's improvement provides further support that PBS strategies, specifically those incorporating curricular modifications, improve problematic behaviors (Carr et al., 1976; Horner, Day, & Day, 1997). More widespread use of PBS may depend on teachers' successful experiences with efficiency and practicality of PBS applications in their classrooms, as well as changes in teachers' perceptions of the program's success.

Figure 3. Frequency of Escape Behavior Across Sessions and Phases

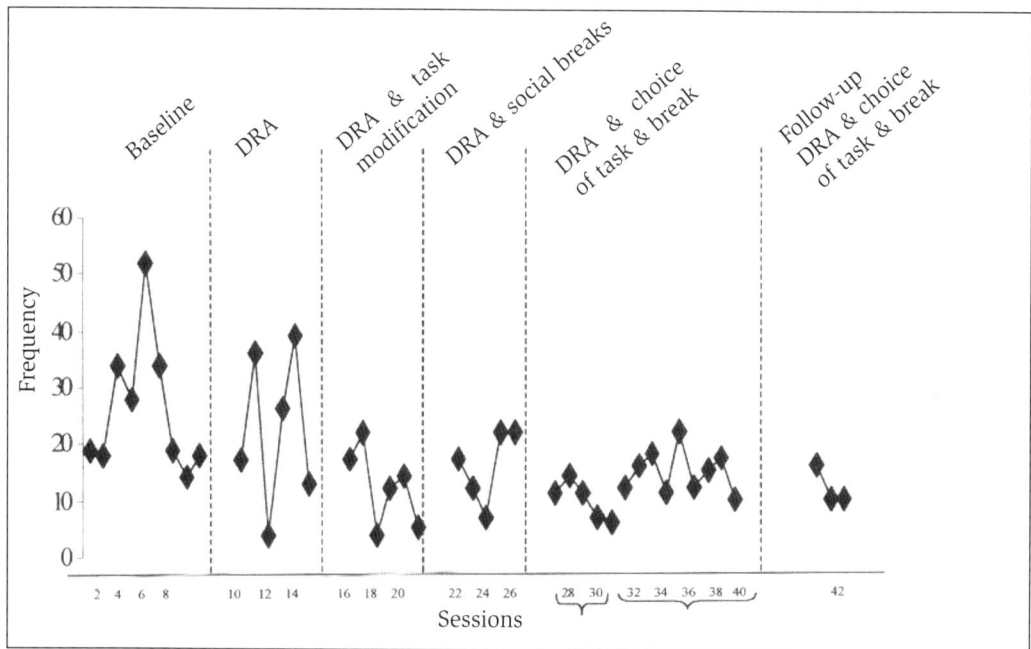

Moreover, researchers and practitioners must continue to address many pragmatic issues if PBS is to become a more routine tool among educators, especially in more inclusive settings, including general education classes where teachers typically manage classroom environments with 20 to 35 students per instructional period. In this study, with just four students in a self-contained classroom, we experienced firsthand the give-and-take necessary to implement FBA and PBS in a manner that balanced the needs of both researchers and practitioners like teachers and administrators.

Indeed, in this case study, we did not pursue certain research-based standards of practice to get PBS into practice within the classroom. For example, based largely on the teacher's preferences and existing daily routines, we limited data collection within each phase of this study to multiple sessions across just 1 or 2 days. In addition, we did not collect interobserver agreement data. Finally, we eliminated a design element (reversal) that would have permitted definitive conclusions about the functional control of the intervention over Callie's escape-motivated behavior. These were three limitations of our study from a research standpoint.

Throughout this article, we have provided tips for "New-to-PBS" professionals, as well as an updated and extended list of PBS resources (see boxes). Our hope is that this article prompts teachers to adapt FBA and PBS for use in their own and colleagues' classrooms, and in other school settings (e.g., playground, cafeteria, and hallways), where research and experience suggest that disruptive behavior is most likely to arise. We propose that by investing

Resources for Positive Behavioral Support

Seek out PBS resources, which are readily available via Web sites, books, journals, conferences, and professional associations.

- **www.pbis.org** Office of Special Education Programs (OSEP) Technical Assistance Center on Positive Behavioral Interventions & Support (U.S. Department of Education). Includes a series of PBS Practices (two-page how-to-do papers plus resource lists) on
    - Conducting FBAs.
    - Collaborative teaming in PBS.
    - Proactive support strategies.
    - Teaching replacement skills.
    - Systems change in PBS.
    - Using competing behavior models.
    - Group action planning and PBS.
    - Addressing cultural and economic diversity in PBS.
- **www.nichcy.org** National Information Center for Children and Youth with Disabilities (NICHCY). On the NICHCY Web site you will find a useful bibliography for using PBS in schools, home, and community. While this document is now out of print, it is still available on the Web site and contains useful information for practitioners. To locate, follow the links starting at the home page: publications, out of print, Resource list (BIB3).
- **www.beachcenter.org** Beach Center on Disability. An organization devoted to improving the quality of life for families and individuals affected with disability. Members of this organization conduct research, provide training and technical assistance, and service at the local, state, and national level. Current research topics include PBS, law and public policy, self-determination, family quality of life, access to the general curriculum, and school-community partnerships reform. To access information regarding PBS, follow links on home page: General topics, Positive Behavior Support, and then select a resource type.
- **http://www.apbsinternational.org** An organization dedicated to the advancement of positive behavior support. Members of this organization receive newsletters, conference discounts, and a subscription to *The Journal of Positive Behavior Interventions*.
- **http://cfs.fmhi.usf.edu/dares/apbs/PBS05CallFinal.pdf** International Conference on Positive Behavior Support; The World of PBS: Science, Value, & Vision
- *Journal of Positive Behavior Interventions*. Pro-Ed
- *Journal of Applied Behavior Analysis*. University of Kansas
- Carr, E. G., Levin, L., McConnachie, G., Carlson, J. I., Kemp, D. C., & Smith, C. E. (1994). *Communication-based interventions for problem behavior: A user's guide for positive change.* (1994) Baltimore, MD: Brookes Publishing.
- Koegel, L. K., Koegel, R. L., & Dunlap, G. (Eds.). (1996). *Positive behavioral support: Including people with difficult behavior in the community.* Baltimore, MD: Paul H. Brookes.
- Luiselli, J. K., & Cameron, M. J. (Eds.). (1998). *Antecedent control: Innovative approaches to behavioral support.* Baltimore, MD: Paul H. Brookes.
- O'Neill, R. E., Horner, R. H., Albin, R. W., Sprague, J. R., Storey, K., & Newton, J. S. (1997). *Functional assessment and program development for problem behavior: A practical handbook.* Pacific Grove, CA: Brooks/Cole.
- Repp, A, C., & Horner, R. H. (1999). *Functional analysis of problem behavior: From effective assessment to effective support.* Belmont, CA: Wadsworth.

time in FBA and PBS now, teachers—and their students—will learn to manage challenging behavior more proactively, and accrue dividends by enhancing engaged academic time and corresponding academic outcomes.

REFERENCES

Alberto, P. A., & Troutman, A. C. (1999). *Applied behavior analysis for teachers.* Upper Saddle River, NJ: Prentice-Hall.

Black, S. (2004). Teachers can engage disengaged students. *The Education Digest, 69,* 39–44.

Carr, E. G., Levin, L., McConnachie, G., Carson, J. I., Kemp, D. C., & Smith, C. E. (1976). Stimulus control of self-destructive behavior in a psychotic child. *Journal of Abnormal Child Psychology, 4,* 139–152.

Carr, E. G., Newsom, C. D., & Binkoff, J. A. (1976). Stimulus control of self-destructive behavior in psychotic child. *Journal of Abnormal Child Psychology, 4,* 139–152.

Clarke, S., Dunlap, G., Foster-Johnson, L., Childs, K. E., Wilson, D., White, R., & Vera, A. (1995). Improving the conduct of students with behavioral disorders by incorporating student interests into curricular activities. *Behavioral Disorders, 20,* 221–237.

Fox, A. M. (1998). Clumsiness in children: Developmental coordination disorder. *Learning Disabilities: A Multidisciplinary Journal, 9,* 57-63.

Gartin, B. C., & Murdick, N. L. (2001). A new IDEA mandate: The use of functional assessment of behavior and positive behavior supports. *Remedial and Special Education, 22,* 344–349.

Horner, R. H., Day, H. M., & Day, J. R. (1997). Using neutralizing routines to reduce problem behavior. *Journal of Applied Behavior Analysis, 30,* 601–614.

Kazdin, A. E. (1982). *Single case research designs.* New York: Oxford University Press.

Kern, L., Mantegna, M., Vorndran, C. M., Bailin, D., & Hilt, A. (2001). Choice of task sequence to reduce problem behaviors. *Journal of Positive Behavior Interventions, 3,* 3–10.

Langdon, C. A. (1999). The fifth Phi Delta Kappa poll of teachers' attitudes toward the public schools. *Phi Delta Kappan, 80,* 611-618.

Miltenberger, R. (2001). *Behavior modification: Principles and procedures* (2nd ed.). Belmont, CA: Wadsworth/Thomson Learning.

O'Neill, R. E., Horner, R. H., Albin, R. W., Sprague, J. R., Storey, K., & Newton, J. S. (1997). *Functional assessment and program development for problem behavior: A practical handbook.* Pacific Grove, CA: Brooks/Cole.

Repp, A. C., & Horner, R. H. (1999). *Functional analysis of problem behavior: From effective assessment to effective support.* Belmont, CA: Wadsworth.

Wheeler, J. J., & Wheeler, W. R. (1995). Reducing challenging behavior through the modification of instructional antecedents: A case study. *B. C. Journal of Special Education, 19,* 4–14.

Originally published in *TEACHING Exceptional Children,* Vol. 37, No. 1, pp. 18–24.

13

Teaching Transitions: Techniques for Promoting Success *Between* Lessons

Kent McIntosh, Keith Herman, Amanda Sanford, Kelly McGraw, and Kira Florence

Even in an otherwise well-functioning classroom, transitions may pose a challenge to teachers and students alike, as student misbehavior is more likely to occur and educational time can be wasted (Sprick, Garrison, & Howard, 1998). In transitions, we demand a lot from students—we ask them to halt their current routine, perform a long chain of tasks, and initiate a new activity, all without breaking classroom rules. The following are some examples of not-so-effective transitions that we have observed over the past year:

- When lining up for recess, two students started pushing each other and lost their recess privileges.
- A class returning from lunch took 30 minutes and two discipline referrals before math instruction started.
- A teacher was reprimanded by several peers and her principal during a whole-school staff meeting for her students' high noise level in the hallway.

Transitions can be particularly difficult for students with autism spectrum disorders (Winterman & Sapina, 2002), attention deficit/hyperactivity disorder (Carbone, 2001), and other behavioral disorders. It is no surprise that children with behavioral challenges can experience difficulties during transitions (Walker, Colvin, & Ramsey, 1995). Children who are easily distracted and overactive often have difficulty monitoring, managing, and directing their own behavior to successfully move from one routine to the next, especially when given detailed, multistep directions.

Adding to the confusion, many classrooms are full of implicit transition expectations—routines that teachers expect students to follow with no instruction. Some students pick up on subtle clues and teach themselves how to transition effectively. Students with disabilities, however, are most likely to learn these routines by mistake—by failing to adhere to the hidden curriculum and being reprimanded. In addition, these expectations vary as students move from room to room.

Rather than assuming that students know (or should know) how to transition appropriately, teachers can enhance their classroom behavior management with explicit instruction and practice in behavioral expectations and routines (Darch, Kame'enui, & Crichlow, 2003). A growing body of evidence emphasizes the importance of using instructional procedures to teach social behavior (Gresham, 2002; Langland, Lewis-Palmer, & Sugai, 1998; Todd, Haugen, Anderson, & Spriggs, 2002).

Fortunately, the strategies needed to teach behavioral expectations are the same as those that effective teachers already use to teach academic skills (Darch et al., 2003; Wolery, Bailey, & Sugai, 1988). These include careful preparation, planning, and design; effective delivery; opportunities to practice; ongoing assessment and evaluation; and performance feedback (Colvin, Kame'enui, & Sugai, 1993). Research suggests that providing clear structure, including specific rules and expectations, increases student attention and reduces hyperactive behaviors among children with and without ADHD (see Gardill, DuPaul, & Kyle, 1996).

Behavioral errors are corrected in the same manner as academic errors. From an instructional model, one might construe misbehavior either as a skill deficit ("can't do") or performance deficit ("won't do"); and both indicate a need for further instruction. Students with skill deficits may benefit from learning the behaviors, and students with performance deficits may benefit from practicing the behaviors to become fluent.

PLANNING FOR TRANSITIONS

Successful transitions require careful planning, teaching, monitoring, and feedback (Sprick et al., 1998). Effective instruction about when and how to perform transitions is essential and may mitigate many problems associated with transitions. As educators, we know a great deal about how best to design and deliver behavioral instruction so that it is more likely to increase student compliance. In this article, we present four techniques to promote smooth transitions: teaching routines, precorrections, positive reinforcement procedures, and active supervision (see box, "Techniques for Effective Transitions").

> **Techniques for Effective Transitions**
>
> These four teaching techniques may help teachers improve their students' transition skills:
> - Teaching Routines—Explicit teaching of expected behavior.
>   - Model the skills (both correct and incorrect examples).
>   - Provide multiple opportunities for student practice.
>   - Monitor and provide feedback.
>   - Reteach as needed.
> - Precorrections—Quick reminders of expected behavior before the transition.
>   - Additional support to firm student skills.
>   - Can be faded or withdrawn as needed.
> - Positive Reinforcement Procedures—Incentives for appropriate behavior.
>   - Specific praise can be more powerful than tangible rewards.
>   - Provide attention contingent on correct behavior.
>   - Ignore or quickly redirect incorrect behavior.
> - Active Supervision—an effective method for monitoring students.
>   - Scan, move, and interact to create a positive classroom culture.
>   - Avoid performing tasks or conversing with other adults in key transitions.

Teaching Routines

Teaching transitions as behavioral routines is an effective method of promoting appropriate classroom behaviors while discouraging inappropriate behaviors. Whereas other strategies like posting expectations can be valuable in reminding students about the rules, teaching with examples and providing practice with feedback shows students exactly how to behave. Although the focus of this article is on transitions, you can use these techniques to teach any behavioral routine, such as raising a hand to ask for help, ignoring other students who are misbehaving, taking notes, or completing independent seatwork.

To provide an example of the process, Figure 1 shows a lesson plan for an especially important transition routine (lining up at the door). In many classrooms, lining up to leave the room can be a context for misbehavior. Instead of viewing students as willfully disobedient or victims of their disabilities, this approach assumes that students may behave more appropriately after learning and practicing expected behavior in lining up. Figure 2 provides a blank reproducible behavioral lesson plan (adapted from Langland et al., 1998).

This process includes five steps (Colvin & Lazar, 1997) useful in teaching any behavior:

1. Provide a rationale.
2. Explain the expected behavior.

Figure 1. Sample Transition Lesson Plan

Lesson for Teaching Expected Behavior
Skill Name
"Lining up right" (to leave the classroom)
Rationale for Teaching the Skill
Lining up right is a key skill in smooth transitions. Tell students, *"When we all line up right, we make more time for activities and recess. Lining up right is safer and helps us all to follow directions."*
Modeling the Skill—Teaching Examples
Teach by *telling and showing* students the correct *and* incorrect (nonexamples) ways to line up: When it is time to leave the room, the teacher (or line leader) will stand at the door and say, "Time to line up right."   1. Stand up and push in their chairs section by section when called (e.g., "Bear section, time to line up right").   (NONEXAMPLE: All students all line up at once instead of section by section, or do not push in chairs.)   2. Walk slowly and quietly to the door.   (NONEXAMPLE: Students run to the door, or bump into each other on the way.)   3. Stand in line quietly, hands at sides, "with two people spaces between you." (teach this idea).   (NONEXAMPLE: Students talk in loud voices, stand directly next to each other, or push.)   4. Students walk quietly in the hallway, with two people spaces, on the right side of the hallway.   (NONEXAMPLE: Students call out, run, walk too closely, or in the middle of the hallway.)
Practice Activities
1. Play "Correct the teacher." After instruction, the teacher performs both examples and nonexamples for the class. Students use thumbs-up and down signals to evaluate the teacher's behavior. If the students signal thumbs-down, the teacher calls on a student to tell the teacher the correct expectation and demonstrate it for the class.   2. Play the "Lining Up Right Game." The class practices lining up right. Every time they line up perfectly, the class gets a point. If the class doesn't line up perfectly, the teacher gets the point, and the class practices the missed step again. Play until the class gets 3 points in a row.
After the Lesson—During the Day or Week
1. Before the class needs to line up, ask a student to tell the class the steps for lining up right.   2. Give specific praise and attention to students who are lining up right ("Keisha, thank you for walking slowly to the line!"). Provide more attention for appropriate behavior than misbehavior.   3. When you see a student line up incorrectly, remind him or her how to do it right and have the student show you the right way to do it.   4. Play the "Lining Up Right Game" at every opportunity to line up. Keep score on the board. Once the class reaches a predetermined point goal, they earn a celebration (preferred activity, extra minute of recess, sticker, etc.).

Note. From "Teaching Respect in the Classroom: An Instructional Approach," by S. Langland, T. Lewis-Palmer & G. Sugai, 1998, *Journal of Behavioral Education, 8,* pp. 245–262. Copyright 1998 by Kluwer Academic/Plenum Publishers. Adapted with permission.

Figure 2. Reproducible Lesson Plan Form

Lesson for Teaching Expected Behavior
Skill Name
Rationale for Teaching the Skill
Modeling the Skill—Teaching Examples
Practice Activities
After the Lesson—During the Day or Week

Note. From "Teaching Respect in the Classroom: An Instructional Approach," by S. Langland, T. Lewis-Palmer & G. Sugai, 1998, *Journal of Behavioral Education, 8,* pp. 245–262. Copyright 1998 by Kluwer Academic/Plenum Publishers. Adapted with permission.

3. Model the expected behavior.
4. Practice the expected behavior.
5. Monitor and provide feedback.

Providing a rationale involves giving students a reason why a rule is important to follow. In Figure 1, the teacher names the behavior, "Line up right," and explains why it is important. Giving a rationale is a short and direct step—one or two sentences often suffice. When reviewing skills in a booster lesson (a lesson designed to firm up previously taught behaviors) the teacher may briefly ask students why walking quietly in the hallway is important. The lesson, however, must focus on performing the skill, not talking about it.

Next, teachers (or, perhaps, trained student volunteers) model the skill the lesson is teaching. Modeling expected behavior is a critical step in demonstrating what the expected behavior looks like. Explicitly showing students what to do provides a clear example of both acceptable and nonacceptable behavior. Providing both examples (correct) and nonexamples (incorrect) of how to perform the behavior further clarifies the line between appropriate and inappropriate behavior, particularly for instructionally naive learners (Kame'enui & Simmons, 1990). The teacher may tell the class, "Here is how *not* to line up right," and stand up before being asked (by a student acting as teacher), then say, "Here is how to line up right," and stand up when asked. Ending with the correct example is prudent. Teachers may identify or ask students to identify the specific transition behavior that is being demonstrated or violated in the examples (e.g., "Who can tell me why this is *not* lining up right?"). Engaging instruction during this step is key in maintaining student attention. Adding humorous nonexamples (as long as they are instructive) can be one way to increase engagement. It is insufficient for students merely to see a demonstration of the behavior—students then need to perform and practice the new skill. Practicing can actively engage students with attention difficulties, increasing the likelihood that they will retain the information (Gardill et al., 1996), but there are additional benefits. Asking students to perform the behavior many times provides checks for understanding, opportunities for praise or corrective feedback, and practice to become fluent with the behaviors. By practicing with teacher guidance and without pressure, students will be better prepared to perform the behavior when more distractions surround them.

The example lesson provides a few activities for practice, including choosing the correct behavior when the teacher models examples and nonexamples and playing games that use repeated practice and performance feedback (see box, "Examples of Transition Routines to Teach").

Precorrections

Once students have learned transition behaviors, some will still benefit from additional support and structure. Precorrections are quick reminders of how to

> **Examples of Transition Routines to Teach**
>
> The following are a few of the types of transitions that could be taught in this format:
>
> - Entering and exiting the classroom at various times of the day.
>   - Start of day/entry activities.
>   - Recess or lunch.
>   - Moving to or from another class.
>   - End of day.
> - Putting materials away and preparing for the next task.
> - Cleaning up a work area.
> - Moving from group to independent work.
> - Turning in homework.
> - Choosing partners for small group activities.
> - Preparing for a lesson.
> - Choosing a book in the library.
> - Returning equipment at the end of recess.
> - Checking in with a mentor before or after school.

perform skills given directly before the opportunity to use them (Kame'enui & Simmons, 1990; Walker et al., 1995). Researchers have shown that precorrections reduce problem behavior during transitions in classrooms and in settings like cafeterias, playgrounds, and hallways (Colvin, Sugai, Good, & Lee, 1997; Kartub, Taylor-Greene, March, & Horner, 2000; Lewis, Sugai, & Colvin, 2000). This technique is especially helpful when teachers can anticipate that students will have difficulty performing skills correctly. You may use precorrections with the whole class or individual students who need more support to be successful.

Examples of precorrections for lining up might include statements such as, "Make sure to wait until I excuse you before you line up," or questions like, "How far apart should you be when you line up?" These precorrections should happen *just before* a teacher asks students to line up. As students become more fluent with transitions, precorrections can be changed to subtle cues like hand signals, or faded or phased out completely.

Positive Reinforcement Procedures

Teachers may use positive reinforcement procedures to encourage students to transition appropriately. A student may obtain verbal praise, good grades, or extra recess for certain kinds of appropriate behavior. If students continue to line up correctly in exchange for acknowledgment for their behavior, you have positively reinforced the correct behavior by your attention. On the other hand, the same is true if students continue to yell in the hallway: They get one-on-one attention when you reprimand them. Effective use of reinforcement requires two skills: providing attention or other incentives for appropriate behavior *and* minimizing any reinforcement for inappropriate behavior (Sprick, Sprick, & Garrison, 1993).

Effective reinforcers may include teacher praise, a preferred activity, a tangible incentive (such as a sticker or candy), or a combination (Alberto & Troutman, 2003). One of the most powerful and readily available reinforcers is teacher attention. For example, simply praising students for pushing in their chairs when they leave their seats may maintain their behavior.

When providing incentives, keep in mind that certain incentives may be aversive to some students. For example, many older students (such as middle and high school students) may not respond favorably to effusive teacher attention or public recognition. In this case, you should provide other incentives, such as homework reduction or a choice of rewards, for appropriate behavior.

Allowing students to earn 1 or 2 extra minutes of recess or a fun group activity may be more acceptable to some educators (and more social for students) than providing tangibles (Alberto & Troutman, 2003). Self-monitoring point sheets (Condon & Tobin, 2001); token economies (Carbone, 2001); or the "Lining Up Right Game" from the provided lesson are examples of positive reinforcement procedures. In the "Lining Up Right Game," students earn points toward a designated incentive with each correct transition.

Schoolwide positive reinforcement procedures, particularly raffles in which students earn tickets for good behavior, have also been used effectively to improve the transition behaviors of an entire school (Kartub et al., 2000).

In addition to providing attention or incentives contingent on appropriate behavior, providing *specific praise* can be even more effective in increasing correct behaviors (Sutherland, Wehby, & Copeland, 2000). Specific praise serves two purposes: first, it tells students exactly what they are doing well, and second, it provides a cue for other students on how to earn the teacher's attention. For example, when you tell a student, "Good job," the student may not know the expectation, or question the sincerity of the praise. When you say, "Thank you for standing quietly with your hands at your sides," the student knows what he or she has done to earn the praise, and other students may try to mimic the appropriate behavior in hopes of receiving praise for their own behavior.

Active Supervision

Active supervision is a specific method for monitoring students in classroom transitions and nonclassroom settings. Researchers have found active supervision effective in both decreasing inappropriate behaviors and increasing appropriate behaviors in school settings (Colvin et al., 1997; DePry & Sugai, 2002; Lewis et al., 2000).

Active supervision is defined by its three behaviors—scanning, moving, and interacting—which increase supervisor awareness and heighten responsiveness to student activity (Colvin et al., 1997). Because of these aspects, active supervision is a good way to promote student safety and well-being in the schools (Colvin & Lazar, 1997; Colvin & Lowe, 1986).

- *Scanning* is a technique used to examine the environment frequently, looking for both appropriate and inappropriate behaviors. This allows teachers to be aware of all the behaviors that students are displaying during transitions. Teachers who use effective scanning glance around the classroom or other setting regularly, looking for multiple opportunities to reward students behaving appropriately. Though recommended ratios vary, you should strive to praise students for appropriate behavior *at least* three times as often as you reprimand them (Sprick et al., 1998).

- *Moving,* as one might guess, consists of walking around the setting, visiting problem areas often, and making one's presence known to students. Instead of using a regular pattern, teachers should move unpredictably, so that students will not know where or when an adult will be in direct proximity.

- *Interacting* includes teaching behaviors, providing precorrections, and even conversing with students informally (DePry & Sugai, 2002). Interaction allows teachers to build a positive relationship with students, prevent inappropriate behavior, and emphasize positive behavior.

You can use active supervision to provide consistent and preventive monitoring of student behaviors, especially during transitions when there may be changes in staff, settings, and behavioral expectations (Colvin et al., 1997). Adequate monitoring requires effort and attention. Using transitions as an opportunity to gather materials or plan for the next activity or spending more time interacting with other adults than with students may negate other efforts to improve transitions. Prior planning and staff training emphasizing the three key behaviors of active supervision may help mitigate these difficulties (see box, "Active Supervision").

REVISTING AND REVIEWING INSTRUCTION

Teaching students transition routines, providing practice activities, and using precorrection, reinforcement, and active supervision allow students to learn how to transition efficiently and effectively and receive support and incentives for appropriate behavior. Defining, teaching, and rewarding correct transitions can result in approximately 80%-90% of students being successful in transitions (Colvin et al., 1997; DePry & Sugai, 2002; Kartub et al., 2000; Taylor-Greene et al., 1997). We recommend teachers revisit expectations and teach "booster" lessons as needed throughout the year, particularly after vacations,

> **Active Supervision**
>
> The following are important active supervision activities:
>
> - Scan.
>   - Examine the environment frequently.
>   - Notice both inappropriate and appropriate behaviors.
> - Move.
>   - Move around the entire area unpredictably.
>   - Visit problem areas frequently.
> - Interact.
>   - Elicit conversations with students.
>   - Provide precorrections and reminders.
>   - Provide positive reinforcers.

long weekends, when new students join the class, or when transition routines start to unravel.

Some students will need additional support to be successful. Students with behavioral challenges may benefit from specific adaptations to get through transitions. Visual structures, such as taping squares on the floor to show students where to stand when lining up, or picture schedules (Winterman & Sapina, 2002) are common and effective adaptations. As with all students, minimizing attention for misbehavior while emphasizing attention for positive behavior is critical.

FINAL THOUGHTS

Though teaching transitions requires time and energy, initial investments in teaching behaviors result in lasting improvements throughout the year (Taylor-Greene et al., 1997; Todd et al., 2002). We encourage teachers to share these techniques with other teachers and paraprofessionals (such as librarians, recess monitors, music teachers, and educational assistants) who work with their students throughout the day. Students with disabilities are more likely to be successful when they know all of their daily routines. Teaching transitions saves considerable teaching time and frustration, especially given how many transitions students experience throughout the school day.

REFERENCES

Alberto, P. A., & Troutman, A. C. (2003). *Applied behavior analysis for teachers* (6th ed.). Upper Saddle River, NJ: Merrill Prentice Hall.

Carbone, E. (2001). Arranging the classroom with an eye (and ear) to students with ADHD. *TEACHING Exceptional Children, 34*(2), 72–81.

Colvin, G., Kame'enui, E. J., & Sugai, G. (1993). Reconceptualizing behavior management and school-wide discipline in general education. *Education and Treatment of Children, 16*, 361–381.

Colvin, G., & Lazar, M. (1997). *The effective elementary classroom: Managing for success.* Longmont, CO: Sopris West.

Colvin, G., & Lowe, R. (1986). Getting good recess supervision isn't child's play. *Executive Educator, 8*, 20–21.

Colvin, G., Sugai, G., Good, R. H., & Lee, Y. (1997). Effect of active supervision and precorrection on transition behaviors of elementary students. *School Psychology Quarterly, 12*, 344–363.

Condon, K. A., & Tobin, T. J. (2001). Using electronic and other new ways to help students improve their behavior: Functional behavioral assessment at work. *TEACHING Exceptional Children, 34*(1), 44–51.

Darch, C. B., Kame'enui, E. J., & Crichlow, J. M. (2003). *Instructional classroom management: A proactive approach to behavior management* (2nd ed.). Upper Saddle River, NJ: Prentice Hall.

DePry, R. L., & Sugai, G. (2002). The effect of active supervision and pre-correction on minor behavioral incidents in a sixth grade general education classroom. *Journal of Behavioral Education, 11*, 255–267.

Gardill, M. C., DuPaul, G. J., & Kyle, K. E. (1996). Classroom strategies for managing students with Attention Deficit/Hyperactivity Disorder. *Intervention in School and Clinic, 32*, 89–94.

Gresham, F. M. (2002). Teaching social skills to high-risk children and youth: Preventative and remedial strategies. In M. R. Shinn, H. M. Walker, & G. Stoner (Eds.), *Interventions for academic and behavior problems II: Preventive and remedial approaches.* Bethesda, MD: National Association of School Psychologists.

Kame'enui, E. J., & Simmons, D. C. (1990). *Designing instructional strategies: The prevention of academic learning problems.* Columbus, OH: Merrill.

Kartub, D. T., Taylor-Greene, S., March, R. E., & Horner, R. H. (2000). Reducing hallway noise: A systems approach. *Journal of Positive Behavior Interventions, 2*, 179–182.

Langland, S., Lewis-Palmer, T., & Sugai, G. (1998). Teaching respect in the classroom: An instructional approach. *Journal of Behavioral Education, 8*, 245–262.

Lewis, T. J., Sugai, G., & Colvin, G. (2000). The effect of pre-correction and active supervision on the recess behavior of elementary school students. *Education and Treatment of Children, 23*, 109–121.

Sprick, R., Garrison, M., & Howard, L. (1998). *CHAMPS: A proactive and positive approach to classroom management.* Longmont, CO: Sopris West.

Sprick, R., Sprick, M., & Garrison, M. (1993). *Interventions: Collaborative planning for students at risk.* Longmont, CO: Sopris West.

Sutherland, K. S., Wehby, J. H., & Copeland, S. R. (2000). Effect of varying rates of behavior-specific praise on the on-task behavior of students with EBD. *Journal of Emotional and Behavioral Disorders, 8*, 2–8.

Taylor-Greene, S., Brown, D., Nelson, L., Longton, J., Gassman, T., Cohen, J., et al. (1997). School-wide behavioral support: Starting the year off right. *Journal of Behavioral Education, 7*, 99–112.

Todd, A., Haugen, L., Anderson, K., & Spriggs, M. (2002). Teaching recess: Low-cost efforts producing effective results. *Journal of Positive Behavior Interventions, 4*, 46–52.

Walker, H. M., Colvin, G., & Ramsey, E. (1995). *Antisocial behavior in school: Strategies and best practices.* Pacific Grove, CA: Brooks/Cole.

Winterman, K. G., & Sapina, R. H. (2002). Everyone's included: Supporting young children with Autism Spectrum Disorders in a responsive classroom learning environment. *TEACHING Exceptional Children, 35*(1), 30-35.

Wolery, M. R., Bailey, D. B., Jr., & Sugai, G. (1988). *Effective teaching: Principles and procedures of applied behavior analysis with exceptional children.* Boston: Allyn & Bacon.

The development of this article was supported in part by Grant No. H325A000101, funded by the U.S. Department of Education, Office of Special Education Programs. Opinions expressed herein do not necessarily reflect the position of the U.S. Department of Education, and such endorsements should not be inferred.

Originally published in *TEACHING Exceptional Children,* Vol. 37, No. 1, pp. 32-38.